second edition

THE SNOBOL4
PROGRAMMING
LANGUAGE

R. E. Griswold
J. F. Poage
I. P. Polonsky

Bell Telephone Laboratories, Incorporated

Prentice-Hall, Inc., Englewood Cliffs, New Jersey

Current printing (last digit):
17 16 15 14

13-815373-6

Library of Congress Catalog Card Number: 70-131996

Printed in the United States of America

Foreword

SNOBOL4 is a computer programming language containing many features not commonly found in other programming languages. It evolved from SNOBOL [1,2,3]*, a language for string manipulation, developed at Bell Telephone Laboratories, Incorporated, in 1962. Extensions to SNOBOL through various versions have made it a useful tool in such areas as compilation techniques, machine simulation, symbolic mathematics, text preparation, natural language translation, linguistics, and music analysis.

The basic data element of SNOBOL4 is a string of characters, such as this line of printing. The language has operations for joining and separating strings, for testing their contents, and for making replacements in them. If a string is a sentence, it can be broken into phrases or words. If it is a formula, it can be taken apart into components and reassembled in another format. A string can appear either as a literal or as the value of a variable. The literal form is indicated by enclosing the string in quotation marks:

`'THIS IS A STRING'`

The string value may be assigned to a variable:

`LINE   =   'THIS IS A STRING'`

A common operation on a string is examination of its contents for a desired structure of characters. This structure, known as a pattern, can be as simple as a string or a given number of characters. A pattern also can be an extremely complicated expression consisting, for example, of a number of alternatives followed by another set of alternatives, all of which must begin a given number of characters from the end of the string. The pattern, as a data type, may also appear either in literal or variable form. The data type of a variable - string, pattern, or any other in the language - depends on the last value assigned to it. There are no type declaration statements for variables as in other programming languages.

SNOBOL4 provides numerical capabilities with both integers and real numbers. Because the language is essentially character oriented, and since most numerical operations involve character counting, integers are more commonly used. Conversion among integers, real numbers, and strings representing integers or real numbers is performed automatically as required. The programmer may, in addition, define other data types, such as complex numbers, and provide operations for them.

Often it is desirable to associate a group of items with one variable name through numerical indexing or some other identifying property. The SNOBOL4 array and table provide these capabilities with more flexibility than most programming languages. An

---

* Numbers in brackets refer to references listed at the end of this manual.

array is a data element consisting of a set of pointers to other data elements, so that each array element may be any data type, even an array. An element of an array is referenced by using an integer index. A table is similar to an array, except that the reference value need not be an integer, but can be any of several other types. Conversion can be made between tables and arrays.

Execution of SNOBOL4 programs is interpretive. Instead of compiling a program into actual computer instructions, the compiler translates the program into a notation the interpreter can easily execute. This makes it fairly simple to provide capabilities such as tracing of new values for variables, an operation that is quite difficult in noninterpretive systems. Another important product of interpretation is flexibility. Functions can be defined and redefined during program execution. Function calls can be made recursively with no special program notation. The language is extendable to new data types needed for a program through data type definition operations. Linked-list nodes and complex numbers are possible programmer-defined data types. Operations on these new data types can be defined as functions.

This book is an instructional and reference guide, and provides many examples of usage of the language. The description of the language is complete and does not require familiarity with earlier versions of the language. Some familiarity with elementary concepts of programming is presumed, however.

M. D. Shapiro

Lafayette, Indiana
May, 1970

Preface

The SNOBOL4 programming language has been developed over a period of years and new language features have been added from time to time during the course of this development. Consequently there are several somewhat different versions of the language in use. The first edition of this book, published in May, 1969, described Version 2. The description in this second edition corresponds to Version 3, released in December, 1969. Version 3 contains a number of features not available in Version 2.

SNOBOL4 has been implemented on several different computers, including the IBM System/360, UNIVAC 1108, GE 635, CDC 3600, CDC 6000 series, PDP-10, Sigma 5/6/7, Atlas 2, and RCA Spectra 70 series. Implementations for other machines are in various stages of completion. These machines have different operating environments and character sets. As a result, implementations of SNOBOL4 vary from machine to machine in details of syntax, operating system interface, and so forth. This book corresponds to the implementation of SNOBOL4 developed at Bell Telephone Laboratories, Incorporated on the IBM System/360 operating under OS. Sections of the manual containing language features particularly dependent upon this implementation make specific reference to this dependency. Program examples in this book were run on an IBM 360 Model 65.

Acknowledgement

The authors' most pleasant responsibility is the acknowledgement of the assistance provided in the course of the design, implementation, and documentation of the SNOBOL4 language.

The ideas of many individuals have helped shape the form of SNOBOL4. Particularly valuable contributions have been made by Messrs. R. B. K. Dewar, B. N. Dickman, D. J. Farber, P. D. Jensen, M. D. McIlroy, R. F. Rosin, M. A. Seelye, and M. D. Shapiro.

The authors have been fortunate in having the assistance of a number of people during various stages of the implementation of SNOBOL4. Mr. R. A. Yates designed and implemented the storage allocation and regeneration techniques used in SNOBOL4. Mr. Yates also contributed many useful ideas to the overall design of the system. Messrs. B. N. Dickman and P. D. Jensen designed and implemented the tracing facilities and provided many helpful suggestions for improving the system. Mr. H. J. Strauss designed and implemented the external function interface. Mr. L. C. Varian's assistance in preparing the initial implementation for the IBM System/360 was particularly valuable.

Mr. J. F. Gimpel has made an important contribution to the organization and presentation of descriptive material in this book. Several of the programs used in the examples are his.

The authors' special thanks go to Mrs. M. T. Hammer and Mrs. L. W. Noll for their help in editing and proofreading the second edition of this book. The authors also would like to express their appreciation to Mrs. R. E. Griswold who has given freely of her time to prepare much of the machine-readable material used in the development of the SNOBOL4 language and its documentation.

This revised edition was phototypeset by Alphanumeric Incorporated using their TEXTRAN*-2 system. The book was designed by Mrs. M. T. Hammer and Mrs. L. W. Noll. Software developed by Mrs. Noll was instrumental in preparing the book in its present form.

---

* Servicemark of Alphanumeric Incorporated

Contents

Chapter 1 - Introduction to the SNOBOL4 Programming Language

Chapter 2 - Pattern Matching

Chapter 3 - Primitive Functions, Predicates, and Operations

Chapter 4 - Programmer-Defined Functions

Chapter 5 - Arrays, Tables, and Defined Data Types

Chapter 6 - Keywords, Names, and Code

Chapter 7 - Types of Data

Chapter 8 - Tracing

Chapter 9 - Input and Output

Chapter 10 - Running a SNOBOL4 Program

Chapter 11 - Programming Details and Storage Management

CHAPTER 1

Introduction to the SNOBOL4 Programming Language

This chapter is an introductory overview of the SNOBOL4 programming language. It describes the format of statements, some of the operations, and some of the types of data handled by the language. Later chapters describe in more detail much of the material in this introductory chapter.

A SNOBOL4 program consists of a sequence of statements. There are four basic types of statements:

(1) the assignment statement,
(2) the pattern matching statement,
(3) the replacement statement, and
(4) the end statement.

The end statement terminates the program.

1.1 Assignment Statements

The simplest type of statement is the assignment statement. It has the form

> *variable*   =   *value*

The assignment statement may be said to have the following meaning: 'Let *variable* have the given *value*.' For example, let V have the value 5, or

> V   =   5

The value may be given by an expression, consisting, for example, of arithmetic operations as in the statement

> W   =   14 + (16 - 10)

which assigns the value 20 to the variable W. Blanks are required around arithmetic operators such as + and -. The value need not be an integer, which is just one type of data handled by SNOBOL4. For example, the value may be a string of characters, indicated by enclosing quotes. An example is the assignment statement

> V   =   'DOG'

which assigns the string **DOG** to the variable **V**. Various types of data and operations that may be performed on them are described later.

Typically a variable is a name such as **V**, **X**, or **ANS**. Variables appearing explicitly in a program must begin with a letter which may be followed by any number of letters, digits, periods, and underscores.

The value of a variable may be used in an assignment statement. Thus

```
RESULT    =    ANS.1
```

assigns to the variable **RESULT** the value of **ANS.1**. (Quotation marks distinguish literal strings from variables.)

Blanks are required to separate the parts of a statement. In an assignment statement, the equal sign must be separated from the variable on the left and the value on the right by at least one blank.

1.2   Arithmetic

1.2.1   Integers

The arithmetic operations of addition, subtraction, multiplication, division, and exponentiation of integers may be used in expressions. The statements

```
M    =    4
N    =    5
P    =    N * M / (N - 1)
```

assign the value **5** to **P**. While blanks are required between the binary operators and their operands, unary operators such as the minus sign must be adjacent to their operands. An example is the statement

```
Q2    =    -P / -N
```

which assigns the value **1** to **Q2**.

Arithmetic expressions can be arbitrarily complex. When evaluating arithmetic expressions, the natural order of operator precedence applies. The unary operations are performed first, then exponentiation (****** or **!**), then multiplication, followed by division, and finally addition and subtraction. All arithmetic operations associate to the left except exponentiation. Hence,

```
X    =    2 ** 3 ** 2
```

is equivalent to

```
X    =    2 ** (3 ** 2)
```

Parentheses may be used to emphasize or alter the order of evaluation of an expression.

In the above examples all the operands are integers and the results are integers. The quotient of two integers is also an integer. The remainder is discarded. Thus

```
Q1   =   5 / 2
Q2   =   5 / -2
```

give Q1 and Q2 the values 2 and -2, respectively.

1.2.2   Real Numbers

Real operands are also permitted in arithmetic expressions. The statements

```
PI      =    3.14159
CIRCUM  =    2. * PI * 5.
```

assign real values to PI and CIRCUM.

If real numbers are mixed with integers in arithmetic expressions, the result is a real number. For example, the value of

```
SUM   =    16.4 + 2
```

is 18.4.

1.3   Strings

Expressions involving operands that are character strings are also permitted in assignment statements. For example, the assignment statement

```
SCREAM   =    'HELP'
```

assigns the string HELP as the value of SCREAM.

The string is specified by enclosing it within a pair of quotation marks. Any character may appear in a string. A pair of double quotation marks can be used instead of single quotation marks. This permits the use of quotation marks within a string as in the statements

```
PLEA        =    'HE SHOUTED, "HELP."'
QUOTE       =    '"'
APOSTROPHE  =    "'"
```

Single quotation marks are used in the examples given in this book where one type of quotation mark is sufficient.

1.3.1   The Null String

The null string, which is a string of length zero, is frequently used in SNOBOL4. With a few exceptions, explained later, all variables have the null string as their initial value. A variable can also be assigned the null string by a statement like

```
NULL    =      ''
```

or, more briefly,

```
NULL    =
```

The variable **NULL** is used in many examples that follow to represent the null string. The null string is different from the following strings, each of which has length one:

```
'0'
' '
```

1.3.2   Strings in Arithmetic Expressions

Numeral strings can be used in arithmetic expressions with integers and real numbers. For example, as a result of the statements

```
Z    =      '10'
X    =      5 * -Z + '10.6'
```

X has the value **-39.4**. Numeral strings representing integers can contain only digits and an optional preceding sign. Numeral strings representing real numbers must have at least one digit before the decimal point. Thus, the following strings cannot be used in arithmetic expressions:

```
'1,253,465'
'.364 E-03'
```

The null string is equivalent to the integer zero in arithmetic expressions.

1.3.3   String-Valued Expressions

Concatenation is the basic operation for combining two strings to form a third. The following statements illustrate the format of an expression involving concatenation.

```
TYPE    =      'SEMI'
OBJECT  =      TYPE 'GROUP'
```

The resulting value of **OBJECT** is the string **SEMIGROUP**. Notice there is no explicit operator for concatenation. Concatenation is indicated by specifying two string-valued operands separated by at least one blank.

```
        FIRST    =      'WINTER'
        SECOND   =      'SPRING'
        TWO.SEASONS   =    FIRST ',' SECOND
```

are equivalent to

```
        TWO.SEASONS   =      'WINTER,SPRING'
```

Strings can also be concatenated with reals and integers as in

```
        ROW   =     'K'
        NO.   =     22
        SEAT  =     ROW NO.
```

which gives **SEAT** the value **K22**.

In an expression involving concatenation and arithmetic operations, concatenation has the lowest precedence. Thus

```
        SEAT   =     ROW NO. + 4 / 2
```

is equivalent to

```
        SEAT   =     ROW (NO. + (4 / 2))
```

or

```
        SEAT   =     'K24'
```

1.3.4   Input and Output of Strings

Three variables provide means for reading and writing data. The variables **OUTPUT** and **PUNCH** are for printing and punching. Whenever either of them is assigned a string, integer or real value, a copy of the value is put out.

```
        OUTPUT   =     'THE RESULTS ARE:'
```

assigns **THE RESULTS ARE:** to **OUTPUT** and also prints it.

```
        PUNCH   =     OUTPUT
```

causes the same line to be punched on a card. The statements

```
        OUTPUT   =
        PUNCH    =
```

cause a blank line to be printed and a blank card to be punched.

The variable **INPUT** is used for reading in strings. Each time the value of **INPUT** is required in a statement, another card is read in and the 80-character string on it is assigned as the value of **INPUT**. Thus

```
        PUNCH   =     INPUT
```

punches a copy of the input card.

Data cards to be read in occur immediately after the end statement that terminates the program.

1.4 Pattern Matching Statements

The operation of examining strings for the occurrence of specified substrings (i.e. pattern matching) is fundamental to the SNOBOL4 language. Pattern matching can be specified in two types of statements:

    (1) the pattern matching statment, and
    (2) the replacement statement.

The pattern matching statement has the form

    subject   pattern

where the two fields are separated by at least one blank. The subject specifies a string that is to be examined, and the pattern can be thought of as specifying a set of strings. The statement causes the subject string to be scanned from the left for the occurrence of a string specified by the pattern.

If

```
    TRADE   =    'PROGRAMMER'
```

the statement

```
    TRADE   'GRAM'
```

examines the value of **TRADE** for an occurrence of **GRAM**. If

```
    PART   =    'GRAM'
```

then an equivalent statement is

```
    TRADE   PART
```

The following example illustrates a pattern matching statement in which the pattern is a string-valued expression.

```
    ROW   =    'K'
    NO.   =    20
    'K24'   ROW  NO. + 4
```

The subject is a literal and the value of the expression is the string **K24**.

Notice that there is no explicit pattern matching operator between the subject and the pattern. The two fields are separated by blanks.

If it is necessary to have concatenation in the subject, the expression must be enclosed within parentheses to avoid ambiguity. An example is

```
TENS    =    2
UNITS   =    5
(TENS UNITS) 30
```

On the other hand, a pattern formed by concatenation does not need parentheses. The following statements are equivalent:

```
TENS UNITS 30
```

```
TENS (UNITS 30)
```

1.5 Replacement Statements

A replacement statement has the form

subject   pattern   =   object

where the fields are separated by at least one blank. Pattern matching is performed as in the pattern matching statement. If the pattern matching operation succeeds, the subject string is modified by replacing the matched substring by the object. For example, if

```
WORD    =    'GIRD'
```

then the replacement statement

```
WORD  'I'    =    'OU'
```

causes the subject string **GIRD** to be scanned for the string **I** and then, since the pattern matches, **I** is replaced by **OU**. Hence **WORD** has as value the string **GOURD**. If the statement is

```
WORD 'AB'    =    'OU'
```

the value of **WORD** does not change because the pattern fails to match.

Another example of the use of replacement statements is given in the following sequence of statements

```
HAND    =    'AC4DAHKDKS'
RANK    =    4
SUIT    =    'D'
HAND  RANK SUIT    =    'AS'
```

which replaces the substring **4D** with the string **AS**.

A matched substring is deleted from the subject string if the object in the replacement statement is the null string. Thus

```
HAND    RANK SUIT    =
```

deletes **4D** from **HAND** leaving it with the string **ACAHKDKS** as value.

1.6   Patterns

The patterns in the preceding examples specify single strings. It is also possible to specify more complex patterns. There are two operations available for constructing such patterns:

   (1) alternation, and
   (2) concatenation.

Alternation is indicated by an expression of the form

        P1 | P2

where the two patterns **P1** and **P2** are separated from the | by blanks. The value of the expression is a pattern structure that matches any string specified by either **P1** or **P2**. For example, the statement

        KEYWORD   =   'COMPUTER' | 'PROGRAM'

assigns to **KEYWORD** a pattern structure that matches either of these two strings. Subsequently, **KEYWORD** may be used wherever patterns are permitted. For example,

        KEYWORD   =   KEYWORD | 'ALGORITHM'

gives **KEYWORD** a new pattern value equivalent to the value assigned by executing the statement

        KEYWORD   =   'COMPUTER' | 'PROGRAM' | 'ALGORITHM'

Using **KEYWORD** in the pattern field, the statement

        TEXT   KEYWORD   =

examines the value of **TEXT** from the left and deletes the first occurrence of one of the alternative strings. If

        TEXT   =   'PROGRAMMING ALGORITHMS FOR COMPUTERS'

the result of the replacement statement is as if the following statement were executed:

        TEXT   =   'MING ALGORITHMS FOR COMPUTERS'

Concatenation of two patterns, **P1** and **P2**, is specified in the same way as the concatenation of two strings:

        P1   P2

That is, the two patterns are separated by blanks. The value of the expression is a pattern that matches a string consisting of two substrings, the first matched by **P1**, the second matched by **P2**. For example, if

```
BASE      =     'BINARY' | 'DECIMAL' | 'HEX'
SCALE     =     'FIXED' | 'FLOAT'
ATTRIBUTE  =      SCALE BASE
```

and

```
DCL    =     'AREAFIXEDDECIMAL'
```

then the pattern match succeeds in the statement

```
DCL    ATTRIBUTE
```

Concatenation has higher precedence than alternation. Thus

```
ATTRIBUTE   =    'FIXED' | 'FLOAT' 'DECIMAL'
```

matches **FIXED** or **FLOATDECIMAL**. The order of evaluation may be altered by using parentheses.

```
ATTRIBUTE   =    ('FIXED' | 'FLOAT') 'DECIMAL'
```

matches either **FIXEDDECIMAL** or **FLOATDECIMAL**.

1.7 Conditional Value Assignment

It is possible to associate a variable with a component of a pattern such that if the pattern matches, the variable is assigned the substring matched by the component. The operator **.** is the conditional value-assignment operator and it is used in an expression of the form

      pattern **.** variable

where the operator is separated from its operands by blanks. For example

```
BASE    =    ('HEX' | 'DEC') . B1
```

assigns to **BASE** a pattern that matches either **HEX** or **DEC**. If **BASE** is used successfully in a pattern match, the value of **B1** is set to the substring matched by **BASE**.

The operator **.** associates to the left, and has higher precedence than concatenation and alternation.

```
A.OR.B   =    A | B . OUTPUT
```

is equivalent to

```
A.OR.B   =    A | (B . OUTPUT)
```

which assigns to **A.OR.B** a pattern that matches the value of **A** or **B**. If **B** matches, the substring matched is printed.

There is also an operator **$** for immediate value assignment which assigns value to a variable if the associated component of the pattern matches regardless of whether the entire pattern matches. Immediate value assignment is discussed in more detail later.

1.8   Flow of Control

A SNOBOL4 program is a sequence of statements terminated by an end statement. Statements are executed sequentially unless otherwise specified in the program. Labels and gotos are provided to control the flow of the program.

A statement may begin with an identifying label, permitting transfer to the statement. For example, the assignment statement

```
START   TEXT    =     INPUT
```

has the label **START**. A label consists of a letter or a digit followed by any number of other characters up to a blank. Blanks separate the label from the subject. A statement with no label must begin with at least one blank. The end statement is distinguished by the label **END**, indicating the end of the program.

Transfer to a labelled statement is specified in the goto field which may appear at the end of a statement and is separated from the rest of the statement by a colon. Two types of transfers can be specified in the goto field: conditional and unconditional.

A conditional transfer consists of a label enclosed within parentheses preceded by an **F** or **S** corresponding to failure or success. An example is the statement

```
        TEXT    =     INPUT      :F(DONE)
```

This statement causes a record to be read in and assigned as the value of **TEXT**. If, however, there is no data in the input file, i.e. an end of file is encountered, no new value is assigned to **TEXT**. Then, because of the failure to read, transfer is made to the statement labelled **DONE**.

A use of the success goto is illustrated in the following program which punches a copy of the input file.

```
LOOP    PUNCH   =     INPUT      :S(LOOP)
END
```

The first statement is repeatedly executed until the end of file is encountered. Then the program flows into the end statement causing the program to terminate.

The success or failure of a pattern match can also be used to control the flow of a program by conditional gotos. For example

```
        COLOR   =     'RED' | 'GREEN' | 'BLUE'
BRIGHT  TEXT    COLOR   =        :S(BRIGHT)F(BLAND)
BLAND
```

All occurrences of the strings **RED**, **GREEN**, and **BLUE** are deleted from the value of **TEXT** before the pattern fails to match. Control then passes to the statement labelled **BLAND**. Both success and failure gotos can be specified in one goto field, and may appear in either order.

An unconditional transfer is indicated by the absence of an **F** or **S** before the enclosing parentheses. For an example of an unconditional transfer, consider the following program that punches and lists a deck of cards.

```
LOOP    PUNCH    =    INPUT      :F(END)
        OUTPUT   =    PUNCH      :(LOOP)
END
```

The goto field in the second statement specifies an unconditional transfer.

1.9   Indirect Reference

Indirect referencing is indicated by the unary operator **$**. For example, if

```
        MONTH    =    'APRIL'
```

then **$MONTH** is equivalent to **APRIL**. That is, the statement

```
        $MONTH   =    'CRUEL'
```

is equivalent to

```
        APRIL    =    'CRUEL'
```

The indirect reference operator can also be applied to a parenthesized expression as in the statements

```
        WORD     =    'RUN'
        $(WORD ':')    =    $(WORD ':') + 1
```

which increment the value of **RUN:**.

In general, the unary operator **$** generates a variable that is the value of its operand. The expression

```
        $('A'  |  'B')
```

is erroneous because the value of the operand of **$** is a pattern, not a string. Indirect reference in a goto is demonstrated by

```
        N    =    N + 1       :($('PHASE' N))
```

If, for example, the assignment statement sets **N** equal to 5', then the transfer is to the statement labelled **PHASE5**.

1.10   Functions

Many SNOBOL4 procedures are invoked by functions built into the system, called primitive functions. Operations that occur frequently are implemented as primitive functions for efficiency. Other primitive functions are used to invoke more complex operations that are fundamental to the language, affect parameters and tables internal to the system, and perform operations that could not be programmed in source language by other means. In addition, facilities are available for a programmer to define his own source-language functions.

1.10.1   Primitive Functions

The primitive function **SIZE** has a single string argument and returns as value an integer that is the length (number of characters) of the string. The statements

```
APE     =     'SIMIAN'
OUTPUT  =     SIZE(APE)
```

print the number **6**.

Arguments to all functions are passed by value, and an arbitrarily complex expression may be used in the argument. Thus the statements

```
N       =     100
OUTPUT  =     SIZE('PART' N + 4)
```

print the number **7**, because the value of the argument is the string **PART104**.

The argument of **SIZE** is supposed to be a string. Therefore, a call of the form

```
SIZE('APE' | 'MONKEY')
```

is erroneous because the value of the argument is a pattern.

DUPL is another function that performs an operation that is frequently required. **DUPL(string,integer)** returns as value a string that consists of a number of duplications of the string argument. The value of

```
DUPL('/*',5)
```

is **/*/*/*/*/*.** **DUPL** returns the null string if the second argument is zero, and fails if it is negative. The statement

```
OUTPUT   =    DUPL(' ',40 - SIZE(S))   S
```

prints the string **S** right justified to column 40 if its length is not greater than 40. Otherwise the statement fails, and **S** is not printed.

REPLACE is a function called with three string-valued arguments.

```
REPLACE(TEXT,CH1,CH2)
```

returns as value a string which is the same as **TEXT**, except that each occurrence of a character appearing in **CH1** is replaced by the corresponding character in **CH2**. For example, the statements

```
STATEMENT   =   'A(I,J)   =   A(I,J) + 3'
OUTPUT      =   REPLACE(STATEMENT,'()','<>')
```

print the line

```
A<I,J>   =   A<I,J> + 3
```

If the last two arguments of the function call do not have the same length, the function fails. Function failure, like input failure, can be used in a conditional transfer.

There are also several functions that return patterns as their values. **LEN** is such a function. **LEN(integer)** returns a pattern that matches any string of the length specified by the integer.

The following example punches a card with the first 40 characters from a card that is read in.

```
INPUT   LEN(40) . PUNCH
```

1.10.2 Predicates

A predicate is a function or operation that returns the null string as value if a given condition is satisfied. Otherwise it fails.

LE is an example of a predicate used for comparing numbers.

```
LE(N1,N2)
```

returns the null string as value if **N1** is a number less than or equal to **N2**. **N1** and **N2** may be either integer or real. Thus

```
PUNCH   =   LE(SIZE(TEXT),80) TEXT
```

punches the string **TEXT** if its length is not greater than 80. The null string value of the predicate does not affect the string that is punched. If the predicate fails, no assignment is made to **PUNCH**, and no card is punched.

The success or failure of a predicate can be used with a conditional goto to control the flow of a program. For example,

```
        SUM   =   0
        N   =   0
ADD     N   =   LT(N,50) N + 1      :F(DONE)
        SUM   =   SUM + N           :(ADD)
DONE    OUTPUT   =   SUM
```

sums the first 50 integers. Iteration continues as long as **N** is less than **50**. When the predicate fails, the conditional transfer to **DONE** is performed and the string **1275** is printed.

There are several predicates for comparing data objects. For example,

        DIFFER(ST1,ST2)

returns the null string as value if the values of two arguments are not identical. Thus

        OUTPUT   =   DIFFER(FIRST,SECOND) FIRST SECOND

concatenates the values of **FIRST** and **SECOND** if they are not the same, and then prints them. The predicate **IDENT** is the converse of **DIFFER**. **IDENT** fails if the values of its arguments are not identical.

For all functions, an omitted argument is assumed to be the null string. Thus

        PUNCH   =   DIFFER(TEXT) TEXT

punches the value of **TEXT** if it is not the null string.

LGT is a predicate that lexically compares two strings.

        LGT(ST1,ST2)

succeeds if **ST1** follows (is lexically greater than) **ST2** in alphabetical order. The statements

```
        OUTPUT   =   LGT(TEXT1,TEXT2) TEXT2      :S(SKIP)
        OUTPUT   =   TEXT1
        OUTPUT   =   TEXT2                        :(JUMP)
SKIP    OUTPUT   =   TEXT1
JUMP
```

print the values of **TEXT1** and **TEXT2** in alphabetical order.

1.10.3 Defined Functions

The SNOBOL4 language provides the programmer with the capability to define functions in the source language. This feature facilitates the organization of a program and may improve its efficiency.

A programmer may define a function by executing the primitive function **DEFINE** to specify the function name, formal arguments, local variables, and the entry point of the function. The entry point is the label of the first of a set of SNOBOL4 statements constituting the procedure for the function.

The first argument of **DEFINE** is a prototype describing the form of the function call. The second argument is the entry point. For example, execution of the statement

        DEFINE('DELETE(STRING,CHAR)','D1')

defines a function **DELETE** having two formal arguments, **STRING** and **CHAR**, and entry point **D1**. The statements

```
D1      STRING CHAR   =            :S(D1)
        DELETE   =    STRING       :(RETURN)
```

form a procedure that deletes all occurrences of **CHAR** from the value of **STRING**. The statement assigning the resulting value to the variable **DELETE** illustrates the SNOBOL4 convention for returning a function value. The function name may be used as a variable in the function procedure. Its value on return from the procedure is the value of the function call. Return from a procedure is accomplished by transfer to the system label **RETURN**.

If the second argument is omitted from the call of **DEFINE**, the entry point to the procedure is taken to be the same as the function name. For example

```
        DEFINE('DELETE(STRING,CHAR)')
```

could have the procedure

```
DELETE STRING CHAR   =            :S(DELETE)
       DELETE   =    STRING       :(RETURN)
```

A call of the function is illustrated in the following statements

```
        MAGIC    =    'ABRACADABRA'
        OUTPUT   =    DELETE(MAGIC,'A')
```

which print **BRCDBR**.

Arguments are passed by value and may be arbitrarily complex expressions. Thus the statement

```
        TEXT    =    DELETE(DELETE(INPUT,'.'),' ')
```

deletes all periods and blanks from the input string.

Functions can also fail under specified conditions. As an example, consider the following version of **DELETE**, which fails if **STRING** does not contain an occurrence of **CHAR**.

```
DELETE STRING    CHAR    =         :F(FRETURN)
D2     STRING    CHAR    =         :S(D2)
       DELETE   =    STRING        :(RETURN)
```

The transfer to the system label **FRETURN** indicates failure of the function call. Consequently,

```
        PUNCH    =    DELETE(INPUT,'*')
```

punches a card only if the input string contains an *****.

Arguments to a function and the value returned can be any type of data object. Consider, for example, the function **MAXNO** where **MAXNO(P,N)** returns a pattern that matches up to **N** adjacent strings matched by the pattern **P**. That is, if

```
        PAT    =    MAXNO('A' | 'B' | 'C' ,2)
```

then in the statement

```
        'EBCDIC'    PAT    'D'
```

the pattern match succeeds with **PAT** matching the string **BC**.

MAXNO has the defining statement

```
        DEFINE('MAXNO(P,N)')
```

and the procedure

```
MAXNO  N   =    GT(N,0) N - 1            :F(RETURN)
       MAXNO  =    NULL | P MAXNO         :(MAXNO)
```

Consider the function **REVERSE** that reverses a string. It has the defining statement

```
        DEFINE('REVERSE(STRING)','R1')
```

and the procedure

```
R1     ONECH   =    LEN(1) . CH
R2     STRING ONECH   =                :F(RETURN)
       REVERSE   =   CH REVERSE    :(R2)
```

There are two variables, **ONECH** and **CH**, used in the function definition in addition to the function name and formal argument. It is prudent to protect these variables so their use outside the function is not affected when the function is called. This is accomplished by declaring them to be local variables in the defining statement:

```
        DEFINE('REVERSE(STRING)ONECH,CH','R1')
```

When the function is called, the current values of the function name, the formal arguments, and the local variables are saved before the procedure is entered. These values are restored upon return from the procedure. This permits the programmer considerable freedom in defining functions. For example, a function can be recursive, i.e. include a call of the function itself. Consider the binomial coefficient $c(n,m)$ which can be defined by equations

```
    c(n,0)   =    1
    c(n,m)   =    n*c(n-1,m-1)/m        for m > 0
```

Computational efficiency can be improved by employing the relation

```
    c(n,m)   =    c(n,n-m)
```

for $m > n/2$.

The corresponding programmer-defined function consists of the defining statement

```
        DEFINE('C(N,M)')
```

and the procedure

```
C        M     =     LT(N - M,M) N - M
         C     =     EQ(M,0) 1                        :S(RETURN)
         C     =     N * C(N - 1,M - 1) / M           :(RETURN)
```

COMB is an example of another recursively defined function. **COMB(STR,N)** lists all combinations of **N** characters from the string **STR**. The defining statement and procedure are

```
        DEFINE('COMB(STR,N,HEAD)CH')
```

and

```
COMB     OUTPUT   =   EQ(N,0) HEAD                    :S(RETURN)
C2       STR LE(N,SIZE(STR)) LEN(1) . CH    =         :F(RETURN)
         COMB(STR,N - 1,HEAD CH)        :(C2)
```

Then

```
        COMB('ABCD',3)
```

prints

```
ABC
ABD
ACD
BCD
```

Notice that **COMB** is defined with three formal arguments but only two values are supplied in the initial call. The missing value is taken to be null.

1.11 Keywords

Several parameters and switches internal to the SNOBOL4 system can be accessed by means of keywords. Keywords are specified by prefixing an ampersand to certain identifiers. For example, if the value of the keyword &DUMP is a nonzero integer when a program terminates, a dump of natural variables is printed. Thus the execution of the statement

```
        &DUMP    =    1
```

indicates that a dump is to be produced.

Strings read in by **INPUT** are 80 characters long. Such strings often contain many unwanted trailing blanks. &TRIM is a keyword that controls the handling of trailing blanks on input of data. If the value of &TRIM is nonzero, trailing blanks are deleted. Thus

```
        &TRIM    =    1
```

causes trimming of trailing blanks. If &TRIM is zero, trailing blanks are not trimmed.

Other keywords are described elsewhere in this book.

1.12   Arrays

Arrays of variables can be created by using the primitive function **ARRAY**. The arguments of **ARRAY** describe the number of dimensions, the bounds of each dimension, and the initial value of each variable in the array. Thus

```
V   =   ARRAY(10,1.0)
```

creates and assigns to V a one-dimensional array of ten variables, each initialized to the real value 1.0. The created variables can be referenced by expressions of the form V<I> where I = 1,...,10. The statement

```
N   =   ARRAY('3,5')
```

creates a 2-dimensional array of variables

```
N<1,1>    N<1,2>    N<1,3>    N<1,4>    N<1,5>

N<2,1>       .         .         .         .

N<3,1>       .         .         .       N<3,5>
```

The omission of the second argument causes each of the variables to have the null string as initial value. The arguments in the call of **ARRAY** can be expressions. Thus

```
&TRIM    =    1
A   =   ARRAY(INPUT)
```

create an array with dimensionality that is data dependent. An array reference, A<I>, that is outside the bounds of the array causes failure that can be used to control program flow. The statements

```
        &TRIM    =    1
        I  =  1
        ST   =   ARRAY(INPUT)
MORE    ST<I>   =   INPUT                            :F(GO)
        I  =  I + 1                                  :(MORE)
GO
```

generate an array ST, and assign values to each of the variables. When all the variables in the array are assigned values, or an end of file is encountered, the transfer to GO is executed.

1.13   Tables

Sets of pairs of associated data objects can be created by the use of tables. A table is similar to a one-dimensional array. However, instead of referencing an element with an integer, any data object can be used.

A table is created by the primitive function **TABLE**. For example

        T   =   TABLE()

creates a table and assigns it as value of **T**.

Elements in the table can be assigned values in a manner similar to array elements. Examples are

        T<'A'>   =   5

and

        T<WORD>   =   T<WORD> + 1

Tables have varying lengths and are dynamically extended if necessary. Some efficiency can be achieved by specifying an estimate of the size of a table at the time it is created. **TABLE(N)** creates a table that initially has room for **N** entries.

1.14   Programmer-Defined Data Types

Integers, reals, strings, patterns, arrays, and tables are types of data objects that are built into the SNOBOL4 language. Facilities are provided in the language to permit a programmer to define additional types of data. This facilitates representation of structural relationships inherent in data.

For example, a simple linear linked list is made up of nodes, each containing a value field and a link field.

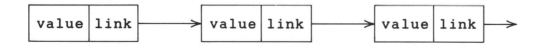

The primitive function **DATA** can be used to define the data type **NODE** and the two field functions, **VALUE** and **LINK**.

        DATA('NODE(VALUE,LINK)')

The statement

        P   =   NODE('S',)

creates a node with value field **S** and the null string in the link field. The value of **P** is a data object with two fields that can be referenced by means of the function calls **VALUE(P)** and **LINK(P)**. The insertion of a node with value **T** at the head of the list is accomplished by the statement

```
P  =  NODE('T',P)
```

The following statement deletes a node from the head of the list

```
P  =  LINK(P)
```

1.15 Program Format

A statement that is longer than one line can be continued onto successive lines by starting the continuation lines with a period or plus sign. An example is

```
    OUTPUT   =    'THE TOTAL NUMBER OF OCCURENCES IS  '
+   SUM<N>
```

Plus signs are used for continuation in examples in this book.

When continuing a statement over a line boundary, the statement may be broken wherever a blank is required.

Several statements may be placed on one line by using semicolons which indicate the ends of statements. An example is

```
    X  =  2;   Y  =  3;   Z  =  10
```

A line beginning with an asterisk is treated as a comment and does not affect the operation of the program.

1.16 Program Example

This is an example of a complete SNOBOL4 program illustrating the use of comment lines, continuation lines, and the end statement. The program reads in data cards that follow the end statement.

```
******************************************************************************
*                                                                            *
*        THIS PROGRAM COUNTS THE NUMBER OF TIMES EACH                         *
*        LETTER IS USED IN INPUT TEXT.                                        *
*                                                                            *
******************************************************************************
         &TRIM    =  1
         CHAR     =  LEN(1) . CH
         LETTERS  =  'ABCDEFGHIJKLMNOPQRSTUVWXYZ'
         COUNT    =  TABLE(30)
READ     OUTPUT   =  INPUT                          :F(DISPLAY)
```

```
          TEXT      =   OUTPUT
NEXT      TEXT      CHAR  =                                        :F(READ)
          COUNT<CH> =   COUNT<CH>   +   1                          :(NEXT)
DISPLAY   OUTPUT    =
LOOP      LETTERS   CHAR  =                                        :F(END)
          OUTPUT    = NE(COUNT<CH>)  CH  ' OCCURS ' COUNT<CH> ' TIMES'
+                                                                 :(LOOP)
END
```

The program output follows, indicating the text read in and the resulting letter count.

```
"THE WORLD OF THE FUTURE WILL BE AN EVER MORE DEMANDING STRUGGLE AGAINST
THE LIMITATIONS OF OUR INTELLIGENCE, ....",
N. WEINER


A OCCURS 5 TIMES
B OCCURS 1 TIMES
C OCCURS 1 TIMES
D OCCURS 3 TIMES
E OCCURS 15 TIMES
F OCCURS 3 TIMES
G OCCURS 5 TIMES
H OCCURS 3 TIMES
I OCCURS 9 TIMES
L OCCURS 7 TIMES
M OCCURS 3 TIMES
N OCCURS 9 TIMES
O OCCURS 6 TIMES
R OCCURS 7 TIMES
S OCCURS 3 TIMES
T OCCURS 9 TIMES
U OCCURS 4 TIMES
V OCCURS 1 TIMES
W OCCURS 3 TIMES
```

1.17   Conclusion

This chapter has presented only an introduction to the main features of SNOBOL4. Detailed descriptions of many features are postponed to subsequent chapters, which provide a guide for the programmer.

Chapter 2, the longest and most involved, describes pattern matching. Primitive functions, predicates, and operators are considered in Chapter 3. Programmer-defined functions are covered in Chapter 4. Arrays, tables, and programmer-defined data types are described in Chapter 5. Chapter 6 discusses keywords and introduces names and code. Chapter 7 contains information on types of data and data type conversion. Tracing facilities are described in Chapter 8, and Chapter 9 covers input and output. The execution of a SNOBOL4 program, including error messages and error control are the subject of Chapter 10. Finally, Chapter 11 discusses matters of efficient programming and related topics.

In addition to numerous examples included in the text, exercises are provided at the ends of chapters.

Appendices at the end of this book provide additional detailed material. Appendix A contains a complete description of the syntax of SNOBOL4. Appendix B describes the differences between Versions 2 and 3 of SNOBOL4. Appendix C illustrates the use of SNOBOL4 in more complicated programs. Appendix D contains solutions to the exercises given at the ends of the chapters.

Exercises

Problem 1.1: Write a program that reads in data cards, prints all cards read in, and punches out a copy of all cards that do not contain an ampersand.

Problem 1.2: Write a program that deletes the first eight characters from each 80-character input card and prints the remainder of the card.

Problem 1.3: Compute and print out the first ten powers of *e* and their sum.

Problem 1.4: Write a program that encodes messages by some simple character replacement (for example, replace **A** by **Z** , **B** by **Y** , etc.). Include punctuation in the encoding.

Problem 1.5: Write a program that reads a deck of cards into an array. Let the first card indicate the number of cards that follow. Print out the cards in reverse order.

Problem 1.6: Hexadecimal digits 0,1,...,9,A,B,C,D,E,F have the decimal equivalents of 0,1,...,15. Using a table to associate hexadecimal digits with corresponding decimal equivalents, define a function that converts a string of hexadecimal characters to its decimal equivalent.

Problem 1.7: Let a binary tree be a data structure composed of nodes that contain three fields: value, left son, right son. A tree has a distinguished node, the root, that is not the left son or right son of any node.

a. Define a data type **BNODE** with fields appropriate for a binary tree.

b. Generate a binary tree with three nodes such that the value of the root node is **+** , the value of the left son is **X** , and the value of the right son is **Y** .

c. Define a function **LLIST** that prints the values of the nodes of a binary tree in the following order.

1. value of the root
2. value of the nodes in the left subtree
3. value of the nodes in the right subtree

CHAPTER 2

Pattern Matching

2.1 Introduction

Strings of characters can be synthesized from smaller strings by concatenation. The converse of synthesis, decomposition of strings into substrings, is performed using pattern matching. Fundamentally, pattern matching is the process of examining a subject string for a substring which is one of a set specified by a pattern. The substring and parts thereof, formed by pattern matching, can be assigned as the values of variables.

There are two types of statements in which pattern matching can occur: the pattern matching statement and the replacement statement. These statements have the respective forms

label   subject   pattern   goto
label   subject   pattern   =   object   goto

The pattern and object may be expressions, as illustrated by

```
LAB1        TEXT        A | B                                :S(LAB2)F(LAB3)
LAB4        STR         C D            =    X '3'            :S(LAB5)F(LAB6)
```

Before matching actually occurs, the expression in the pattern field is evaluated. Its value can be a string. It also can be a pattern structure, which may be thought of as a set of strings. The string or pattern structure is used to drive a pattern matching procedure (the scanner) which performs the actual matching. Should any string specified by the pattern field appear as a substring of the subject, pattern matching succeeds.

The primary purpose of this chapter is to consider in detail those SNOBOL4 language features that programmers may use to write expressions that, when evaluated, yield pattern structures. These features include the pattern-building operations of concatenation and alternation, primitive pattern structures built into the system, primitive functions whose values are pattern structures, value assignment operations, and the unary operator *, which produces an unevaluated expression.

Pattern structures representing sets of fixed strings such as those built by

```
BASE  =  'BINARY'  |  'DECIMAL'  |  'HEX'
SCALE  =  'FIXED'  |  'FLOAT'
ATTRIBUTE  =  SCALE BASE
```

are basic to pattern matching. Additional language features provide natural ways to talk about more complicated sets of strings, such as:

all strings of a specified length,
all characters up to the first comma,
the longest string of blanks,
any number of repetitions of a string,
any string balanced with respect to parentheses, and
any string at all.

For many users of SNOBOL4, a knowledge of how patterns are actually matched is of little importance. The success or failure of matching is all that matters. However, by understanding the scanning procedure, a programmer can write more efficient patterns and make use of features such as immediate value assignment and unevaluated expressions that can actually change a pattern during matching. Thus, the secondary purpose of this chapter is to describe how the scanner works.

2.2 Alternation and Concatenation

A brief introduction to the pattern building operations of alternation and concatenation appears in Chapter 1. There, alternation and concatenation are used to build pattern structures that match sets of strings.

Alternation, indicated by the binary operator |, builds a single pattern structure from its two arguments. If P1 and P2 are strings or pattern structures, the statement

        P3 = P1 | P2

builds a new structure and assigns it as the value of P3. P3 matches any string matched by P1 or P2.

No explicit operator is used to indicate concatenation. Concatenation is implied when two elements of an expression are separated by one or more blanks. If P4 and P5 are strings, the statement

        P6 = P4 P5

assigns to P6 a string which is the value of P4 followed by the value of P5. If either P4 or P5 is a pattern structure, the statement above builds a pattern structure and assigns it as the value of P6. P6 matches any string that can be formed from a string matched by P4, followed by a string matched by P5.

Alternation and concatenation can be used to build pattern structures that match large numbers of strings. Consider the following statements.

```
P  =  'BE'  |  'BEA'  |  'BEAR'
Q  =  'RO'  |  'ROO'  |  'ROOS'
R  =  'DS'  |  'D'
S  =  'TS'  |  'T'
PAT  =  P  R  |  Q  S
```

Concatenation has higher precedence than alternation, so the structure for **PAT** is built as if

```
PAT  =  (P  R)  |  (Q  S)
```

had been written. **PAT** matches any of the twelve strings:

BEDS	ROTS
BED	ROT
BEADS	ROOTS
BEAD	ROOT
BEARDS	ROOSTS
BEARD	ROOST

2.3 Scanning

Matching a pattern structure against a subject string is done by a procedure called the scanner. The pattern structure behaves like a program that indicates to the scanner how to examine the subject string.

At any instant during scanning, the scanner uses two pieces of information:

(1) where in the subject string it should be looking, and
(2) what component of the pattern structure it should match.

The scanner has a pointer called the cursor which is positioned to the left of the character that the scanner must match. A second pointer called the needle points at the component to be matched.

Consider the following example, in which the string of characters **READS** is matched by a pattern structure that is the value of **BR**.

```
BR  =  ('B'  |  'R')  ('E'  |  'EA')  ('D'  |  'DS')
'READS'  BR
```

For illustrative purposes, it is convenient to think of components of a pattern structure as a set of beads that the scanner is trying to thread using the needle. A bead diagram representing **BR** is shown below.

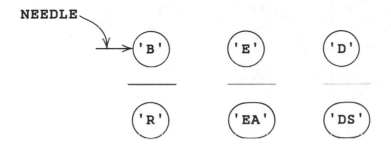

In bead diagrams, left-to-right order of concatenation is preserved. Alternation is represented top to bottom. The needle points at the bead that the scanner is currently trying to match. If a bead matches, the needle passes through and moves upward as far as it can go without crossing a horizontal line. If a bead does not match, the needle moves down to an alternative bead, provided one exists. Downward movement may not cross a horizontal line. If no alternative exists, the needle is pulled back through the last successfully matched bead, and an alternative is sought there.

The following figure illustrates the steps in matching **BR** against **READS**. The arrow pointing at **READS** represents the cursor, while the arrow pointing at the beads represents the needle. Failure in the fifth step causes the needle to be pulled back. The cursor is moved back at the same time.

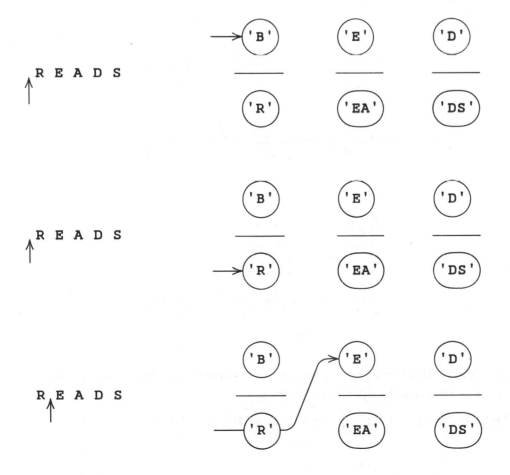

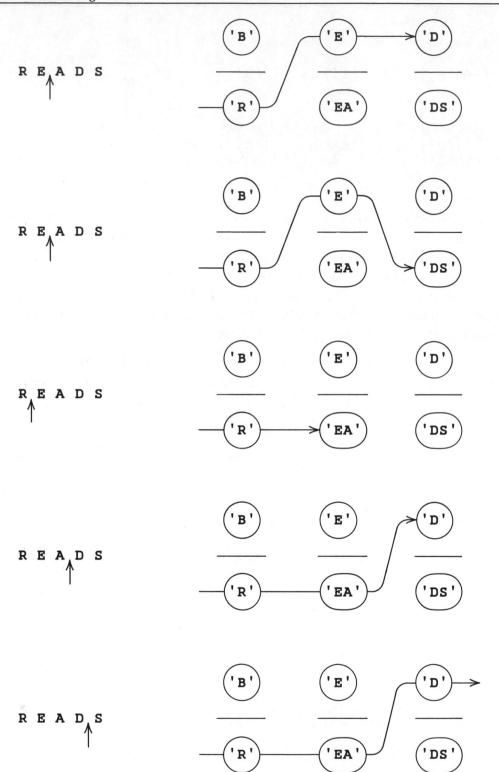

Bead diagrams graphically illustrate one important control that the programmer has over the scanner. In a pattern-valued expression such as

BR = ('B' | 'R') ('E' | 'EA') ('D' | 'DS')

alternatives are matched by the scanner in left-to-right order (top to bottom in the bead diagram). Thus, the scanner attempts to match **B** before **R**, **E** before **EA**, and **D** before **DS**. By positioning alternatives correctly a programmer can control the order in which the scanner looks at them.

The bead diagram for the pattern structure **PAT** developed in the previous section follows.

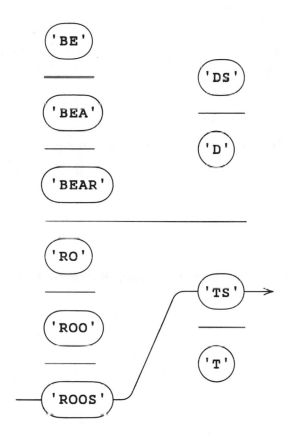

A successful match in the statement

        'ROOSTS'   **PAT**

requires eleven steps.

2.4   Modes of Scanning

Two keywords, **&ANCHOR** and **&FULLSCAN**, give the programmer additional control over the scanner. The scanner operates in an unanchored or anchored mode, depending on the value of **&ANCHOR**. When unanchored, a pattern can match anywhere in the subject string. When anchored, a pattern can match only beginning at the first character.

For efficiency, tests are made during scanning to prevent the scanner from looking at alternatives that cannot possibly succeed. &FULLSCAN can be used to turn these tests off, leading to complete, but possibly inefficient, pattern matching. Discussion of &FULLSCAN is deferred until the end of this chapter, since it is useful only with more sophisticated patterns.

2.4.1   Unanchored Mode

The keyword &ANCHOR initially has the value zero, signifying the unanchored mode of scanning. The scanner may look anywhere in the subject string for an appropriate substring. Consider the following example.

    'A BIG BOY'   'BIG' | 'LITTLE'

Pattern matching succeeds. The steps involved are shown below using a bead diagram.

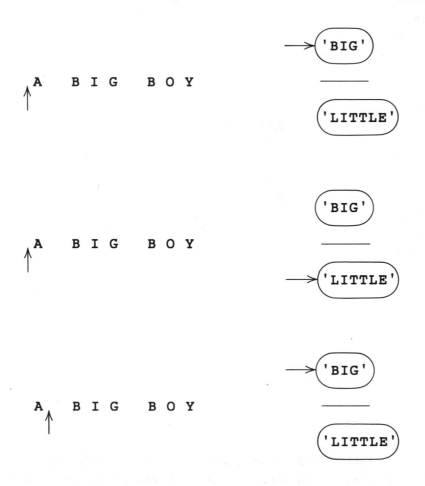

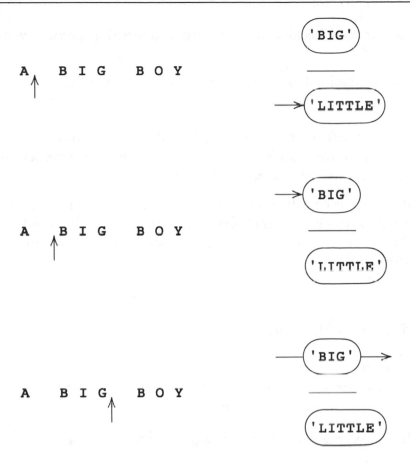

The cursor is initially at the left of the subject string. When all possible alternatives fail, the cursor is moved one character to the right. All possible alternatives are tried with the cursor beginning in the new position. Again, all alternatives fail. The cursor is moved again and this time the first alternative succeeds.

In the unanchored mode, the origin of pattern matching is moved by changing the initial position of the cursor. Thus, the scanner matches, if possible, a substring anywhere in the subject string. If more than one valid substring exists, the scanner finds the leftmost one.

2.4.2 Anchored Mode

Frequently it is necessary to know if a pattern matches when its origin is at the first character of the subject string. As an example, suppose a program is desired that reads any SNOBOL4 program and prints only those lines that are not comments (i.e. do not have * in column 1). At first glance, the following statements might seem to suffice.

```
BEGIN   LINE   =   INPUT                              :F(END)
        LINE   '*'                                    :S(BEGIN)
        OUTPUT   =   LINE                              :(BEGIN)
END
```

This program does not work as intended because a card with * appearing anywhere at all in it is rejected.

If &ANCHOR has a nonzero value obtained by executing a statement such as

    &ANCHOR = 1

the pattern match is anchored at the left of the subject string. When the scanner is in the anchored mode, the initial position of the cursor is not moved. Thus the scanner, when anchored, only matches * against the first character of LINE.

The anchored mode of scanning is generally more efficient than the unanchored mode, since the scanner examines fewer possibilities. Anchored scanning should be used where possible. It is, of course, possible to switch modes during execution of a program simply by changing the value of &ANCHOR.

2.5   Value Assignment through Pattern Matching

Pattern matching may be viewed as a means of decomposing a string into substrings. To be useful, a substring found by the scanner often must be assigned as the value of a variable. Consider the pattern BR used in an earlier section.

    BR = ('B' | 'R') ('E' | 'EA') ('D' | 'DS')

Used in a pattern matching statement such as

    STR BR   :S(L1)F(L2)

where the subject string may be anything, success of matching indicates only that one of the valid strings appears somewhere in STR. It does not indicate which string matches or where it matches. On failure, no indication is given of how nearly successful the scanner was. There are two ways of assigning a substring found by the scanner to a variable: conditional value assignment and immediate value assignment.

2.5.1   Conditional Value Assignment

The binary operator . is used to indicate conditional value assignment. The value of the expression

        P . V

is a pattern in which V is associated with the pattern P. This pattern is the same as P, except that upon successful completion of pattern matching, the substring matched by P is assigned as the value of the variable V. Thus, by associating several variables with portions of a pattern, it is possible to ascertain what the overall pattern matches, and also which components of the pattern are used in the match. For example, rewriting BR as

    BR = (('B' | 'R') ('E' | 'EA') ('D' | 'DS')) . BRVAL

associates the variable **BRVAL** with the entire pattern. On successful completion of matching, the entire substring matched is assigned as value of **BRVAL**. Rewriting still further, variables can be associated with pieces of the pattern.

```
      BR  =  (('B' | 'R') . FIRST  ('E' | 'EA') . SECOND
+              ('D' | 'DS') . THIRD) . BRVAL
```

A successful match causes the entire substring to be assigned as the value of **BRVAL**. **B** or **R** becomes the value of **FIRST**, **E** or **EA** becomes the value of **SECOND**, and **D** or **DS** becomes the value of **THIRD**. Failure to match leaves the values of all variables unchanged.

2.5.2 Immediate Value Assignment

The binary operator **$** signifies immediate value assignment. The expression

```
        P   $   V
```

associates a variable **V** with a pattern **P** so that whenever **P** matches a substring, the substring immediately becomes the new value of **V**. It is possible, by using **$**, to associate variables with parts of a large pattern, to see how far scanning progressed in the event of failure. Value assignment is done for those parts of the pattern that match, even if the overall match fails. Suppose **BR** is rewritten using **$** instead of . where shown.

```
      BR  =  (('B' | 'R') $ FIRST  ('E' | 'EA') $ SECOND
+              ('D' | 'DS') $ THIRD) . BRVAL
```

In the following statement, pattern matching fails.

```
      'BEATS'   BR                                    :S(L1)F(L2)
```

However, since immediate assignment is performed whenever the associated part of the pattern matches, the following assignments are made.

```
      FIRST  =  'B'
      SECOND =  'E'
      SECOND =  'EA'
```

Values of **THIRD** and **BRVAL** are unchanged. If conditional assignment is used, values of all four variables are unchanged. In the following example, the pattern matches.

```
      'BREADS'   BR                                   :S(L1)F(L2)
```

Values assigned both during and after scanning are:

```
      FIRST  =  'B'
      FIRST  =  'R'
      SECOND =  'E'
      SECOND =  'EA'
      THIRD  =  'D'
      BRVAL  =  'READ'
```

The outcome is the same as if conditional value assignment had been used. Immediate value assignment is less efficient in this case because two redundant assignments are made. As a general rule, conditional value assignment should be used whenever possible. Immediate value assignment should be used only in those cases where intermediate results are important.

2.5.3   Precedence

The operators **.** and **$** have the same precedence and associate to the left. They have higher precedence than alternation and concatenation. Thus, in the statement

```
    BR  =  (('B' | 'R') $ FIRST  ('E' | 'EA') $ SECOND
+          ('D' | 'DS') $ THIRD) . BRVAL
```

the outer parentheses are required to associate **BRVAL** with the entire pattern, while additional parentheses are not required to associate **FIRST**, **SECOND**, and **THIRD**.

2.5.4   Association with the Variable OUTPUT

Since **OUTPUT** is a variable, it may be associated with any portion of a pattern. A successful match involving the pattern

```
    ('BED' | 'BUG' | 'BOMB')  .  OUTPUT
```

causes the successful alternative to be printed. Using **$** to associate **OUTPUT** with several parts of a pattern achieves the effect of tracing the progress of the scanner. By constructing **BR** as

```
    BR  =  ('B' | 'R') $ OUTPUT  ('E' | 'EA') $ OUTPUT
+          ('D' | 'DS') $ OUTPUT
```

the output resulting from execution of the statement

```
    'READS'  BR                                    :S(L1)F(L2)
```

is

```
R
E
EA
D
```

2.5.5   Value Assignment in Replacement Statements

Value assignment is a necessity in some kinds of replacement statements. In the following replacement statement **E** or **EA** is replaced with **I** only if the overall pattern **BR** matches. In effect, the replacement statement changes **BED** and **BEAD** into **BID**, **BEDS** and **BEADS** into **BIDS**, etc.

```
BR  -  ('B' | 'R') . FIRST  ('E' | 'EA')  ('D' | 'DS') . LAST
STR  BR  =  FIRST  'I'  LAST
```

The replacement statement works properly because conditional assignment is done after pattern matching, but before the object expression is evaluated.

2.5.6   Association of Several Variables with One Pattern

Earlier examples illustrated how variable association may be nested. It is also possible to associate more than one variable with a single pattern structure. The statement

```
PAT  =  P1 $ V1 . V2
```

builds a pattern structure where variables **V1** and **V2** are both associated with the pattern **P1**, **V1** as immediate assignment and **V2** as conditional assignment. Changing the order of association to

```
PAT  =  P1 . V2 $ V1
```

has no effect on the value assignment. If **PAT** is involved in a successful pattern match, **V1** and **V2** are assigned the same value. If the pattern match fails, the value of **V1** might be changed but the value of **V2** is not.

2.6   The Null String in Pattern Matching

The null string is the string of zero length. Attempts by the scanner to match the null string always succeed. The variable **NULL** has the null string as its initial value and, by convention, is used in this chapter to represent the null pattern that matches a string of zero length. Pattern matching in the statement

```
STR  NULL                                    :S(ON)F(ERROR)
```

always succeeds, even if **STR** itself has the null string as value.

The variable **NULL** is frequently used in more complex patterns. For example, a pattern that matches the eight strings

```
C            BC
D            BD
AC           ABC
AD           ABD
```

can be written as

    (NULL | 'A') (NULL | 'B') ('C' | 'D')

Matching a pattern of the form

    NULL $ X $ Y PAT

sets the values of X and Y to the null string before matching of PAT begins.

A number of patterns described in this chapter match the null string. Where bead diagram representations of the patterns are given, NULL is used to indicate the null string.

2.7 Cursor Position

The unary operator ə is called the cursor position operator. Its operand is a variable. The value of əX is a pattern structure that matches the null string and assigns the current cursor position as an integer value of the variable X. Assignment of the cursor postion to the operand of the ə operator takes place as immediate value assignment. Value is assigned when the cursor position operator is encountered during pattern matching, not following successful completion.

Execution of the following statements assigns the integers 0, 1, 2, 3, 4, and finally 5 to the variable HEAD.

    &ANCHOR = 0
    'TEST AT OPERATOR' əHEAD 'AT'

Pattern matching succeeds when the cursor is initially positioned to the left of the AT. The cursor position at this point is 5, the final value assigned to HEAD.

The following program reads a collection of input strings one at a time, prints them, matches for a pattern, and underlines the substrings matched. The cursor position operator is used to locate the beginning and end of the matched substring. From the cursor positions a second line is constructed, consisting of dashes in the position of the matched substring.

```
        &TRIM  =  1
        P  =  ('B' | 'R') ('E' | 'EA') ('D' | 'DS')
        PATTERN  =  əX  P  əY
LOOP    OUTPUT  =  INPUT                             :F(END)
        OUTPUT  PATTERN                             :F(NOPAT)
        OUTPUT  =  DUPL(' ',X)  DUPL('-',Y - X)
BLLINE  OUTPUT  =                                   :(LOOP)
NOPAT   OUTPUT  =  'P FAILED TO MATCH.'             :(BLLINE)
END
```

For the input data

```
THE BEADS ARE RED.
BRED AND BORED.
BEAUTY AND THE BEAST.
```

the program output is

```
THE BEADS ARE RED.
    ----


BRED AND BORED.
  ---


BEAUTY AND THE BEAST.
P FAILED TO MATCH.
```

2.8 LEN

LEN(integer) is a primitive function whose value is a pattern structure that matches any string of the specified length. The argument of LEN must have a nonnegative integer value when pattern matching is performed. In the following example, pattern matching succeeds only if the subject STR has in it somewhere an open parenthesis separated from a closed parenthesis by exactly five characters.

```
        STR   '('  LEN(5)  ')'                          :S(L1)F(L2)
```

LEN can be used to break out fixed-length fields from strings. In the following example dates from data cards such as

```
1290 SEP. 27 CHINA, CHIHLI              100,000
1293 MAY  20 JAPAN, KAMARKURA            30,000
1531 JAN. 26 PORTUGAL, LISBON            30,000
```

are reformatted as

```
SEP. 27, 1290    CHINA, CHIHLI              100,000
MAY  20, 1293    JAPAN, KAMARKURA            30,000
JAN. 26, 1531    PORTUGAL, LISBON            30,000
```

A program that performs this transformation is

```
        &ANCHOR  =   1
        DATE  =  LEN(4) . YR ' ' LEN(4) . MO  ' '  LEN(2) . DAY
LOOP    CARD  =   INPUT                              :F(END)
        CARD  DATE  =  MO ' ' DAY ', ' YR ' '        :F(NOGOOD)
        OUTPUT  =  CARD                              :(LOOP)
NOGOOD OUTPUT  =  CARD '  IMPROPERLY FORMATTED.'     :(LOOP)
END
```

LEN is used to match the various pieces of the data, assigning the strings found to the variables YR, MO, and DAY. YR, MO, and DAY are assigned values after pattern matching but before the entire substring matched by DATE is replaced. Only the date portion of CARD is reformatted.

2.9 SPAN and BREAK

SPAN and BREAK are primitive functions whose values are pattern structures that match runs of characters. Patterns described by

    a run of blanks,
    a string of digits, and
    a word (run of letters)

can be formed using SPAN as

```
SPAN(' ')
SPAN('0123456789')
SPAN('ABCDEFGHIJKLMNOPQRSTUVWXYZ')
```

Patterns described by

    everything up to the next blank,
    everything up to the next punctuation mark, and
    everything up to the next number,

can be formed using BREAK as

```
BREAK(' ')
BREAK(',.;:!?')
BREAK('+-0123456789')
```

Arguments of BREAK and SPAN must be nonnull strings when pattern matching is performed.

The pattern structure for SPAN matches the longest string beginning at the cursor that consists solely of characters appearing in the argument. SPAN may be thought of as streaming from the cursor until a character not included in the argument is found. SPAN must match at least one character, or it fails.

BREAK generates a pattern structure that matches the longest string beginning at the cursor that does not contain a character of the argument. Thus, regarding its argument as a list of 'break' characters, BREAK streams from the cursor up to, but not including, the first break character. BREAK must find a break character, or it fails. If the cursor is positioned immediately to the left of a break character, BREAK matches the null string.

A bead diagram for the statement

```
'IT RUNS.'      BREAK(' ') SPAN(' ') BREAK('.') '.'
```

illustrates how the cursor is moved by **SPAN** and **BREAK**.

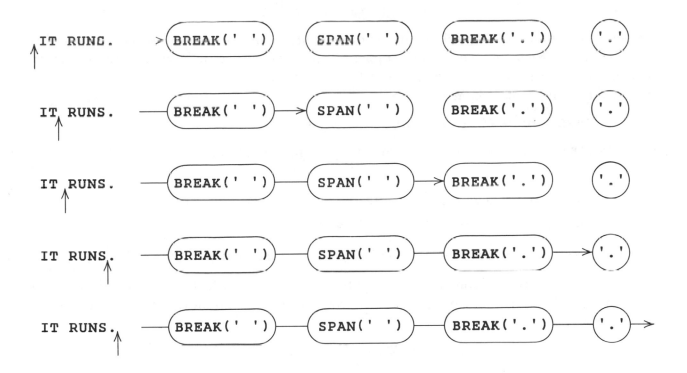

The next program illustrates the use of both **BREAK** and **SPAN**. It compresses tabulated data, leaving fields separated by single colons rather than an arbitrary number of blanks. For example, if the input is

```
ACTINIUM      AC    89    227*        1899    DEBIERNE
ALUMINUM      AL    13     26.9815    1825    OERSTED
AMERICIUM     AM    95    243*        1944    SEABORG
ANTIMONY      SB    51    121.75      1450    VALENTINE
```

the output is

```
ACTINIUM:AC:89:227*:1899:DEBIERNE
ALUMINUM:AL:13:26.9815:1825:OERSTED
AMERICIUM:AM:95:243*:1944:SEABORG
ANTIMONY:SB:51:121.75:1450:VALENTINE
```

A program that performs this transformation is

```
        &ANCHOR  =  1;    &TRIM   =    1
        FIELD  =  BREAK(' ') . CHARS  SPAN(' ')
LOOP    CARD  =   INPUT                              :F(END)
INLOOP  CARD  FIELD  =   CHARS  ':'                  :S(INLOOP)
        PUNCH  =  CARD                               :(LOOP)
END
```

Each input card is repeatedly examined for a run of blanks, and the blanks are replaced by a colon. When blanks no longer exist, the compression is complete and a new card is punched.

Some care must be exercised in using **BREAK**, since it does not match the break character that stops the streaming. Suppose a program is wanted which restores, to some degree, the compressed data generated above. Each field of the compressed data can be broken out using a statement such as

```
    CARD  BREAK(':') . FLD  ':'  =
```

Since **BREAK(':')** does not 'consume' the colon, the literal is included to remove the break character.

SPAN never matches a string shorter than the maximum span. For example,

```
    '9824761.'  SPAN('0123456789')  '6'
```

cannot succeed since **SPAN** always matches up to the decimal point.

In the event that components of the pattern beyond **BREAK** fail, **BREAK** does not skip over the break character to continue streaming. In the anchored mode the following statement never succeeds.

```
    '123,427,642.00'  BREAK('.,')  LEN(1)  '0'
```

BREAK('.,') matches **123** and that is all. Similarly, **SPAN** does not skip over a matched span of characters if components of the pattern beyond **SPAN** fail.

2.10 ANY and NOTANY

ANY(string) and **NOTANY(string)** are primitive functions whose values are pattern structures that match single characters. **ANY** matches any character appearing in its argument. **NOTANY** matches any character not appearing in its argument. Thus, the pattern structure for **ANY('AEIOU')** matches any vowel. The pattern for **NOTANY('AEIOU')** matches any character that is not a vowel. Arguments of **ANY** and **NOTANY** must be nonnull strings when pattern matching is performed.

ANY and **NOTANY** are fast ways of looking for one of a set of single characters. For example,

```
    ANY('AEIOU')
```

is preferable to

```
    'A' | 'E' | 'I' | 'O' | 'U'
```

The call

```
    NOTANY('STRUCTURE')
```

is valid even though the characters **T**, **R**, and **U** appear twice. The order of characters is irrelevant. **NOTANY('CERSTU')** is equivalent to **NOTANY('STRUCTURE')**.

A complete syntactic recognizer for SNOBOL4 statements is included in Appendix C. **ANY** is used in patterns to recognize several of the syntactic elements.

Identifiers begin with a letter which may be followed by any number of letters, digits, periods, and underscores. A binary operator is one or more blanks (for concatenation) or a binary symbol surrounded by blanks. A label begins with a letter or digit which may be followed by anything up to a blank or semicolon.

If the following assignments are made

```
OPSYMS   =   '+-*/.$&@|?¬#%!'
LETTERS  =   'ABCDEFGHIJKLMNOPQRSTUVWXYZ'
DIGITS   =   '0123456789'
ALPHANUMERICS   =   LETTERS   DIGITS
```

patterns to recognize identifiers, binary symbols, binary operators, and labels are

```
IDENTIFIER  =   ANY(LETTERS) (NULL | SPAN(ALPHANUMERICS '._'))
BINARYSYM   =   ANY(OPSYMS)  |  '**'
BINARYOP  =  SPAN(' ')  (NULL | BINARYSYM SPAN(' '))
LABEL   —   ANY(ALPHANUMERICS)  BREAK('; ')
```

2.11   TAB, RTAB, and REM

TAB(integer) and **RTAB(integer)** are primitive functions whose values are pattern structures that match all characters from the current cursor position up to a specific point in the subject string. **TAB(N)** matches up through the **N**th character of the subject string. **RTAB(N)** matches up to but not including the **N**th character from the right end of the subject string. Stated another way, **TAB(N)** insures that **N** characters are matched by positioning the cursor to the right of the **N**th character. **RTAB(N)** insures that all but **N** characters are matched by positioning the cursor to the left of the **N**th character from the end. For example, in the statement

```
'SNOBOL4'  LEN(2)  TAB(6)
```

the pattern matches the substring **SNOBOL** with **TAB(6)** matching **OBOL**. In a similar statement,

```
'SNOBOL4'  LEN(2)  RTAB(1)
```

the substring **SNOBOL** is once again matched with **RTAB(1)** matching **OBOL**.

RTAB(0) is particularly useful for matching everything to the end of the subject string. For convenience, the variable **REM** has as its initial value the pattern structure for **RTAB(0)**. Thus, the pattern

```
LAST8   =   RTAB(8)  REM . L8
```

matches the entire subject and assigns the last eight characters as the value of **L8**.

TAB and **RTAB** require integer arguments when pattern matching is performed. If the argument of **TAB** or **RTAB** is negative, a program error occurs. An argument that would require moving the cursor left causes failure. The statement

```
STR  LEN(5)  TAB(4)
```

fails because the cursor cannot be moved back by **TAB(4)**.

TAB and **RTAB** are particularly valuable in breaking fields out of structured data. The following data is part of the 1964 list of congressmen from New Jersey.

```
   Column 4                  Column 30   Column 36
       ↓                         ↓           ↓
 1 WILLIAM T. CAHILL            REP       COLLINGSWOOD
 2 THOMAS C. MCGRATH, JR.       DEM       MARGATE CITY
 3 JAMES J. HOWARD              DEM       WALL
        .
        .
        .
14 DOMINICK V. DANIELS          DEM       JERSEY CITY
15 EDWARD J. PATTEN             DEM       PERTH AMBOY
```

Suppose a new deck of cards is desired, listing only the names left justified at column 1, and the post office address right justified at column 44. The following program reads the cards, breaks out the **NAME** and **PO** fields, formats and punches a new deck.

```
        &ANCHOR = 1;   &TRIM  =  1
        NAMEANDPO = TAB(3) (TAB(29) . NAME) TAB(35) (REM . PO)
LOOP    CARD = INPUT                               :F(END)
        CARD NAMEANDPO                             :F(ERROR)
        NAME = TRIM(NAME)
        OUTPUT = NAME DUPL(' ',44 - (SIZE(NAME) + SIZE(PO)))  PO
        PUNCH = OUTPUT                             :(LOOP)
END
```

Fields are broken out of the input cards using the pattern **NAMEANDPO**. The **NAME** field has trailing blanks that are trimmed before the output line is formatted. The post office address is obtained using **REM** and does not have trailing blanks since the input card was initially trimmed. **DUPL** is used to insert the proper number of padding blanks between **NAME** and **PO** on output. Output from the program is

```
WILLIAM T. CAHILL               COLLINGSWOOD
THOMAS C. MCGRATH, JR.          MARGATE CITY
JAMES J. HOWARD                         WALL
        .
        .
        .
DOMINICK V. DANIELS             JERSEY CITY
EDWARD J. PATTEN                PERTH AMBOY
```

A bead diagram illustrating the match of **NAMEANDPO** and the first data card is shown below.

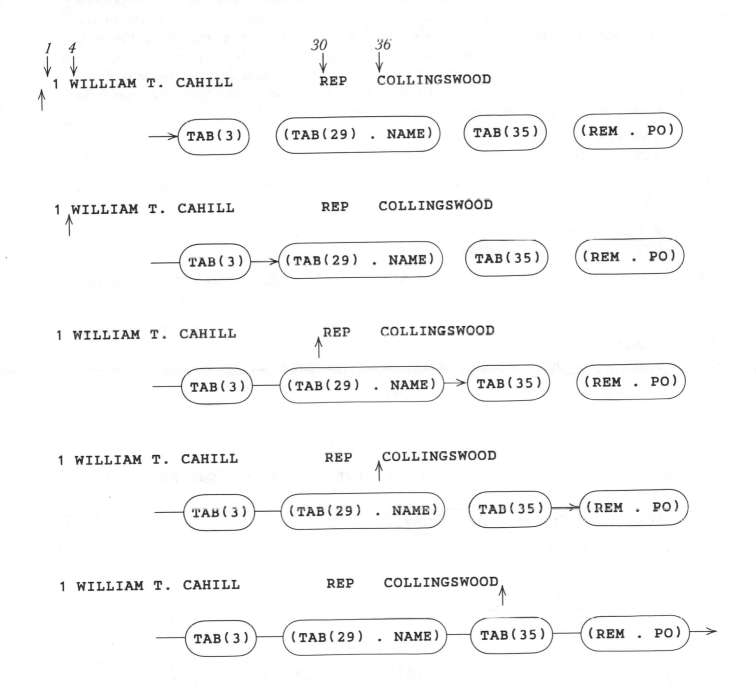

2.12 POS and RPOS

POS(integer) and RPOS(integer) are primitive functions whose values are pattern structures. These pattern structures match the null string if the cursor is at a point in the subject string specified by the integer argument. POS(N) succeeds, matching the null string, only if the cursor is positioned just at the right of the Nth character. RPOS(N) succeeds, matching the null string, only if the cursor is positioned just at the left of the Nth character from the end of the subject string. POS and RPOS never cause the cursor to be moved; they test its position. For example, in the statements

```
        &ANCHOR  =   1
        STR  SPAN(' ')  POS(7)
```

pattern matching succeeds only if the first seven characters are blanks and the eighth is not a blank. In the following example,

```
        &ANCHOR  =   1
        STR  SPAN(' ')  RPOS(7)
```

pattern matching succeeds only if the seventh character from the end of STR is nonblank and everything preceeding it is blank.

POS(0) is a pattern that succeeds only if the cursor is at the left of the subject string. RPOS(0) succeeds only if the cursor is at the right of the subject string. POS(0) and RPOS(0) can serve as left and right anchors for any pattern P, as in

```
        ENTIRE  =  POS(0)  P  RPOS(0)
```

In the statement

```
        STR  ENTIRE
```

pattern matching succeeds only if P matches all of STR. If, at the time ENTIRE is built, P has the value

```
        'CAR'  |  'CART'  |  'CARTE'
```

Matching in the statement

```
        'CARTE'  ENTIRE
```

is illustrated by the bead diagram:

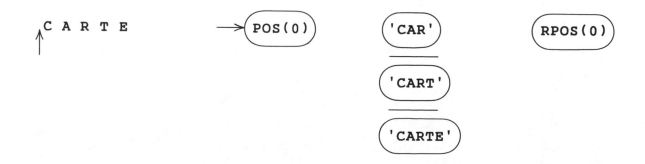

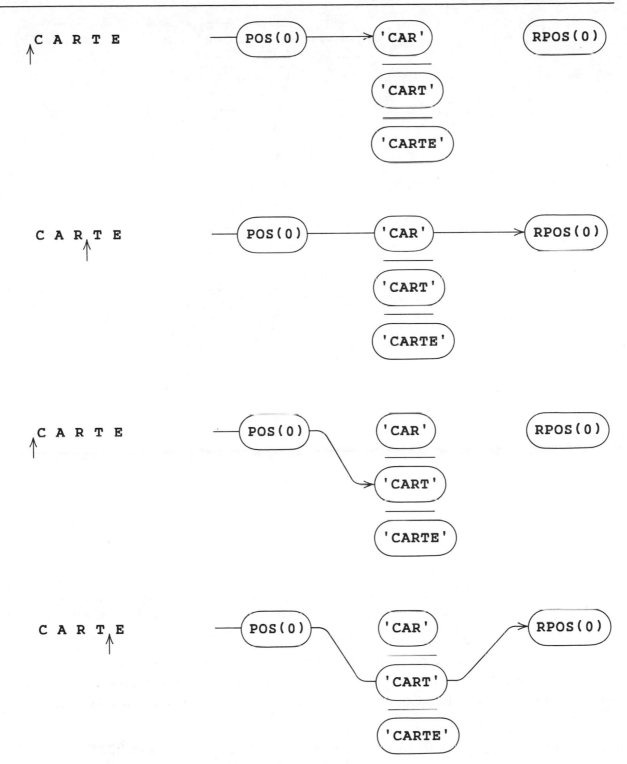

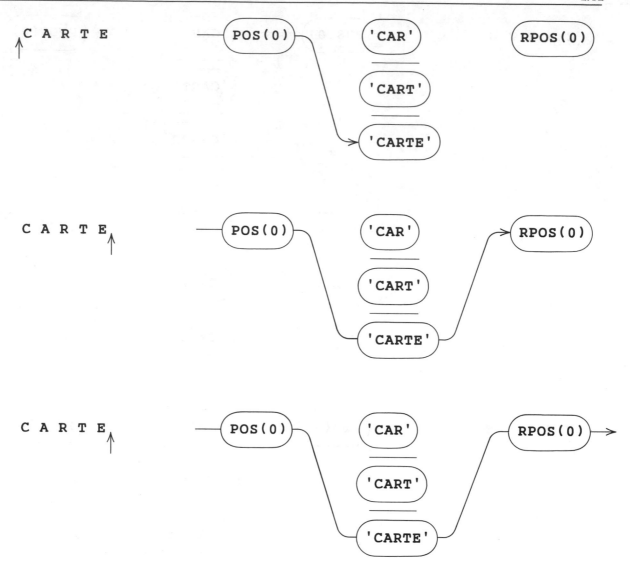

Arguments for **POS** and **RPOS** must have nonnegative integer values when pattern matching is performed. Negative or noninteger arguments cause a program error.

The following program uses **POS**, **RPOS**, **SPAN**, and **BREAK** to list cards that do not conform to a specified format. Cards, to be valid, must have four columns of data right justified at columns 10, 20, 30, and 40. Data in any field must contain no more than nine nonblank characters.

SPAN and **BREAK** are used to locate fields on a card while **POS** and **RPOS** verify the location of the fields. A number indicating the position of an invalid card in the input deck is concatenated onto the front of an invalid card before printing.

```
       &ANCHOR  =   1
       FIELD   =   SPAN(' ')  BREAK(' ')
       FORMAT  =   POS(0) FIELD POS(10) FIELD POS(20) FIELD
+                  POS(30) FIELD POS(40) SPAN(' ') RPOS(0)
       OUTPUT  =   'CARDS WITH IMPROPER FORMAT ARE:'
```

```
         OUTPUT  =
LOOP    N  =  N + 1
         CARD  =   INPUT                               :F(END)
         CARD  FORMAT                                  :S(LOOP)
         OUTPUT =  '#' N DUPL(' ',3 - SIZE(N)) CARD    :(LOOP)
END
```

Input supplied to the program for test purposes is

```
XXXXXXXX    XXXXXX    XXXX      X
            XXXXXX    XXXX      X
XXXXXXXXX   XXXXXX    XXXX      X
XXXXXXXXX             XXXX      X
XXXXXXXXX   XXXXXX    XXXX      X
XXXXXXXXX   XXXXXX    XXXX
XXXXXXXXX   XXXXXX    XXXX      X
XXXXXXXXX   XXXXXX    XXXX      XX
XXXXXXXXX   XXXXXX    XXXX      X
XXXXXXXXXX  XXXXXX    XXXX      X
XXXXXXXXX   XXXXXX    XXXX      X
XXXXXXXXX   XXXXXX    XXXX      X          X
```

Output from the program is

```
#2                  XXXXXX    XXXX      X
#4   XXXXXXXXX                XXXX      X
#6   XXXXXXXXX    XXXXXX    XXXX
#8   XXXXXXXXX    XXXXXX    XXXX      XX
#10  XXXXXXXXX    XXXXXX    XXXX      X
#12  XXXXXXXXX    XXXXXX    XXXX      X          X
```

2.13 FAIL

FAIL is a variable whose initial value is a primitive pattern that always fails to match. FAIL causes the scanner to seek alternatives.

Consider the following statements.

```
&ANCHOR  =   0
'MISSISSIPPI'  ('IS' | 'SI' | 'IP' | 'PI') $ OUTPUT   FAIL
```

Normally, the pattern would match the first IS, print it, and terminate successfully. However, FAIL causes the scanner to back up after printing the IS to look for another alternative. SI is found and printed, and again FAIL causes the scanner to back up. Thus, FAIL causes the scanner to find and print all six substrings of MISSISSIPPI that the pattern

```
('IS' | 'SI' | 'IP' | 'PI')
```

matches before terminating in failure.

In general, the behavior of the scanner during any pattern match may be observed using a statement of the form

```
STR  PAT $ OUTPUT   FAIL
```

FAIL is generally used when a programmer wishes to force the scanner to try a number of alternatives even though some may succeed. In the following example, strings are read from cards and printed only if

(1) the string contains at least one **A**,
(2) the string contains at least one **B**, and
(3) the string does not contain a **C**.

The behavior is similar to the logical **AND**.

```
        &ANCHOR  =  1;   &TRIM   =   1
        OUTPUT   =   'ACCEPTABLE WORDS ARE:'
        OUTPUT   =
        PAT  =  (BREAK('A') $ A | BREAK('B') $ B |
+               BREAK('C') $ C)  FAIL
LOOP    STRING  =  ' ' INPUT                        :F(END)
        A  =
        B  =
        C  =
        STRING  PAT
        (DIFFER(A)  DIFFER(B)  IDENT(C))            :F(LOOP)
        OUTPUT  =  STRING                           :(LOOP)
END
```

For the input strings

```
ALPHA
BETA
ABRACADABRA
ABSOLUTELY
AWFUL
ALBEIT
```

the output is

```
ACCEPTABLE WORDS ARE:

 BETA
 ABSOLUTELY
 ALBEIT
```

PAT uses **BREAK** to look for the characters **A**, **B**, and **C**. If one is found, the corresponding variable is assigned a nonnull value. **FAIL** forces the scanner to check all three alternatives of **PAT**, whether they succeed or not. Thus, if the string contains an **A** and **B** but not **C**, the values of the variables **A** and **B** will be nonnull and the value of **C** will be null. **DIFFER** and **IDENT** are used to check the values of **A**, **B**, and **C**.

2.14 FENCE

The variable **FENCE** has a primitive pattern structure as its initial value. **FENCE** matches the null string when encountered by the scanner moving left to right through a pattern. If a subsequent failure causes the scanner to back up to FENCE, seeking an alternative, the pattern match is terminated. Considering **FENCE** as a bead, the needle passes freely from left to right. Attempting to pull the needle back through **FENCE** causes failure of pattern matching.

Consider the following statements:

```
&ANCHOR  =   1
'BERATES'  ('BE' | 'GE' | 'FRE')  ('TS' | 'T')
```

BE matches, and both **TS** and **T** fail. At this point the scanner backs up and tries **GE** and **FRE**, both of which fail. Looking at the pattern, it is obvious that **GE** and **FRE** should not be tried because the first two characters are known to be **BE**.

Inserting **FENCE** between the groups of alternatives eliminates the problem.

```
'BERATES'  ('BE' | 'GE' | 'FRE')  FENCE  ('TS' | 'T')
```

Now, if **BE** matches, **FENCE** keeps the scanner from needlessly backing up to look at **GE** and **FRE**.

FENCE can be used to temporarily anchor the scanner in a program that otherwise operates in the unanchored mode. Inserting **FENCE** before **PAT** in the statement

```
STR   (FENCE PAT)
```

causes pattern matching to fail if **PAT** does not match beginning with the first character of **STR**.

2.15 ABORT

ABORT is a variable whose initial value is a primitive pattern structure that causes immediate failure of the entire pattern match. No alternatives are tried, and the statement fails.

ABORT is useful in constructing conditional pattern matching statements. For instance, in processing SNOBOL4 source decks as data, the following pattern ignores comment cards, but matches all others against the pattern **CARD**.

```
CARDFORM  =  '*'  ABORT  |  CARD
```

Similarly, the pattern

```
SHORTPAT  =  LEN(12)  ABORT  |  PAT
```

permits an attempt to match **PAT** only if the subject string is less than 12 characters long.

In general, a pattern described by a statement of the form, 'has characteristics of P but not Q,' can be implemented by

```
PNOTQ  =  Q  ABORT   |   P
```

2.16 Unevaluated Expressions

The unary operator * postpones the evaluation of its operand. If E is an expression, then *E is an unevaluated expression. The unevaluated expression is evaluated when

(1) the scanner encounters *E as part of a pattern structure, or
(2) *E is used as the argument of the primitive function EVAL.

In this chapter, unevaluated expressions, often simply called expressions, are considered only in the context of pattern matching. Chapter 3 describes EVAL in more detail.

If an unevaluated expression appears as part of a pattern, the expression is evaluated when encountered during pattern matching. If evaluation of the expression is successful, the value becomes part of the pattern structure and pattern matching continues. If evaluation of the expression fails, the scanner backs up, seeking alternatives. Failure during evaluation of an expression does not necessarily cause failure of the entire pattern match.

A typical use for unevaluated expressions is motivated by the following example. Two strings are read as input data and a list is made of the words appearing in both strings. The list is generated by obtaining words one at a time from the first string using the pattern WORD and using the pattern

```
' '  W  ANY(' .,')
```

to determine if each word appears in the second string.

```
       &ANCHOR  =  0;    &TRIM   =    1
       WORD  =  BREAK(' .,') . W  SPAN(' .,')
       STRING1  =  INPUT  ' '                             :F(ERROR)
       STRING2  =  ' '  INPUT  ' '                        :F(ERROR)
LOOP   STRING1  WORD  =                                   :F(OUTPUT)
       STRING2  ' '  W  ANY(' .,')                        :F(LOOP)
       LIST  =  LIST  W  ', '                             :(LOOP)
OUTPUT OUTPUT  =  LIST
END
```

For the input strings

```
THESE TWO STRINGS ARE ALMOST ALIKE.
THE TWO STRINGS AREN'T ALIKE.
```

the printed output is

```
TWO, STRINGS, ALIKE,
```

As programmed above, a pattern structure for

```
' '   W   ANY(' .,')
```

must be built during each pass through the loop because of the structure for **ANY**. Constructing the pattern outside of the loop is not appropriate either, since the value of **W** changes for each iteration of the loop. Using an unevaluated expression in place of the variable **W** does permit the pattern structure to be constructed outside of the loop. As illustrated below, the pattern structure for **FINDW** contains *W in place of **W**. The expression *W is not evaluated until needed in pattern matching. The value of **W** used during pattern matching is the current value, in this case the value just assigned by matching **WORD**.

```
        &ANCHOR  =  0;   &TRIM  =   1
        WORD  =   BREAK(' .,') . W SPAN(' .,')
        FINDW  =   ' '  *W ANY(' .,')
        STRING1  =   INPUT  ' '                      :F(ERROR)
        STRING2  =   ' '  INPUT  ' '                 :F(ERROR)
LOOP    STRING1  WORD  =                             :F(OUTPUT)
        STRING2  FINDW                               :F(LOOP)
        LIST  =   LIST  W  ', '                      :(LOOP)
OUTPUT  OUTPUT  =   LIST
END
```

Unevaluated expressions are valid arguments for primitive pattern-valued functions. A pattern structure for the function is built, but the argument remains unevaluated until pattern matching is performed.

The following program is similar to the one above, except that characters common to two strings are sought rather than words. Each character of the first string is obtained using the pattern **CHAR**. The pattern **FINDCH** uses the unevaluated expression *CH as the argument of **BREAK**. When **FINDCH** is used in pattern matching, the current value of **CH**, that just obtained by matching **CHAR**, becomes the break character.

```
        &ANCHOR  =  1;   &TRIM  =   1
        CHAR  =   LEN(1) . CH
        FINDCH  =   BREAK(*CH)
        STRING1  =   INPUT                           :F(ERROR)
        STRING2  =   INPUT                           :F(ERROR)
LOOP    STRING1  CHAR  =                             :F(OUTPUT)
        STRING2  FINDCH                              :F(LOOP)
        LIST  =   LIST  CH                           :(LOOP)
OUTPUT  OUTPUT  =   LIST
END
```

For the input strings

```
TWO STRINGS FOR TESTING
ABCDEFGHIJKLMNOPQRSTUVWXYZ
```

the output string is

TWOSTRINGSFORTESTING

In pattern matching, unevaluated expressions can be used in a variety of ways as illustrated by the following examples.

2.16.1   Example 1

PAIR is a pattern that matches any two consecutive identical characters. PAIR uses LEN(1) to match any character, and immediate value assignment to assign the character as value of X. The expression *X is then evaluated and must match the same character as LEN(1).

```
        PAIR  =  (LEN(1) $ X  *X) . OUTPUT
        'COOK'  PAIR
        'COMMON'  PAIR
        'AARON'  PAIR
        'CHICKADEE'  PAIR
END
```

Output from the program is:

```
OO
MM
AA
EE
```

2.16.2   Example 2

Given any subject string STR and any pattern P, BIGP finds the longest substring of STR that P matches.

```
        BIGP  =  (*P $ TRY *GT(SIZE(TRY),SIZE(BIG))) $ BIG FAIL
```

BIGP uses two variables, BIG and TRY. During pattern matching, the value of BIG is the longest substring found. Before pattern matching, BIG must be initialized to the null string. TRY is assigned every substring that the pattern P matches. If TRY is longer than BIG, the value of BIG is updated.

BIGP utilizes unevaluated expressions in two ways. *P allows BIGP to be constructed without specifying the value of P. The value of P is determined during pattern matching. The predicate *GT(SIZE(TRY),SIZE(BIG)) is evaluated during pattern matching whenever *P matches a substring. It compares the size of TRY with the size of BIG. If the new substring is shorter, the predicate fails. Failure of a predicate or function during pattern matching causes the scanner to back up seeking alternatives. If the new substring is longer, the predicate succeeds, returning the null string as value. This null string is immediately matched. The variable **BIG** is then assigned the new substring as value. **FAIL** causes the scanner to back up and look for another substring matched by **P**.

The following is a test program for **BIGP**.

```
      BIGP  =  (*P $ TRY  *GT(SIZE(TRY),SIZE(BIG))) $ BIG  FAIL
       STR  =  'IN 1964 NFL ATTENDANCE JUMPED TO 4,807,884; '
+               'AN INCREASE OF 401,810.'
      P  =  SPAN('0123456789,')
      BIG  =
      STR  BIGP
      OUTPUT  =  'LARGEST NUMBER IS  '  BIG
      P  =  SPAN('ABCDEFGHIJKLMNOPQRSTUVWXYZ')
      BIG  =
      STR  BIGP
      OUTPUT  =  'LARGEST WORD IS  '  BIG
END
```

The output is

```
LARGEST NUMBER IS  4,807,884
LARGEST WORD IS  ATTENDANCE
```

2.16.3   Example 3

Recursive definitions of patterns are possible using unevaluated expressions. The pattern structure for

```
      P  =  P  'Z'  |  'Y'
```

is constructed using the previous value of **P**. If **P** was null, the new value of **P** matches the strings **Y** and **Z**.

If the value of **P** is left unevaluated as in

```
      P  =  *P  'Z'  |  'Y'
```

the value of **P** at pattern matching time (which is ***P 'Z' | 'Y'**) replaces ***P**, giving rise to a recursive definition. The pattern **P** matches either **Y** or anything matched by **P** followed by **Z**. Therefore, since **P** matches **Y**, it also matches **YZ**. Since **P** matches **YZ**, it also matches **YZZ**, etc. Thus, **P** matches strings of the form

```
      Y
      YZ
      YZZ
      YZZZ
       .
       .
       .
```

A test program for the recursive definition of P follows.

```
      P  =  *P  'Z'  |  'Y'
      PO  =  P . OUTPUT
      'Y'  PO
      'YZZZ'  PO
      'XYZ'  PO
      'YZZX'  PO
      'AYZZZZB'  PO
END
```

Output from the program is

```
Y
YZZZ
YZ
YZZ
YZZZZ
```

2.16.4   Example 4

Recursive definitions can be quite complicated, as in the following example, which recognizes a simple class of arithmetic expressions.

```
      &ANCHOR  =  1
      VARIABLE  =  ANY('XYZ')
      ADDOP  =  ANY('+-')
      MULOP  =  ANY('*/')
      FACTOR  =  VARIABLE  |  '('  *EXP  ')'
      TERM  =  FACTOR  |  *TERM  MULOP  FACTOR
      EXP  =  ADDOP  TERM  |  TERM  |  *EXP  ADDOP  TERM
LOOP  STRING  =  TRIM(INPUT)                           :F(END)
      STRING  EXP RPOS(0)                              :F(NOGOOD)
      OUTPUT  =  STRING  '  IS AN EXPRESSION.'         :(LOOP)
NOGOOD OUTPUT  =  STRING  '  IS NOT AN EXPRESSION.'    :(LOOP)
END
```

Output for typical data is

```
X+Y*(Z+X)  IS AN EXPRESSION.
X+Y+Z  IS AN EXPRESSION.
XY  IS NOT AN EXPRESSION.
```

2.16.5   Example 5

A useful form of recursive pattern definition is one that seeks repetitions of a basic pattern. In the following example, input cards are read and leadering (consisting of alternating blanks and periods) is inserted for runs of three or more blanks.

The pattern **P** matches an odd number of blanks by seeking repetitions of two blanks followed at the end by a single blank. **PAT** uses **P** to match an odd number of blanks that is at least three in length. The actual replacement of blanks by leadering takes place in the statement labelled **LOOP1** that is executed once for each span of blanks in a card.

```
        &TRIM  =  1
        P  =  ' '  *P  |  ' '
        PAT  =  aY  ' '  P  aX
LOOP    CARD  =  INPUT                            :F(END)
        OUTPUT  =  CARD
LOOP1   CARD  PAT  =  DUPL(' .',(X - Y) / 2)  ' '  :S(LOOP1)
        OUTPUT  =  CARD                           :(LOOP)
END
```

For the input data

```
INSERT                    LEADERING
TRY TWO   BLANKS
TRY THREE    BLANKS
TRY FOUR     BLANKS
TRY FIVE      BLANKS
TRY          SEVERAL      BREAKS
FINALLY, TRY

                                    A RIGHT JUSTIFIED ONE.
```

the output is

```
INSERT                    LEADERING
INSERT . . . . . . . . . LEADERING
TRY TWO   BLANKS
TRY TWO   BLANKS
TRY THREE    BLANKS
TRY THREE . BLANKS
TRY FOUR     BLANKS
TRY FOUR .   BLANKS
TRY FIVE      BLANKS
TRY FIVE . . BLANKS
TRY          SEVERAL      BREAKS
TRY . . . . SEVERAL . . . BREAKS
FINALLY, TRY
FINALLY, TRY

                                    A RIGHT JUSTIFIED ONE.
. . . . . . . . . . . . . . . . . . . . . . . . A RIGHT JUSTIFIED ONE.
```

2.17 ARB

ARB is a variable whose initial value is a primitive pattern structure that matches zero or more characters. When first encountered by the scanner moving from left to right, **ARB** matches the null string. When 'backed into' on subsequent occasions, **ARB** increases the size of the substring it matches by one. **ARB** fails only when it can no longer increase the length of the substring it matches.

ARB can be used in the construction of patterns typified by the statement, 'any string containing both **CAT** and **DOG**.' Nothing is said about the order in which they appear or their separation. A suitable pattern is

            CATANDDOG = 'CAT' ARB 'DOG' | 'DOG' ARB 'CAT'

Matching **CATANDDOG** against the strings

            CATALOG FOR SEADOGS
            DOGS HATE POLECATS
            CATDOG

ARB matches the substrings

            ALOG FOR SEA
            S HATE POLE

and the null string, respectively.

The pattern structure for **ARB** has implicit alternatives. When 'backed into' because of failure, **ARB** attempts to find another suitable substring rather than fail. Only when all implicit alternatives have failed is the needle passed to an explicit alternative or back to a previously successful component.

The following definition of **ARB** is equivalent to the initial definition given to **ARB**.

            ARB = NULL | LEN(1) *ARB

A bead diagram for **ARB** is

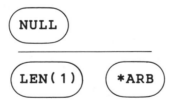

If the bead for ***ARB** is replaced with the bead diagram for **ARB**, an expanded bead diagram for **ARB** becomes

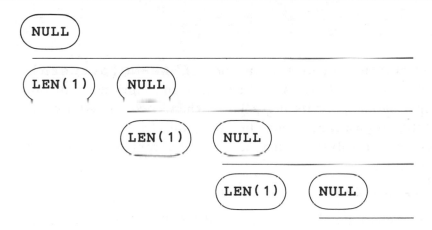

It can be seen from the bead diagram that

    (1) the null string is matched on the first attempt,

    (2) subsequent attempts increase the substring matched by one character, and

    (3) failure occurs when the size of the substring cannot be increased.

ARB, although natural, cannot be used with impunity. For example, it should not be used as the first component of a pattern unless associated with a variable for value assignment. The statement

```
      STR   ARB   PAT
```

should be replaced by

```
      STR   PAT
```

which, when executed in the unanchored mode, behaves in exactly the same way, but is much faster.

ARB should not be used to break fields out of a string if they are separated by known delimiters. For example, the statement

```
      STR   BREAK(',') . FIELD   ','   =
```

is faster than the statement

```
      STR   ARB . FIELD   ','   =
```

although they accomplish the same thing.

2.18 ARBNO

ARBNO is a mnemonic for 'arbitrary number of.' **ARBNO(pattern)** is a primitive function whose value is a pattern structure that matches zero or more consecutive occurrences of strings matched by its argument. When encountered by the scanner in the forward direction, **ARBNO(pattern)** matches the null string. When 'backed into,' it tries to increase the length of the substring matched by its argument. In the statements

```
&ANCHOR  =  1
SUBSTR  ARBNO(LEN(3))  RPOS(0)
```

the pattern match succeeds only if the length of **SUBSTR** is zero or a multiple of three.

The value of **ARBNO(P)** is a pattern structure with implicit alternatives. It is equivalent to the pattern structure defined in the statement

```
ARBNOP  =  NULL  |  P  *ARBNOP
```

A bead diagram having a form similar to that for **ARB** illustrates the implicit alternatives of **ARBNOP** or **ARBNO(P)**.

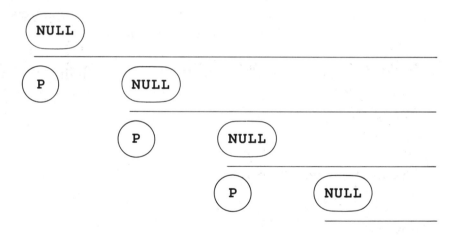

In the following example the argument of **ARBNO** has several alternatives.

```
&ANCHOR  =  1
P  =  '1234'  |  '123'  |  '234'  |  '341'  |  '412'
ARBNOTEST  =  ARBNO(P)  $  OUTPUT  RPOS(0)
'123412341'  ARBNOTEST
END
```

The following bead diagram for **ARBNOTEST** illustrates how alternatives are handled. The output from the program above is a blank line (resulting from the null string), and then

```
1234
12341234
1234123
123
123412
123412341
```

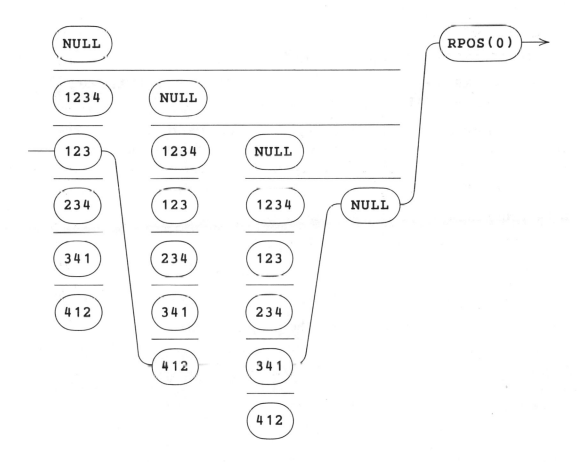

BREAK and **SPAN** can frequently be used in place of **ARBNO**. For example,

        ARBNO(' ')

can usually be replaced by

        SPAN(' ')

or, if necessary,

        NULL | SPAN(' ')

ARBNO is relatively slow and should be avoided if some other pattern will suffice.

2.19   BAL

The initial value of the variable **BAL** is a primitive pattern structure that matches any nonnull string of characters which is balanced with respect to parentheses. **BAL** matches

```
X
XYZ
(A+B)
A(B*C)(E/F)G+H
```

BAL does not match

```
)A+B(
((A+B)
```

A pair of patterns that are equivalent to **BAL** are

```
BALEXP  =  NOTANY('()')  |  '(' ARBNO(*BALEXP) ')'
BAL  =  BALEXP  ARBNO(BALEXP)
```

The value of **BALEXP** matches a single balanced expression that consists of a single character that is neither an open nor closed parenthesis, or it matches an arbitrary number of balanced expressions (possibly none) enclosed in parentheses. **BAL** itself matches the concatenation of one or more single balanced expressions.

Insight into the behavior of **BAL** can be gained from use of the following pattern:

```
ALLBAL  =  BAL $ OUTPUT  FAIL
```

When used in the unanchored mode, a statement such as

```
'((A+(B*C))+D)'  ALLBAL
```

prints out every balanced expression. The output for this case is

```
((A+(B*C))+D)
(A+(B*C))
(A+(B*C))+
(A+(B*C))+D
A
A+
A+(B*C)
+
+(B*C)
(B*C)
B
B*
B*C
*
```

```
*C
C
+
+D
D
```

BAL facilitates the manipulation of algebraic and functional expressions. Programs using **BAL** to translate algebraic expressions from Polish to infix notation, and vice versa, appear in Chapter 4.

2.20 SUCCEED

The variable **SUCCEED** has a pattern structure as its initial value. **SUCCEED** matches the null string when first encountered by the scanner moving left to right through a pattern. If a subsequent failure causes the scanner to back up to **SUCCEED**, seeking an alternative, **SUCCEED** again matches the null string. Thus, **SUCCEED** always matches the null string, both in the forward direction and when alternatives are sought. **SUCCEED** has a bead representation where all implicit alternatives are the null string.

Since the number of implied alternatives is infinite, the scanner can never back through **SUCCEED**.

Practical uses for **SUCCEED** seem limited. However, the light-hearted programmer can use **SUCCEED** and **FAIL** to produce pattern matches that never terminate:

```
SAWTOOTH  =  SUCCEED  (LEN(1)  ARB) $ OUTPUT  FAIL
```

Since **FAIL** repeatedly causes the scanner to back up and retry **ARB**, the subpattern

    LEN(1)   ARB

matches first one character, then two, and so on up to the length of the subject string. Each substring matched by this subpattern is printed. Eventually **ARB** cannot match a longer string and fails, causing the scanner to back into **SUCCEED**. **SUCCEED** matches the null string and the entire process repeats itself.

If the pattern **SAWTOOTH** is used in the statement

    'XXXXXX'   SAWTOOTH

pattern matching does not terminate, and the following output is produced.

```
X
XX
XXX
XXXX
XXXXX
XXXXXX
X
XX
XXX
XXXX
XXXXX
XXXXXX
X
XX
 .
 .
 .
```

SAWTOOTH can never succeed because of **FAIL**, and can never fail because of **SUCCEED**.

2.21   Quickscan Mode

In the quickscan mode, the scanner uses a number of heuristics to avoid looking at alternatives that cannot possibly lead to a successful match. Hence, the scanner operates on the assumption that the programmer is not interested in how matching is done, but only in the outcome. Typically, patterns concerned with how matching is done employ immediate value assignment or unevaluated expressions. Patterns that do not use these features can and should be used in the quickscan mode. Patterns using immediate value assignment and unevaluated expressions may produce unexpected results in the quickscan mode. This section describes the heuristics used by the scanner to speed up pattern matching. It points out where unexpected results may arise and what can be done about them. The keyword **&FULLSCAN** initially has a zero value, signifying the normal or quickscan mode of pattern matching.

This chapter, so far, has been concerned with the basic components of patterns. No consideration has been given to the context in which a component occurs. The basic notion of the quickscan mode is quite simple: Before a component or bead is matched, its context is examined to see if matching should be attempted, terminated, or an alternative sought. The easiest question to answer is whether the number of characters remaining in the subject string is sufficient to successfully complete a match. Consider the following example.

```
BD  =  ('BE' | 'B')  ('AR' | 'A')  ('DS' | 'D')
'BEAD'  BD
```

Four of the possible strings matched by **BD** are too long: **BEARDS**, **BEARD**, **BEADS**, and **BARDS**. The scanner should avoid them if possible. In the bead diagram which follows, a number is associated with each bead. The number represents the minimum number of characters necessary to match that bead and anything that follows. If the number is greater than the number of characters remaining in the subject string, the scanner does not attempt to match the bead against the subject string.

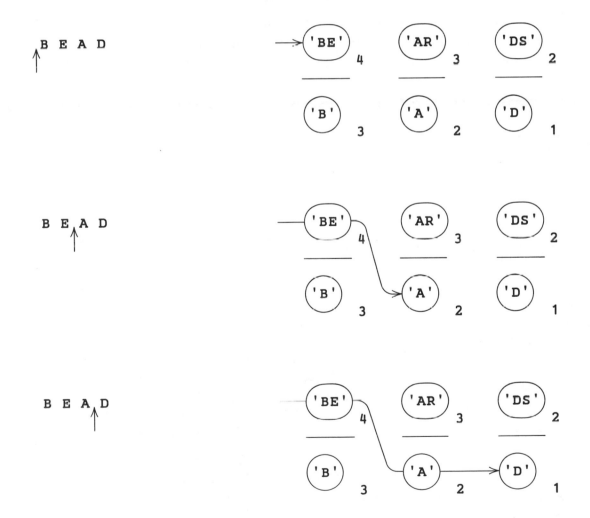

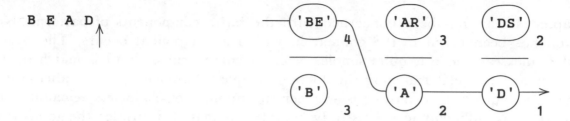

The components **AR** in step 2 and **DS** in step 3 are not tried. **AR** cannot match since two characters remain in the subject string and at least three are necessary. Similarly, **DS** is not tried because one character remains and at least two were required.

In the unanchored quickscan mode, the scanner does not move the initial position of the cursor if insufficient characters remain in the subject string. Consider the following example.

```
&ANCHOR  =   0
'BATS'   BD
```

Matching fails with the cursor initially positioned to the left of the subject string. It is then moved to the left of the **A**. Since three characters remain in the subject string, only **B** is tried. Failing to match **B**, the scanner recognizes that further repositioning of the cursor is useless.

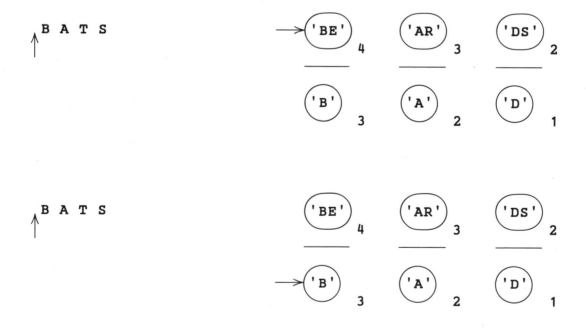

B A T S

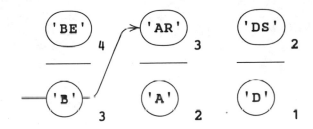

B A T S

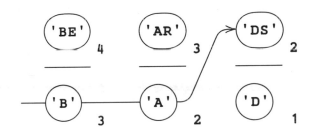

B A T S

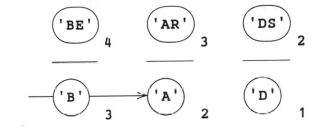

B A T S

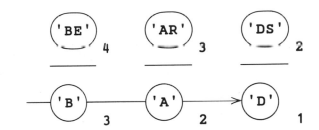

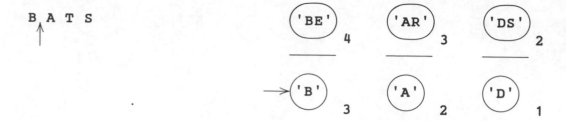

In the quickscan mode, the scanner distinguishes between two kinds of failure: (1) failure to match, as when **X** is compared to **T**; and (2) failure because too few characters remain in the subject string. In the latter case, the scanner does not allow **ARB** to match a longer substring, nor does it move the initial position of the cursor in unanchored mode. Consider the following pattern matching statement executed in the unanchored mode:

        'CAT'   ARB   'X'

Clearly the match cannot succeed. When the scanner reaches the state shown in the diagram below, **ARB** can no longer extend the substring it matches. **ARB** indicates failure because of too few characters. The scanner does not reposition the cursor, and matching fails.

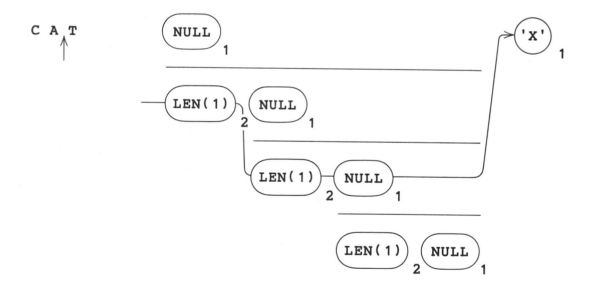

A similar situation arises in the anchored mode for such patterns as

        'CAT'   ARB   ARB   'X'

The first **ARB** matches the null string. The second **ARB** matches the null string, then **C**, and finally **CA** before it fails for lack of room. The scanner does not seek an implicit alternative for the first **ARB**, and terminates pattern matching in failure.

In the quickscan mode, the scanner recognizes a special case for **ARBNO**. When backed
into, **ARBNO(P)** tries to extend the substring matched by finding another instance of **P**. If
P is null or has null alternatives, behavior like **SUCCEED** may result. The scanner tries to
prevent this. When backed into, **ARBNO(P)** examines the substring matched by the last
instance of **P**. If this substring is null, **ARBNO** does not try to find an additional instance
of **P**, but backs up to the last instance of **P** and seeks an alternative to the null string.

For example, in the quickscan mode, **ARBNO(NULL)** looks like **NULL | NULL**. The first
NULL appears because **NULL** is always attempted independently of the argument to
ARBNO. The second **NULL** comes from the argument.

Behavior of **ARBNO(NULL | 'X')** can be deduced from the output generated by the
following statement.

            '*XXX'   ('*'   ARBNO(NULL | 'X')) $ OUTPUT   FAIL

The output is

```
*
*
*X
*X
*XX
*XX
*XXX
*XXX
```

Left recursion in a pattern structure, as illustrated by

            P = *P 'Z' | 'Y'

could be a problem because it might put the scanner in a loop. In the quickscan mode,
recursive loops are broken whenever possible. Most looping problems are avoided by a
look-ahead feature that compares the number of characters remaining with the number of
characters required together with the assumption that any unevaluated expression matches
at least one character.

As an example, consider the following statement:

            'YZZ' P

It is convenient to think that whenever the bead for ***P** is encountered, it expands into a
bead diagram for the current definition of **P**. The process is illustrated by the following
diagram.

Y Z Z

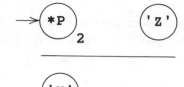

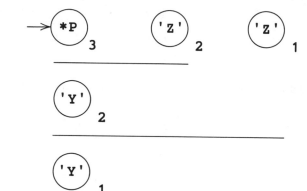

Y Z Z

Y Z Z

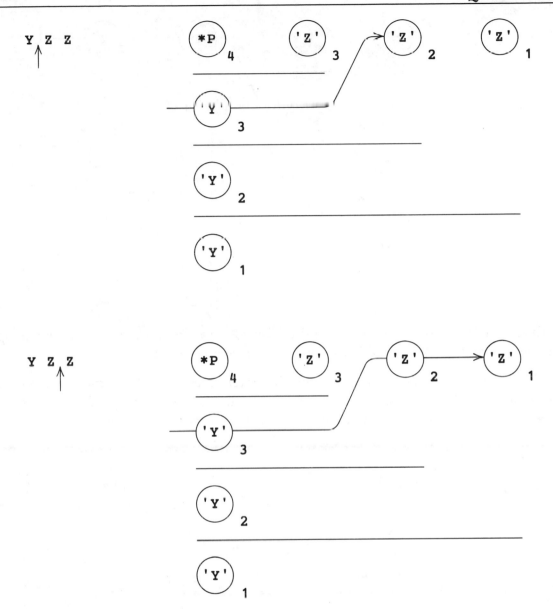

The final state is

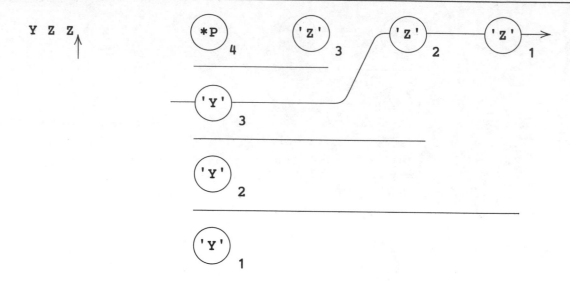

When the minimum number of characters required by *P reaches four, the recursive loop is broken and the alternative Y is tried, leading to a successful match.

The assumption that *P matches at least one character does not affect the outcome of the previous example. Had zero characters been assumed, one more iteration of the loop would have been required, and the final diagram would have been as follows.

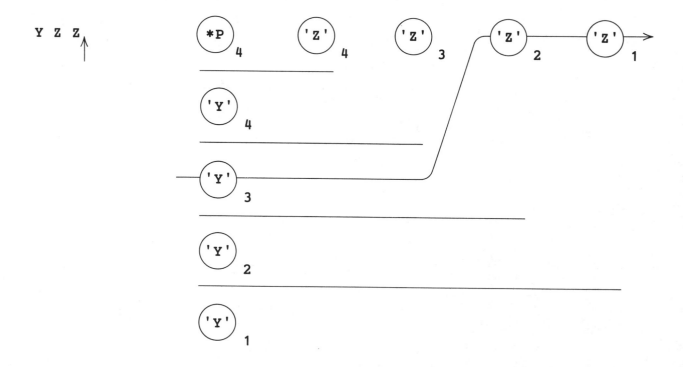

However, the one-character assumption keeps the following equivalent statements from looping.

```
P  =  *P  *Q  |  'Y'
Q  =  'Z'
```

If both ***P** and ***Q** can match the null string, the bead diagram grows without limit. With the one-character assumption, the two equivalent examples above behave similarly.

Assuming a one-character minimum for unevaluated expressions can lead to difficulties:

```
PAT  =  *W  *X  *Y  *Z
```

The shortest string **PAT** matches is of length four. The following match, straightforward as it seems, fails.

```
W  =  'C'
X  =  'A'
Y  =  'T'
Z  =
'CAT'  PAT
```

As seen in the next section, the match succeeds if the fullscan mode is used.

Patterns such as **BIGP**, described in the section on unevaluated expressions, can produce unexpected results in the quickscan mode.

```
BIGP  =  (*P $ TRY  *GT(SIZE(TRY),SIZE(BIG))) $ BIG   FAIL
```

The expression ***GT(SIZE(TRY),SIZE(BIG))** is assumed to require one character when, in fact, it matches the null string. Therefore, the quickscan mode prevents ***P** from matching any substring which includes the last character of the subject string. Hence, in the statements

```
P  =  SPAN('0123456789,')
'1234.56  789,312'  BIGP
```

the final value of **BIG** is **1234** rather than the expected **789,312**. Again, as seen in the next section, the fullscan mode prevents such difficulties.

In summary, the following heuristics are used in the quickscan mode to improve the efficiency of pattern matching:

(1) continual comparison of the number of characters remaining in the subject string against the number of characters required,

(2) repositioning of the cursor in the unanchored mode only if sufficient characters remain,

(3) refusal to extend the substring matched by **ARB** or to reposition the cursor if failure is caused by too few characters,

(4) refusal to extend substring matched by **ARBNO(P)** if the last match of **P** was the null string, and

(5) assumption that unevaluated expressions must match at least one character.

2.22   Fullscan Mode

In the fullscan mode, all heuristics to improve pattern matching efficiency are turned off. Each component of a pattern is matched independently of its context. Furthermore, when unanchored, the initial position of the cursor is moved through the entire subject string. The fullscan mode of pattern matching is entered by assigning a nonzero value to the keyword **FULLSCAN**.

The following example, which prints all possible nonnull substrings of a subject, suggests applications of the fullscan mode.

```
        &ANCHOR   =   0
        &FULLSCAN =   1
        '12345'  (LEN(1) ARB) $ OUTPUT   FAIL
END
```

Output from the program is:

```
1
12
123
1234
12345
2
23
234
2345
3
34
345
4
45
5
```

If &**FULLSCAN** had been zero, the initial position of the cursor would not have been moved, and only the first five lines would have been printed.

An example, which can only be done in the fullscan mode, is back referencing. This pattern succeeds only if a subject string has two identical nonoverlapping substrings of length 3:

```
        BACKR   =   LEN(3) $ X   ARB   *X
```

The statement

```
        'ABCDEFGBCDA'   BACKR
```

succeeds and **X** has the value **BCD**. The statement above does not work in the quickscan mode. When **LEN(3)** matches **ABC**, **ARB** eventually matches **DEFGBCD** and then fails because **X** is assumed to match one character. The condition is recognized in the quickscan mode, preventing the initial position of the cursor from being moved. Hence, matching fails without **BCD** ever being matched by **LEN(3)**.

In the fullscan mode, the tests of **ARBNO** for null arguments are turned off. **ARBNO(NULL)** and **ARBNO(NULL | 'X')** behave like **SUCCEED**. The statement

```
        '*XXX'  ('*'  ARBNO(NULL  |  'X')) $ OUTPUT  FAIL
```

causes the scanner to loop, generating output lines consisting of a single *****.

Recursive patterns such as

```
        P  =  *P  'Z'  |  'Y'
```

do not work because the recursive loop is not broken.

Patterns such as

```
        PAT  =  *W  *X  *Y  *Z
```

work for subject strings having fewer than four characters because the one-character assumption no longer holds.

The following example compares the results of a program run in the quickscan and fullscan modes.

2.22.1   Example

This program prints combinations of characters taken three at a time from a subject string.

```
        DEFINE('F(X,Y,Z)')
        COMB3  =  LEN(1) $ A  ARB  LEN(1) $ B  ARB  LEN(1) $ C
+               *F(A,B,C)  FAIL
        '123456'  COMB3                                 :(END)
F       OUTPUT  =  X Y Z                                :(RETURN)
END
```

Output from Quickscan	*Output from Fullscan*
123	123
124	124
125	125
	126
	134
	135
	136
	145
	146
	156
	234
	235
	236
	245
	246
	256
	345
	346
	356
	456

Exercises

Exercise 2.1: Count the total number of punctuation marks in text, given on a series of input cards. Define a punctuation mark to be a period, comma, colon, semicolon, question mark, exclamation mark, left parenthesis, right parenthesis, apostrophe, or quotation mark.

Exercise 2.2: Write a pattern that matches words beginning with C or CR, followed by O or OO or EE, followed by P or PS. Construct the pattern so that each successful step in the pattern matching is explicated by a printed output.

Exercise 2.3: Write a program that identifies and prints all words of a given length. Assume that the length is given on the first input card and that text occurs on following cards. Make appropriate assumptions about the format of the first card, the characters that are assumed to delimit words, and how the text appears on successive cards.

Exercise 2.4: Let the label for an assembly language statement begin in column 1 and consist of at most eight characters, of which the first is a letter and the remainder are letters or digits. The label is followed by at least one blank. A statement without a label begins with a blank. Write a program that reads in assembly language statements and prints those statements with invalid labels.

Exercise 2.5: Construct a pattern that matches a SNOBOL4 string literal.

Exercise 2.6: Write a recognizer for strings of the form

ABC, AABBCC, AAABBBCCC, ...

Exercise 2.7: Write a pattern that matches strings that are repetitions of a nonnull substring (e.g. 1111111, 123123123, abcdefabcdefabcdef).

Exercise 2.8: Construct a pattern that matches strings that are FORTRAN format Hollerith field specifications (i.e. a positive integer n, followed by the letter H, and followed by n characters).

Exercise 2.9: Write a program that determines whether a string is palindromic, i.e., whether it reads the same forward and backward (e.g. MADAM).

CHAPTER 3

Primitive Functions, Predicates, and Operations

3.1 Introduction

A function is an operation upon a number of arguments. The value of a function is computed by a procedure. There are two types of functions: primitive and programmer-defined. Primitive functions are implemented by procedures built into the SNOBOL4 system. Procedures for programmer-defined functions, described in the next chapter, are included in the source program.

Syntactically, a function call is recognized as an identifier used for a function name, followed by a list of arguments separated by commas and enclosed in parentheses. An example is

```
IDENT(A,'TREE')
```

An argument of a function call may be any expression. Execution of a function call causes the expressions for the arguments to be evaluated and the values passed to the procedure. Thus, the procedure gets only the values of the arguments and not the expressions. Consider the following statements:

```
A   =   'APPLE'
B   =   'SEED'
APPLE   =   'FRUIT'
SEED   =   'TREE'
APPLESEED   =   'FRUITTREE'
IDENT($A $B,$(A B))
```

FRUITTREE is the value of each argument to **IDENT**. The two strings **FRUITTREE** are all that the procedure for **IDENT** knows of its arguments.

A variable such as **C** is an expression, albeit a trivial one. Thus, if

```
C   =   'CLAW'
D   =   'TIGER'
```

the call

```
IDENT(C,D)
```

passes the strings **CLAW** and **TIGER**, the values of **C** and **D**, as arguments to the procedure

76

for **IDENT**. Furthermore, since the procedure for **IDENT** knows nothing about **C** and **D**, it cannot possibly change their values.

Any omitted argument is assigned the null string as value. Thus, **IDENT(E)** compares the value of **E** and the null string. The use of too many arguments in the call of a primitive function is an error.

A function call is an expression and has a value. The value of a function call may be of any data type. A programmer must always be aware that a function call has a value, even if it is the null string. Otherwise, as later examples illustrate, unexpected results may arise.

A function call may succeed or fail, depending upon the outcome of the associated procedure. If the procedure for a function is successful, the value computed by the procedure becomes the value of the function call. If the procedure fails, the function call fails.

This chapter only describes a few primitive functions. Others dealing with pattern matching, input and output, arrays, and programmer-defined data types, and so forth, are described in other chapters. A list of functions appears in Chapter 7 and page references are included in the index.

3.2   Numerical Predicates

Several primitive functions are concerned with testing relations between arguments. These functions, which succeed or fail depending on whether the relation is true or false, are called predicates. If a predicate is successful, the value of the call is the null string.

3.2.1   LT, LE, EQ, NE, GE, and GT

A predicate, such as **GE(X,Y)**, succeeds if **X** stands in the given relation to **Y**. The arguments to numerical predicates may be integers or reals. Thus, if

```
X   =   17.0
Y   =   '3'
```

then **GE(X,Y)** succeeds and **LT(X,Y)** fails. If an argument is omitted, it is assigned the null string, which is treated as zero. If **M** is **2**, then **EQ(M)** fails, but **EQ(M - 2)** succeeds and returns the null string. If a real number is compared with an integer, the integer is converted to real before the comparison.

Numerical predicates frequently are used for loop control. For example, if **N** has as its value the number of times a loop has been executed and **M** is the limit on **N**, the following statement checks **N** against **M**, and increments **N** if it is less than **M**.

```
N   =   LT(N,M)   N + 1                          :S(LOOP)F(OUT)
```

Evaluation of the object expression takes place before assignment is made. Thus, the evaluation of `LT(N,M)` takes place before `N` is incremented. If `LT(N,M)` succeeds, the value is the null string. Concatenation of the null string with `N + 1` does not affect `N + 1`, so `N` is properly incremented. Furthermore, since the statement succeeds, control passes to `LOOP`. If `LT(N,M)` fails, `N` is not incremented and control passes to the statement labelled `OUT`.

Placement of predicates in a statement is important. Consider the following statement, which looks as if it might be suitable for loop control.

```
N  LT(N,M)  =  N + 1                            :S(LOOP)F(OUT)
```

The statement does not properly increment `N`. If `N` is `2` and `M` is `4`, the value of `N` after execution of the statement is `32`. The predicate `LT(N,M)`, situated where it is, is treated as a pattern. Since `LT(N,M)` is null, the pattern matches the null string. The null string matched in the value of `N` is replaced by `N + 1`, leading to the unexpected result `32`.

3.2.2 INTEGER

It is frequently desirable to test whether the value of a variable is an integer. The predicate test `INTEGER(X)` succeeds if the value of `X` is an integer and fails otherwise. Thus,

```
INTEGER(X)
```

succeeds for

```
X  =  3
X  =  '3'
```

but fails for

```
X  =  'INT'
X  =  '3.0'
```

`INTEGER` is typically used to check data coming from the input stream. The following statements reject cards which do not contain a single integer left justified on the card.

```
        &TRIM    =    1
LOOP    CARD  =  INPUT                :F(END)
        INTEGER(CARD)                 :S(PROCESS)F(REJECT)
```

Since the null string is equivalent to the integer `0`, a blank card passes the integer test.

3.3 Object Comparison Predicates

There are several types of data predefined in the SNOBOL4 language. Programmer-defined data types can be added, as described in Chapter 5. Some data values, such as numbers, can be represented in different ways as different types of data. SNOBOL4 includes predicates to test whether two objects are identical or different.

3.3.1 IDENT and DIFFER

IDENT and DIFFER are functions of two arguments which may be of any data type. For the function call IDENT(X,Y) to succeed or for DIFFER(X,Y) to fail, the values of the arguments, X and Y, must be truly identical. The value of a function argument is a pointer to a data object or, in the case of integers and real numbers, the value is the data object itself.

Each distinct string of characters appears in storage once and only once. Execution of

```
X  =  'BCD'
Y  =  'B'  'CD'
```

results in X and Y having the same value. The string BCD appears once, and both X and Y point to it. IDENT(X,Y) therefore succeeds.

Pattern structures behave differently. Execution of the statements

```
X  =  A  |  B
Y  =  A  |  B
```

constructs two equivalent but physically distinct pattern structures. Thus, X and Y have different values, since they point to different copies of the pattern structure A | B. IDENT(X,Y) therefore fails.

However, if

```
X  =  A  |  B
Y  =  X
```

then IDENT(X,Y) succeeds since X and Y point to the same data object.

Integers and real numbers are data objects rather than pointers to data. Execution of

```
X  =  3
Y  =  2 + 1
```

assigns 3 to both X and Y. Comparison of X and Y by IDENT(X,Y) succeeds because the data objects are identical. Similarly, if

```
X  =  3.0
Y  =  3.0
```

then IDENT(X,Y) succeeds.

IDENT and DIFFER must be used with care when their arguments have different data types. If

```
X   =   3
Y   =   '3'
```

EQ(X,Y) succeeds as illustrated earlier because numeral strings are acceptable in arithmetic contexts. IDENT(X,Y) fails because the value of X is an integer, but the value of Y is a string.

Similarly, for

```
X   =   3.0
Y   =   3
```

IDENT(X,Y) fails because the values are not identical.

3.3.2 LGT

Lexical ordering of strings can be tested using the predicate LGT(X,Y). LGT(X,Y) succeeds, returning the null string, if the value of X is lexically greater than Y. Stated another way, LGT(X,Y) succeeds if X follows Y alphabetically. The order of the characters is implementation dependent. For example, on the IBM 360 the EBCDIC encoding is used with the blank preceding letters and letters preceding digits. The value of &ALPHABET is a string of all characters in lexical order.

Consider, as an example, the problem of alphabetizing the characters in a string. That is, the string LABORATORIES is to be transformed into the string AABEILOORST. The following program performs the transformation using an interchange sorting technique.

```
            &ANCHOR  =  1;    &FULLSCAN   =   1
            FLIP  =  LEN(*I) . HEAD  LEN(1) $ X  LEN(1) $ Y  *LGT(X,Y)
            STR  =  'LABORATORIES'
            OUTPUT  =  STR
            LIMIT  =  SIZE(STR)  -  2
LOOP        STR  FLIP  =  HEAD  Y  X
            I  =  LT(I,LIMIT)  I  +  1                        :S(LOOP)
            I  =  0
            LIMIT  =  GT(LIMIT,0)  LIMIT  -  1                :S(LOOP)
            OUTPUT  =  STR
END
```

Output is

```
LABORATORIES
AABEILOORRST
```

Sorting is performed in the statement labelled LOOP. The pattern FLIP matches two adjacent characters, assigning them as values of the variables X and Y. *LGT(X,Y) is then evaluated to test the order of the characters. If the order is correct, LGT(X,Y) fails and the characters are not interchanged. If `LGT(X,Y)` succeeds, pattern matching succeeds and the two characters are interchanged as the replacement is performed.

The variable `I` is used to determine which two characters are compared by `LGT(X,Y)` and the variable `LIMIT` controls the number of passes made over the string `STR`.

3.4 Additional Primitive Functions

3.4.1 SIZE

`SIZE` is a function that determines the length of a string. Its value is the number of characters in its argument.

3.4.2 REPLACE

One-for-one character replacement in a string may be accomplished using the function `REPLACE`. The value of `REPLACE(X,Y,Z)` is the string resulting from replacement in `X` of each character appearing in `Y` by the corresponding character in `Z`. As a result of executing the following statements,

```
BINARY  =  '111001'
ONESCOMP  =  REPLACE(BINARY,'01','10')
```

`ONESCOMP` has the value `000110`, obtained from `BINARY` by replacing all zeroes with ones, and ones with zeroes. The value of the variable `BINARY` remains unchanged.

`REPLACE` normally succeeds, but it fails if

(1) the second and third arguments have different lengths, or
(2) the second or third argument is null.

Multiple occurrences of characters in the third argument are valid. Thus,

```
REPLACE(S,'.,;:?!','        ')
```

replaces all punctuation marks with blanks.

In the case of the multiple occurrence of a character in the second argument, the rightmost correspondence holds. Thus, following execution of the statement

```
TEXT  =  REPLACE('FEET','EE','AO')
```

the variable `TEXT` has value `FOOT`.

An example of the usefulness of `REPLACE` is the following program that converts a deck of cards prepared on an 026 keypunch (BCD) to a deck using 029 keypunch code (EBCDIC).

```
LOOP     PUNCH  =  REPLACE(INPUT,'#ə%<ɛ',"='()+")   :S(LOOP)
END
```

029 graphics are used in the example above.

3.4.3 TRIM

TRIM is a primitive function whose argument must be a string or an integer. The value of **TRIM** is a string which is the argument value with all trailing blanks removed. Thus, the statements

```
TEXT  =  'A PRIMITIVE FUNCTION
SHORTTEXT  =  TRIM(TEXT)
```

gives **SHORTTEXT** the value **A PRIMITIVE FUNCTION**. The value of **TEXT** is not changed.

It is not necessary to use the function **TRIM** to delete trailing blanks from input since this operation is performed automatically under the control of **&TRIM**.

3.4.4 DUPL

DUPL is a primitive function of two arguments, the first of which is a string and the second an integer. The value of **DUPL** is a string consisting of the first argument repeated the number of times specified by the second argument.

DUPL is used in many of the examples in Chapters 1 and 2 to generate strings of blanks for formatting output lines. A typical example is the following one where a string is right justified to column 50.

```
OUTPUT  =  DUPL(' ',50 - SIZE(STR))  STR
```

Another use of **DUPL** is to generate, with one line of program, several lines of output. For example, if the page width for printing is 132 characters, five lines containing periods in columns 10 and 50 can be generated by

```
OUTPUT  =  DUPL(DUPL(' ',9) '.' DUPL(' ',39) '.' DUPL(' ',82),5)
```

3.4.5 REMDR

REMDR is a primitive function of two integer arguments. The value of **REMDR** is an integer that is the remainder of dividing the first argument by the second. Thus,

```
OUTPUT  =  REMDR(15,4)
```

prints the integer 3. The sign of **REMDR** is the sign of the dividend or first argument. Thus,

```
REMDR(-15,4)
REMDR(15,-4)
REMDR(-15,-4)
```

have the values −3, 3, and −3 respectively.

3.4.6 DATE and TIME

DATE and **TIME** are primitive functions requiring no arguments. The value of **DATE( )** is an 8-character string of the form month/day/year. For July 11, 1970 the value of **DATE( )** is 07/11/70.

The value of **TIME( )** is an integer that is the elapsed time in milliseconds from the beginning of program execution. Compilation time is not included. On IBM 360 equipment, the standard interval clock is updated only sixty times a second, so timing is approximate at best.

3.4.7 EVAL

EVAL is a primitive function whose argument must be an unevaluated expression, string, integer, or real. If the argument is an unevaluated expression, the expression is evaluated to obtain the value of **EVAL**. If the argument is a string, the value of **EVAL** is the value of the expression represented by the string. Integer and real arguments are simply returned as values without modification.

In the following example, the value of **S** is a string, and the value of **U** is an unevaluated expression. Both output statements print the integer **15**.

```
S      =    'X + SIZE(X) * 10'
U      =    *(X + SIZE(X) * 10)
X      =    5
OUTPUT  =    EVAL(S)
OUTPUT  =    EVAL(U)
```

Any string or unevaluated expression that is a syntactically correct expression in SNOBOL4 may be evaluated by **EVAL**. A syntactic error in the argument of **EVAL** causes failure of **EVAL**. Thus, evaluation of **E** in the statements

```
E      =    '5+6'
SUM    =    EVAL(E)
```

fails since blanks are required around the +.

3.4.8 APPLY

APPLY is a primitive function that creates and executes a function call. APPLY($F,a_1,\ldots,a_n$) calls the function F with the arguments $a_1,\ldots,a_n$. The value of APPLY is the value returned by the function it calls. The function F may be any function, primitive or programmer-defined. Use of APPLY on a primitive function must specify the correct number of arguments. Omission of trailing arguments is not permitted.

An important use of APPLY is to call various functions, depending on the current value of data. Execution of the statements

```
X   =   'REMDR'
Y   =   6;   Z   =   5
OUTPUT   =   APPLY(X,Y,Z)
```

calls REMDR(6,5) and prints 1. Subsequent execution of

```
X   =   'DUPL'
OUTPUT   =   APPLY(X,Y,Z)
```

calls DUPL(6,5) and prints 66666.

3.5 Negation (¬) and Interrogation (?)

Two predicates, specified by the unary operators ¬ and ?, test the success or failure resulting from evaluation of expressions. The negation operator ¬ fails if its operand succeeds, and succeeds if its operand fails. A null string is returned as value on success. The interrogation operator ? is the converse of ¬. It succeeds, returning the null value, if its operand succeeds. It fails if its operand fails.

Negation may be used to complement a predicate. For example, the following program reads an input deck and prints those cards that contain integers.

```
          &TRIM   =   1
LOOP      CARD   =   INPUT                          :F(END)
          OUTPUT   =   INTEGER(CARD)   CARD         :(LOOP)
END
```

Suppose the converse program, one that prints all cards that are not integers, is desired. No predicate is available which succeeds when its argument is not an integer. However, the negation operator together with the predicate INTEGER suffices. Thus, the following program lists all noninteger cards.

```
          &TRIM   =   1
LOOP      CARD   =   INPUT                          :F(END)
          OUTPUT   =   ¬INTEGER(CARD)   CARD        :(LOOP)
END
```

Complicated Boolean functions on the states of variables can be constructed using predicates and negation. For example, suppose the integer **N** is to be incremented, provided at least one of the variables **X**, **Y**, or **Z** is null. The following statement tests the variables and, if the condition is satisfied, increments **N**,

$$N = \neg(\text{DIFFER}(X) \quad \text{DIFFER}(Y) \quad \text{DIFFER}(Z)) \quad N + 1$$

If **X**, **Y**, and **Z** are nonnull, the expression succeeds but the negation operation fails, and **N** is not incremented. If any variable is null, the corresponding **DIFFER** fails, causing the expression to fail. Negation succeeds and **N** is incremented.

Interrogation is used primarily to convert a function that returns a nonnull value into a predicate that succeeds or fails, but returns a null value. Thus, in the following statement, **N** is incremented if **F(X)** succeeds, but the value of **F(X)** is not concatenated with **N + 1**.

$$N = \text{?F(X)} \quad N + 1 \qquad \qquad :S(ON)F(OUT)$$

3.6 External Functions

The primitive functions described in this chapter and elsewhere in this book are built into the SNOBOL4 language. There is a facility whereby a library of functions, called external functions, can be accessed during program execution [4]. External functions are written in FORTRAN or assembly language and provide a means for extending the SNOBOL4 language. External functions are typically used for:

(1) Complicated numerical computations.

(2) Specialized input and output operations.

(3) Creating and operating on data types not provided by the SNOBOL4 language itself.

Since external functions are not part of the SNOBOL4 system, the availability and access to various external functions varies from installation to installation. This chapter does not describe how to create external functions, but only how to use those that may be available. The external functions described in the following sections are hypothetical, and are not necessarily available at any installation.

3.6.1 Loading and Calling External Functions

To use an external function, it must be added to the SNOBOL4 system by loading it during program execution. This is accomplished by executing the primitive function

```
LOAD(prototype,library)
```

The prototype describes the external function which is then loaded from the given library. The prototype of the function consists of the function name, the data type for each argument, and the data type of the value returned. In the prototype, the name comes first, followed by the argument data types within parentheses, and finally the data type of the returned value. For example

        LOAD('SIN(REAL)REAL','SNOLIB')

loads an external function **SIN** which expects one real argument and returns a real value. The function is loaded from the library **SNOLIB**. The second argument may be omitted, implying a standard (public) library.

After execution of the **LOAD** function, the function **SIN** is available for use like any primitive function. For example,

        Z   =   SIN(0.79)

assigns 0.7104 to Z, assuming **SIN** expects its argument in radians.

The data types in the load prototype must correspond to those expected by the external function.

Another example of an external function is

        LOAD('LOG(REAL,INTEGER)REAL')

where **LOG** is an external function in which the second (integer) argument specifies the base of the logorithm.

In the call of an external function, omitted trailing arguments are taken to be null strings. Extra arguments are ignored.

External functions may introduce new data types into the SNOBOL4 system. The load prototype may specify these new data type names. A typical example is an external function that creates bit strings having data type **BIT**.

        LOAD('BITSTRING(STRING)BIT')

An example of use is

        X   =   BITSTRING('1110011')

which converts a string of characters into a corresponding string of bits.

In load prototypes, data type specifications unknown to SNOBOL4 system are ignored and left to be handled by the external functions. Such data types can be omitted from the prototype altogether:

        LOAD('BITSTRING(STRING)')

is equivalent to the example above.

3.6.2   Unloading Functions

External functions may be unloaded when they are no longer needed. This is accomplished by the primitive function **UNLOAD**, which unloads the named function. For example

        UNLOAD('SIN')

would unload **SIN** described in the previous section. When an external function is unloaded, it becomes 'undefined' and the space it occupies is freed.

UNLOAD is not restricted to external functions: Any function can be unloaded and consequently undefined. The space occupied is reclaimed only for external functions, however.

3.7   OPSYN and Operator Definition

It is sometimes convenient to provide synonyms for existing functions or operators. The primitive function **OPSYN** can be used for this purpose. The general format of **OPSYN** is

        OPSYN(new,old,n)

3.7.1   Function Synonyms

If **n** is omitted (or zero), **new** and **old** are treated as function names and the new function name becomes a synonym for the old function. For example,

        OPSYN('SAME','IDENT')

makes **SAME** a synonym for the function **IDENT**.

A call using a synonym for a primitive function must have the correct number of arguments. Trailing arguments may not be omitted. For example,

        SAME(X)

is erroneous.

3.7.2   Operator Synonyms

If the third argument of **OPSYN** is 1, the two arguments are interpreted as unary operators if possible. For example,

        OPSYN('$','*',1)

makes the unary operator **$** a synonym for *****. After execution of this function call, **$X** behaves like ***X**.

If either argument is not one of the unary operators, it is interpreted as a function name. Therefore

      OPSYN('$','F',1)

makes **$** a synonym for the function **F**. Subsequently **$X** results in a call of **F(X)**.

Conversely,

      OPSYN('F','*',1)

makes the function **F** a synonym for the unary operator *****. Subsequently **F(X)** behaves like ***X**.

If neither argument is a unary operator, the effect of **OPSYN** is the same as if the third argument were zero.

If the third argument is **2**, the arguments are interpreted as binary operators if possible. The result is similar to the case for unary operators. Thus

      OPSYN('+','F',2)

causes **N + M** to call **F(N,M)**.

Any type of function can appear as an argument to **OPSYN**. However, an invocation of a primitive function by a synonym must have the correct number of arguments.

Operators given in the first two arguments of **OPSYN** must be given precisely. In

      OPSYN('||','F',1)

the first argument is not interpreted as a unary operator even though it starts with one. If the binary operator of concatenation is to be **OPSYN**ed, it must be given as a single blank.

Any string that cannot be interpreted as an operator is taken to be a function name without checking that the string meets the syntactic requirements for a function name. The first argument, **||**, in the call of **OPSYN** above is an example. Such functions cannot be called explicitly, but may be invoked implicitly by **APPLY** since **APPLY** does not check the syntax of its first argument either.

3.7.3   Summary of Operators

In addition to the operators with defined meanings, a number of undefined operators are provided. The operators can be defined through the use of **OPSYN**. Tables summarizing operators follow.

Unary Operators

Graphic	Definition
¬	negation
?	interrogation
$	indirect reference
.	name
!	*none*
%	*none*
*	unevaluated expression
/	*none*
#	*none*
+	positive
−	negative
ə	cursor position
|	*none*
ɛ	keyword

Binary Operators

Graphic	Definition	Associativity	Precedence
¬	*none*	right	12
?	*none*	left	12
$	immediate value assignment	left	11
.	conditional value assignment	left	11
!,**	exponentiation	right	10
%	*none*	left	9
*	multiplication	left	8
/	division	left	7
#	*none*	left	6
+	addition	left	5
−	subtraction	left	5
ə	*none*	left	4
blank	concatenation	left	3
|	alternation	left	2
ɛ	*none*	left	1

Note that the sets of unary and binary operators are the same except for concatenation and the alternative graphic for exponentiation.

Any operator that does not have a primitive definition can be defined using **OPSYN**. Similarly the primitive definition of any operator can be changed. The precedence and associativity of binary operators is not changed by their redefinition.

Exercises

Exercise 3.1: Assume source cards to an assembler have fields beginning in columns 1, 8, 16, and 36. Write a program to reformat these cards so that the fields begin in columns 1, 10, 20, and 40. Pad with blanks to achieve this, and keep only the first 80 characters of the result.

Exercise 3.2: Assume source cards to an assembler consist of four fields in free format separated by blanks. The first field always begins in column 1. Typical cards might be

```
X             L        1,0(1)      LOAD
Y        ST    1,0(3)               SAVE
```

Write a program to reformat these cards with the four fields starting in columns 1, 10, 20, and 40. Assume the fields are short enough to fit in this format. This program should allow the first and the last fields to be omitted, but assume that the second and third fields are always present.

Exercise 3.3: Refine the program in Exercise 3.2 above to allow for the possibility of a quoted literal (as in SNOBOL4) in the third field, and assume such literals may contain imbedded blanks. Assume that quotation marks do not occur in other fields. For simplicity assume only one kind of quotation mark. Furthermore, comment cards, identified by an asterisk in column 1, should be passed through unchanged.

Exercise 3.4: Let a sequence of integers be given left justified on data cards. Write a program that reads in the cards and prints the largest number.

Exercise 3.5: Write a program that reads in an integer **N** from a data card, and prints the value of **N** factorial. Have the program test the data and print an appropriate comment if the input is not a positive integer.

Exercise 3.6: A permutation can be thought of as a rearrangement of objects. Thus a permutation can be represented by a pair of strings such as **(abc,cab)** indicating that **a** is replaced by **c**, **b** is replaced by **a**, and **c** is replaced by **b**.

If the permutation is applied to the first string in the pair, the index of the permutation is the number of such iterated applications required to obtain the original string. For example, the index of **(abc,cab)** is three.

Write a program that reads in a permutation and determines its index.

Exercise 3.7: Any string of a specified length can be reversed with a single call of the function **REPLACE**. Write a call of **REPLACE** that reverses any string of length 7. (The authors are indebted to Mr. Morris M. Siegel for calling this technique to their attention.)

Exercise 3.8: Define a unary operator that is synonymous with the primitive function SIZE.

Exercise 3.9: Define a new operator for addition which has higher precedence than subtraction.

CHAPTER 4

Programmer-Defined Functions

4.1 Introduction

A programmer may define his own functions. A program with programmer-defined functions must include:

> (1) a call to the primitive function **DEFINE** for each programmer-defined function, and

> (2) a procedure, written in SNOBOL4, for each function.

4.2 The Primitive Function **DEFINE**

Procedures are written using formal arguments, and must adhere to special conventions for returning. Execution of the primitive function **DEFINE** communicates to the SNOBOL4 system:

> (1) the name of the function,
> (2) a list of formal arguments used in the programmer-defined procedure,
> (3) a list of variables local to the programmer-defined procedure, and
> (4) the entry point of the procedure.

Programmer-defined functions are defined by executing the primitive function **DEFINE**. The first argument of **DEFINE** is a prototype for the call of the function being defined. The second argument is a label specifying the entry point to the programmer-defined function. For example, execution of

```
DEFINE('F(X,Y)L1,L2','FENTRY')
```

defines a function **F** with two formal arguments, **X** and **Y**. Two local variables **L1** and **L2** are used in the procedure whose entry point is the statement labelled **FENTRY**. Extra commas in the lists of formal arguments and local variables are ignored.

Often local variables are not needed, so it is permissible to omit the list of local variables. An example is

```
DEFINE('G(Z)','GENT')
```

It is also permissible to omit the second argument, in which case the entry point is assumed to be the same as the function name. Thus,

```
DEFINE('COUNT(N)')
```

defines the function **COUNT** with entry point **COUNT**. Functions can be defined without any formal arguments. For example,

```
DEFINE('MARK()')
```

defines the function **MARK** with no formal arguments.

The **DEFINE** function returns the null string as value.

4.3 Procedures for Programmer-Defined Functions

A procedure for a programmer-defined function is a set of SNOBOL4 statements. The label, given explicitly or implicitly in the arguments of the associated **DEFINE** function, specifies the statement to which control is passed when a call is made to the function. Thus, during execution of the statement labelled **ZSET** in the example below, the call to **UNION** causes control to be passed to **UN**. Execution of **ZSET** is temporarily suspended while the value of **UNION** is being computed. Once the value of **UNION** has been computed, control returns to statement **ZSET** where computation is resumed, using the value returned.

```
        DEFINE('UNION(X,Y)CH','UN')
           .
           .
           .
ZSET    Z  =  SET1  UNION(SET2,SET3)  SET4
           .
           .
           .
UN      UNION  =  X
ULOOP   Y LEN(1) . CH  =                              :F(RETURN)
        UNION  BREAK(CH)                              :S(ULOOP)
        UNION  =  UNION  CH                           :(ULOOP)
```

The defining statement must be executed before the call is made. The procedure is called and should not be flowed into. The procedure may be transferred around or placed out of the way of program flow.

The statements constituting the procedure are written using the formal arguments, whose values are supplied by arguments of a call.

Variables used in procedures should be declared local if their values outside the procedure should not be changed by the function call. In **UNION**, the value of the variable **CH** changes continually during evaluation. The global value of **CH** might be altered as a result of the call if **CH** were not declared as a local variable. Upon entry to a procedure, all local variables are given null string values.

All statement labels, including labels in procedures, are global. Transfer can be made from a statement in one procedure to a statement in another.

The name of a function may be used as a variable in the procedure. The value of the function call is the current value of the function name when the procedure returns. Thus, in the example above, the value of the call **UNION(SET2,SET3)** is the value of the variable **UNION** when the statement **ULOOP** fails, causing return to the statement **ZSET**.

Return of control from a procedure to the calling statement is accomplished by transferring to one of the three system labels: **RETURN**, **FRETURN**, or **NRETURN**.

4.3.1 RETURN

Transfer to **RETURN** indicates that the function call is successful. The value of the function call is set to the value of the function name. Execution continues in the calling statement using the returned value.

4.3.2 FRETURN

Transfer to **FRETURN** indicates failure of the function call.

An example using both **RETURN** and **FRETURN** is the function **PAL**, which checks its argument to see if it is a palindromic string. **PAL** compares the argument string and its reverse. If they are identical, **PAL** transfers to **RETURN**, indicating success. Otherwise **PAL** transfers to **FRETURN**, indicating failure.

```
        &TRIM   =   1
        DEFINE('PAL(STR)CH,S1,S2')
            .
            .
            .
TEST    PHRASE  =   INPUT                              :F(END)
        PAL(PHRASE)                                    :S(GOOD)F(NOGOOD)
            .
            .
            .
```

```
PAL     S1  =   STR
PALL    S1  LEN(1) . CH =                          :F(PTEST)
        S2  =   CH  S2                             :(PALL)
PTEST   IDENT(STR,S2)                              :S(RETURN)F(FRETURN)
          .
          .
          .

END
```

4.3.3 NRETURN

By transferring to the label **NRETURN**, a programmer-defined function may return a computed name rather than a value. A call to a function that returns a computed name may be used as the subject of an assignment statement. For example,

```
        F(X,Y)  =   X  Y
```

is a valid statement provided the function **F** returns by name using **NRETURN**. A further description of names is included in Chapter 6.

4.4   Execution of Programmer-Defined Functions

When a call to a programmer-defined function is made, the arguments of the call are evaluated first. Before execution of the procedure begins, the values of the following variables are saved in the following order:

    (1) the name of the function,
    (2) all formal arguments, and
    (3) all local variables.

New values are assigned to these variables as follows:

    (1) the name of the function is assigned the null string,
    (2) the formal arguments are assigned their values, and
    (3) all local variables are assigned the null string.

Consider the function **UNION** specified in the defining statement

```
        DEFINE('UNION(X,Y)CH','UN')
```

and called by **UNION(SET2,SET3)**. Values of the variables **UNION**, **X**, **Y**, and **CH** at the time of a call are saved. New values for these variables are assigned as if the following statements had been executed.

```
        UNION  =
        X  =  SET2
        Y  =  SET3
        CH  =
```

Then control passes to the statement labeled **UN**.

When return from a procedure is made using **RETURN**,

   (1) the value of the function call is set to the value of the function name, and

   (2) the values of all variables saved at the time of the call are restored in reverse order.

When return is made using **FRETURN**,

   (1) the values of all variables saved at the time of the call are restored, in reverse order, and

   (2) the call fails.

When return is made using **NRETURN**,

   (1) the function call becomes a variable whose name is taken from the value of the function name, and

   (2) the values of all variables saved at the time of the call are restored, in reverse order.

A programmer-defined function may be called with more or fewer arguments than specified in the corresponding defining statement. If too few arguments are specified, the trailing omitted arguments are assigned null strings. If too many arguments are specified, the extra arguments are evaluated, but their values are ignored.

4.4.1   Example - Union, Intersection, and Negation

This example includes three functions that perform the union, intersection, and negation of sets of characters, and a short test program. Notice that the procedures follow the defining statements in the listing. However, by transferring around the procedures, the defining statements are executed one after another. The test program then makes calls to the procedures.

```
START
UNION   DEFINE('UNION(X,Y)CH','UN')              :(INTER)
UN      UNION  =  X
ULOOP   Y  CHAR  =                               :F(RETURN)
        UNION  CHTEST                            :S(ULOOP)
```

```
          UNION  =  UNION  CH                          :(ULOOP)
INTER     DEFINE('INTER(X,Y)CH','IN')                  :(NEG)
IN        X  CHAR  =                                   :F(RETURN)
          Y  CHTEST                                    :F(IN)
          INTER  =  INTER  CH                          :(IN)
NEG       DEFINE('NEG(X)CH,HEAD','NG')                 :(PATDEF)
NG        NEG  =  UNIVERSE
NLOOP     X  CHAR  =                                   :F(RETURN)
          NEG  CHLOC  =  HEAD                          :(NLOOP)
PATDEF    CHAR  =  LEN(1) . CH
          CHTEST  =  BREAK(*CH)
          CHLOC  =  BREAK(*CH) . HEAD  LEN(1)
TEST      UNIVERSE  =  'ABCDEFGHIJKLMNOPQRSTUVWXYZ'
          VOWELS  =  'AEIOU'
          OUTPUT  =  'VOWELS  =  "'  VOWELS '"'
          CONS  =  NEG(VOWELS)
          OUTPUT  =  'CONS  =  "'  CONS '"'
          WORD  =  'COMPILER'
          OUTPUT  =  'VOWELS IN "' WORD '" ARE:  "'
+                    INTER(WORD,VOWELS)  '"'
          OUTPUT  =  'CONSONANTS IN "' WORD '" ARE:  "'
+                    INTER(WORD,CONS)  '"'
          OUTPUT  =  'UNION OF "NIGHT" AND "HOWL" IS "'
+                    UNION('NIGHT','HOWL')  '"'
END
```

Output from the program is:

```
VOWELS  =  "AEIOU"
CONS  =  "BCDFGHJKLMNPQRSTVWXYZ"
VOWELS IN "COMPILER" ARE:  "OIE"
CONSONANTS IN "COMPILER" ARE:  "CMPLR"
UNION OF "NIGHT" AND "HOWL" IS "NIGHTOWL"
```


4.5   Redefinition of Programmer-Defined Functions

Programmer-defined functions can be defined at any time during execution of a program. It is also possible, having defined a function at one point, to redefine it at a subsequent time. For example, a function can be initialized when it is first called, and its entry point redefined for subsequent calls.

In the previous example, the pattern CHLOC is used only in the function procedure for NEG. The following procedure for NEG includes the assignment statement that constructs CHLOC.

```
NG        CHLOC  =  BREAK(*CH) . HEAD  LEN(1)
          DEFINE('NEG(X)CH,HEAD','NG2')
NG2       NEG  =  UNIVERSE
```

```
NLOOP  X  CHAR  =                                          :F(RETURN)
       NEG  CHLOC  =  HEAD                                 :(NLOOP)
```

The original **DEFINE** for **NEG** specifies the starting label **NG**. On the first call of **NEG**, the pattern structure for **CHLOC** is constructed and **NEG** is redefined with the starting label **NG2**. Subsequent calls of **NEG** do not execute the statement that constructs **CHLOC**.

4.6 Recursive Functions

Many functions are conveniently defined recursively. For example, factorials may be defined as

```
fact(0)  =  1
fact(n)  =  n*fact(n-1)    for  n > 0
```

Using Pascal's triangle, a recursive definition for the binomial coefficients is easily deduced.

```
            1

          1   1

        1   2   1

      1   3   3   1

    1   4   6   4   1

  1   5   10  10  5   1
```

```
binc(n,0)  =  1
binc(n,n)  =  1
binc(n,k)  =  binc(n-1,k-1)+binc(n-1,k)    0 < k < n
```

A recursive procedure has the property that the function itself is called in the procedure. While convenient, recursive procedures may lead to computational inefficiencies. Nevertheless, recursion is frequently the most natural way of expressing a function, and may considerably simplify programming.

Programmer-defined functions in SNOBOL4 may be recursive. Since values of the function name, arguments, and local variables are all saved when a function is called, a procedure can include recursive coding.

4.6.1   Example - Decimal to Binary Conversion

The next program converts decimal integers to their binary representation by successive divisions. For example, to compute the binary representation of **57**, it is repeatedly divided by **2** and the remainders are concatenated.

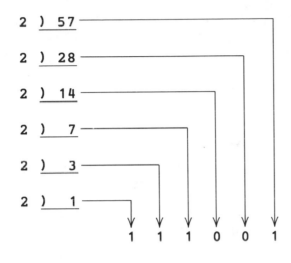

$$57_{10} \quad = \quad 111001_2$$

The binary representation of **57** is the binary representation of **28** (11100_2) followed by the remainder of **57/2**. A recursive definition of the process is

$$\text{binary(57)} \quad = \quad \text{binary(28)} \quad \text{remainder(57/2)}$$

where concatenation is implied.

In SNOBOL4, the results of integer division are truncated. Thus, **57 / 2** is **28**. Thus, the recursive definition can be written in the more general form

$$\text{binary(n)} \quad = \quad \text{binary(n/2)} \quad \text{remdr(n,2)} \qquad \text{for} \quad n > 1$$

(where **remdr(n,2)** is the remainder of **n/2**) with the terminal cases

```
binary(1)  =  1
binary(0)  =  0
```

A defining statement and procedure for **BINARY** are

```
         DEFINE('BINARY(N)')                           :(BINEND)
BINARY BINARY  =  GT(N,1)  BINARY(N / 2)  REMDR(N,2)
+                                                     :S(RETURN)
         BINARY  =  N                                  :(RETURN)
BINEND
```

On entry to **BINARY**, the value of **N** is tested by the predicate **GT(N,1)**, which fails for the two terminal cases **N = 0** and **N = 1**. Thus, the first statement fails for terminal cases and **N** is returned as the value of **BINARY**. If **N** is greater than **1**, a recursive call is made to **BINARY** with **N / 2** as the argument. The value of **BINARY(N / 2)** then has the remainder of **N / 2** concatenated with it, to get the final value of **BINARY(N)**.

The following diagram illustrates the recursive calls made during evaluation of **BINARY(57)**. The recursion plunges six levels before reaching the terminal case of **N = 1**. On returning, the value of **BINARY** evolves.

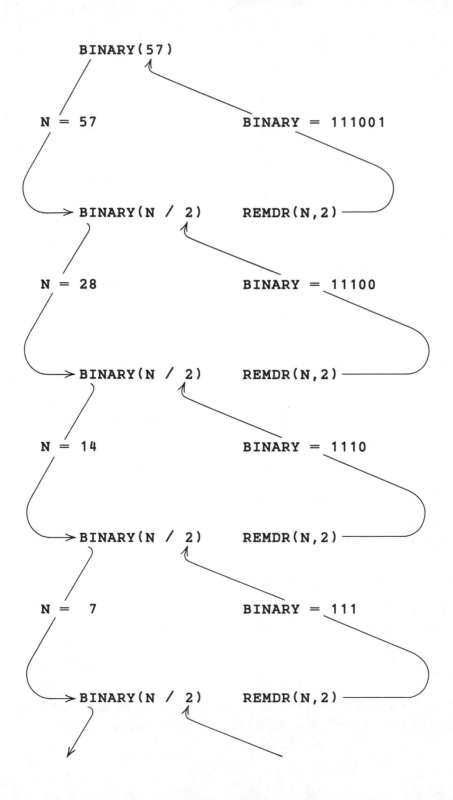

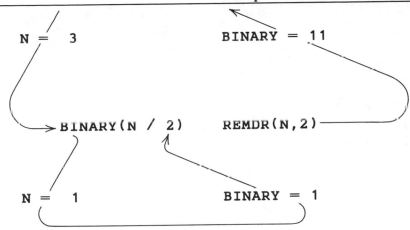

It is important to notice the necessity of preserving values before a function call and restoring them upon completion. At the first level down, **BINARY(28)** is called with **N** having value **57**. During the course of evaluating **BINARY(28)**, **N** takes on values **28**, **14**, **7**, **3**, and **1**. Following evaluation of **BINARY(28)**, **N** must once again have the value **57** in order to compute the remainder of **57 / 2**.

An improvement is possible in the definition of **BINARY**. SNOBOL4 permits use of a function name as one of the formal arguments in a function definition. Thus,

```
DEFINE('BINARY(BINARY)')
```

is a valid statement. The procedure of **BINARY** can be rewritten substituting **BINARY** for **N**.

```
BINARY BINARY  =  GT(BINARY,1)  BINARY(BINARY / 2)
+                         REMDR(BINARY,2)                        :(RETURN)
```

The second statement would become

```
BINARY  =  BINARY
```

which is redundant. For the terminal cases recognized by the failure of **GT(BINARY,1)**, **BINARY** has the proper value, **0** or **1**, and an unconditional **RETURN** is made.

```
        DEFINE('BINARY(BINARY)')
        OUTPUT  =  '     0  =  '  BINARY(0)
        OUTPUT  =  '    13  =  '  BINARY(13)
        OUTPUT  =  '    57  =  '  BINARY(57)
        OUTPUT  =  '   472  =  '  BINARY(472)
        OUTPUT  =  '  8192  =  '  BINARY(8192)
        OUTPUT  =  '13279  =  '  BINARY(13279)
        OUTPUT  =  '99999  =  '  BINARY(99999)      :(END)
BINARY BINARY  =  GT(BINARY,1)  BINARY(BINARY / 2)
+                         REMDR(BINARY,2)                        :(RETURN)
END
```

```
    0  =  0
   13  =  1101
   57  =  111001
  472  =  111011000
 8192  =  10000000000000
13279  =  11001111011111
99999  =  11000011010011111
```

4.6.2 Example - Polish to Infix Translation

Arithmetic expressions such as

```
        X + Y
      A / B / C
  V - W - X + Y * Z
```

are written using an infix notation. They can also be written in Polish prefix notation [5,6], resembling conventional functional notation. Here the binary operators appear to the left of their arguments. Prefix notation for the expressions is

```
        +(X,Y)
      /(/(A,B),C)
  +(-(-(V,W),X),*(Y,Z))
```

Conversion from Polish prefix form to infix form, and vice versa, can be performed using recursive programmer-defined functions. The first of the two following programs converts strings from Polish to infix form. The recursive rules for specifying the function **INF** are:

(1) If the argument to **INF** is a simple variable, then

```
    INF(VAR)  =  VAR
```

(2) If the argument to **INF** is a Polish expression of the form **OP(EX1,EX2)**, then

```
    INF(OP(EX1,EX2))  =  (INF(EX1)  OP  INF(EX2))
```

The conversion consists of finding the operator and its two arguments, which may be expressions. The operator is inserted between its two arguments and parentheses are placed around the resulting expression. Of course, the arguments are still in Polish form, so each must be converted to infix by a recursive call of **INF**.

The following diagram depicts the conversion of /(/(A,B),C) to ((A/B)/C).

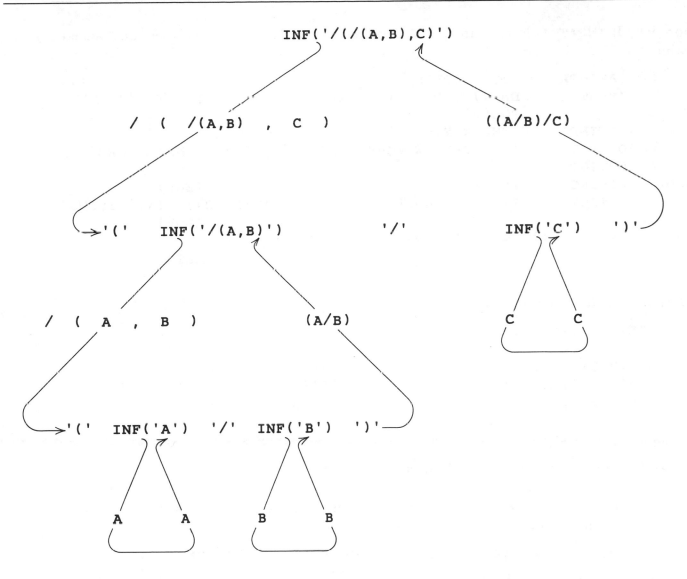

In the following program, the procedure for **INF** consists of one line. The pattern **INPAT** is used to break a Polish expression into an operator and two arguments.

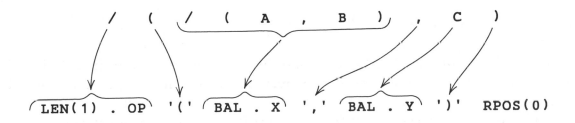

If **INPAT** matches **INF**, it matches the entire string, which is then rearranged into infix notation. If **INPAT** fails to match, **INF** must be a variable and is returned unchanged as value.

```
          &ANCHOR  =   1;    &TRIM    =    1
          INPAT  =   LEN(1) . OP  '('  BAL . X  ','  BAL . Y  ')'
+                    RPOS(0)
          DEFINE('INF(INF)X,Y,OP')
          OUTPUT  =  '      PREFIX FORM'  DUPL(' ',25)  'INFIX FORM'
          OUTPUT  =
LOOP      STRING  =   INPUT                               :F(END)
          OUTPUT  =   STRING  DUPL(' ',36 - SIZE(STRING))  INF(STRING)
+                                            :(LOOP)
INF       INF INPAT  =  '('  INF(X)  OP  INF(Y)  ')'
+                                            :(RETURN)
END
```

Output from the program follows.

PREFIX FORM	INFIX FORM
`-(*(A,+(B,C)),/(D,E))`	`((A*(B+C))-(D/E))`
`-(-(-(-(-(A,B),C),D),E),*(F,G))`	`(((((A-B)-C)-D)-E)-(F*G))`
`-(+(A,*(B,G)),/(D,P))`	`((A+(B*G))-(D/P))`

4.6.3 Example - Infix to Polish Translation

Conversion of arithmetic expressions from infix to Polish form is harder than the converse. A function **POL**, which performs the conversion, is of the form:

```
POL(EX1 OP EX2)  =  OP '(' POL(EX1) ',' POL(EX2) ')'
```

Ambiguities can arise when attempting to separate an unparenthesized expression into two expressions and an operator. For example, the expression

```
A - B * C - D
```

can be separated many ways, including

```
(A - B) * (C - D)
```

```
(A - (B * C)) - D
```

Normal conventions for the precedence and association of operators require that multiplication and division have precedence over addition and subtraction, and that operators associate to the left. Thus, of the choices above, the first is incorrect because subtraction is given higher precedence than multiplication, and the second is correct.

In defining the function **POL**, the precedence of multiplicative over additive operators can be assured by dealing with the additive operators first. For example:

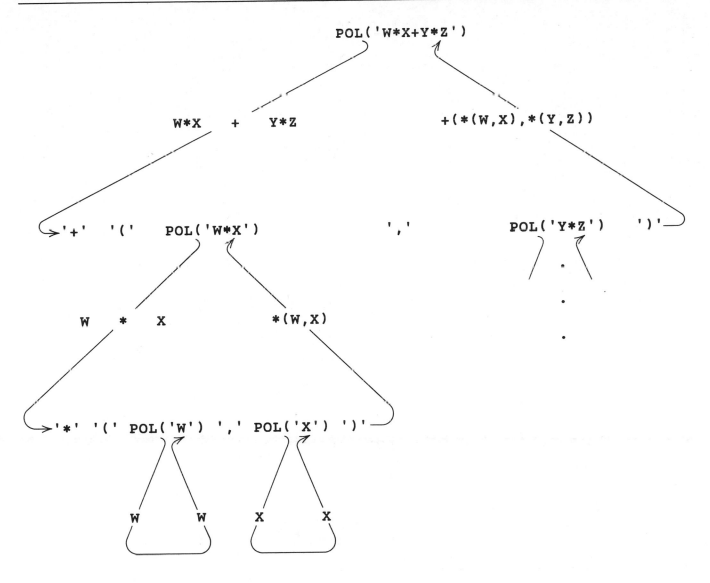

Left association of operators is assured by selecting the rightmost operator in a string of operators having equal precedence. For example

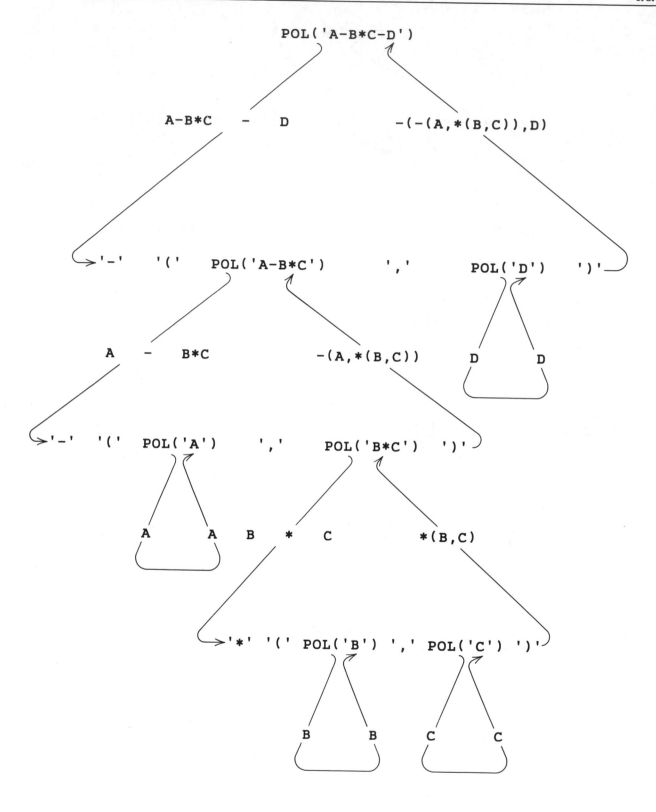

Thus, the rules prescribing the behavior of **POL** are:

(1) Remove any enclosing parentheses from the infix string.

(2) If possible, separate the argument into two expressions balanced with respect to parentheses and separated by the rightmost additive operator. The value of **POL** then becomes

```
OP '(' POL(EX1) ',' POL(EX2) ')'
```

If this is not possible, perform Step 3.

(3) If possible, separate the argument into expressions balanced with respect to parentheses and separated by the rightmost multiplicative operator. The value of **POL** then becomes

```
OP '(' POL(EX1) ',' POL(EX2) ')'
```

If this is not possible, perform Step 4.

(4) The infix string must be a simple variable, which becomes the value of **POL**.

A complete program for infix-to-Polish conversion and test results follow.

```
        &ANCHOR  =  1;    &TRIM  =   1
        PMPAT  =  (ARBNO(BAL ANY('+-')) $ X FAIL  |  *DIFFER(X)
+               TAB(*(SIZE(X) - 1))) . X  LEN(1) . OP  REM . Y
        MDPAT  =  (ARBNO(BAL ANY('*/')) $ X FAIL  |  *DIFFER(X)
+               TAB(*(SIZE(X) - 1))) . X  LEN(1) . OP  REM . Y
        STRIP  =  '(' BAL . POL ')'  RPOS(0)
        DEFINE('POL(POL)X,Y,OP')
        OUTPUT =  '     INFIX FORM' DUPL(' ',26) 'PREFIX FORM'
        OUTPUT =
LOOP    STRING  =  INPUT                              :F(END)
        OUTPUT  =  STRING  DUPL(' ',36 - SIZE(STRING)) POL(STRING)
+                                           :(LOOP)
POL     POL   STRIP                                   :S(POL)
        POL   PMPAT  =  OP  '(' POL(X) ',' POL(Y) ')'
+                                           :S(RETURN)
        POL   MDPAT  =  OP  '(' POL(X) ',' POL(Y) ')'
+                                           :(RETURN)
END
```

INFIX FORM	PREFIX FORM
((A*(B+C))-(D/E))	-(*(A,+(B,C)),/(D,E))
A-B-C-D-E-F*G	-(-(-(-(-(A,B),C),D),E),*(F,G))
((A+(B*G))-(D/P))	-(+(A,*(B,G)),/(D,P))

The pattern **STRIP** removes the outer parentheses from the infix expression. The patterns

PMPAT and MDPAT separate the infix expression into two expressions and an operator according to the convention for left association. The patterns are identical except that PMPAT looks for addition or subtraction and MDPAT looks for multiplication or division.

PMPAT has three parts, corresponding to the first balanced expression, the operator, and the second balanced expression. The pattern for the first expression is complicated by the fact that the operator must be the rightmost in the string of operators. Consider the pattern for the first expression:

```
     (ARBNO(BAL ANY('+-'))  $ X   FAIL  |  *DIFFER(X)
+     TAB(*(SIZE(X) - 1))) . X
```

It consists of two alternatives. The first,

```
     ARBNO(BAL ANY('+-'))  $ X   FAIL
```

is used to locate the rightmost operator by matching a sequence of balanced strings followed by additive operators. FAIL forces ARBNO to match the longest such string and eventually causes failure of the alternative. Thus, for the expression A-B*C-D, the last match of the first alternative is

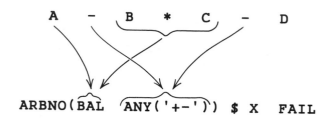

On entry to the second alternative

```
     *DIFFER(X)   TAB(*(SIZE(X) - 1))
```

the value of X is checked to see if it is the null string. If so, no match is possible. If it is not null, the first balanced expression must be all but the last character of X. The first expression is matched by

```
     TAB(*(SIZE(X) - 1))
```

The remainder of PMPAT consists of the expression

```
     LEN(1) . OP   REM . Y
```

LEN(1) is used to match the operator and REM matches the remainder of the string, which is the second balanced expression.

4.6.4   Example - Tower of Hanoi

The Tower of Hanoi is a game derived from the ancient Tower of Brahma, a ritual allegedly practiced by Brahman priests to predict the end of the world. At the time of creation, 64 golden discs of decreasing size appeared stacked on a diamond needle. Nearby were two other diamond needles, both empty. The Brahman priests, created at the same time, were set to the task of moving the discs from their original needle to a second needle using, when necessary, the third needle as temporary storage. Before all 64 discs are moved to the second needle and stacked in decreasing size, the end of the world will be upon us.

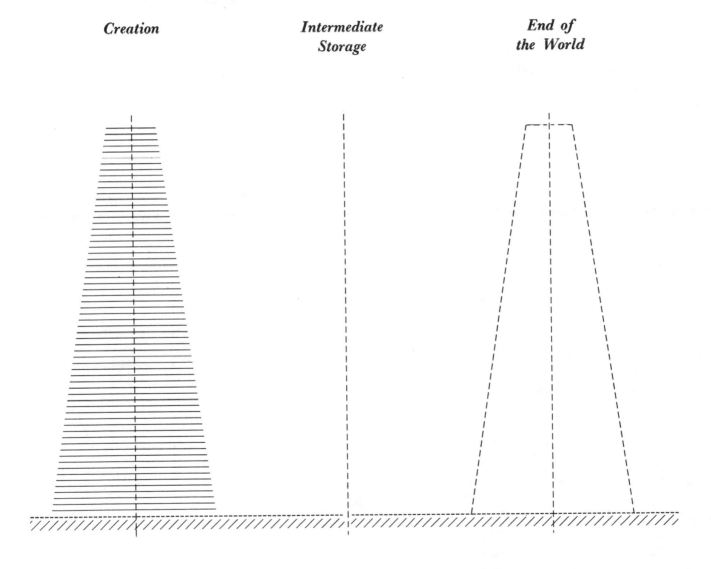

Creation   *Intermediate*   *End of*
                           Storage   *the World*

Movement of the discs is governed by the rules:

(1) only one disc may be moved at a time,
(2) a disc may be moved from any needle to any other, and
(3) at no time may a larger disc rest upon a smaller disc.

A solution to the Tower of Hanoi is a recursive function that prints out the steps necessary to move **N** discs from one needle to another (where **N** is hopefully a good deal smaller than 64). A program that defines the function **HANOI** and tests it by moving 5 discs from needle **A** to needle **C** follows.

```
        DEFINE('HANOI(N,NS,ND,NI)')                         :(HANOI.END)
HANOI   EQ(N,0)                                             :S(RETURN)
        HANOI(N - 1,NS,NI,ND)
        OUTPUT = 'MOVE DISC ' N ' FROM ' NS ' TO ' ND
        HANOI(N - 1,NI,ND,NS)                               :(RETURN)
HANOI.END
TEST    HANOI(5,'A','C','B')
END
```

```
MOVE DISC 1 FROM A TO C
MOVE DISC 2 FROM A TO B
MOVE DISC 1 FROM C TO B
MOVE DISC 3 FROM A TO C
MOVE DISC 1 FROM B TO A
MOVE DISC 2 FROM B TO C
MOVE DISC 1 FROM A TO C
MOVE DISC 4 FROM A TO B
MOVE DISC 1 FROM C TO B
MOVE DISC 2 FROM C TO A
MOVE DISC 1 FROM B TO A
MOVE DISC 3 FROM C TO B
MOVE DISC 1 FROM A TO C
MOVE DISC 2 FROM A TO B
MOVE DISC 1 FROM C TO B
MOVE DISC 5 FROM A TO C
MOVE DISC 1 FROM B TO A
MOVE DISC 2 FROM B TO C
MOVE DISC 1 FROM A TO C
MOVE DISC 3 FROM B TO A
MOVE DISC 1 FROM C TO B
MOVE DISC 2 FROM C TO A
MOVE DISC 1 FROM B TO A
MOVE DISC 4 FROM B TO C
MOVE DISC 1 FROM A TO C
MOVE DISC 2 FROM A TO B
```

```
MOVE DISC   1  FROM   C TO B
MOVE DISC   3  FROM   A TO C
MOVE DISC   1  FROM   B TO A
MOVE DISC   2  FROM   B TO C
MOVE DISC   1  FROM   A TO C
```

The program logic can be seen by induction. Clearly, moving no discs requires no steps. Moving one disc from needle **A** to needle **C** requires one step.

```
MOVE DISC   1   FROM   A TO C
```

Moving two discs from **A** to **C** requires three steps.

```
MOVE DISC   1   FROM   A TO B
MOVE DISC   2   FROM   A TO C
MOVE DISC   1   FROM   B TO C
```

Moving three discs from **A** to **C** requires seven steps.

```
MOVE DISC   1   FROM   A TO C
MOVE DISC   2   FROM   A TO B
MOVE DISC   1   FROM   C TO B
MOVE DISC   3   FROM   A TO C
MOVE DISC   1   FROM   B TO A
MOVE DISC   2   FROM   B TO C
MOVE DISC   1   FROM   A TO C
```

The general solution is:

```
MOVE N-1 DISCS FROM   A TO B
MOVE DISC   N   FROM   A TO C
MOVE N-1 DISCS  FROM   B TO C
```

The implementation is simple. **HANOI** is defined with four arguments:

(1) **N** is the number of discs to be moved,
(2) **NS** is the starting needle,
(3) **ND** is the destination needle, and
(4) **NI** is the intermediate storage needle.

On entry to **HANOI**, the value of **N** is compared with zero. If **N** is zero, no discs are moved and the function returns. If **N** is not zero, **HANOI** is called recursively to move **N-1** discs from the starting needle to the intermediate storage needle. Having done that, the command to move the **N**th disc from the starting needle to the destination needle is printed. Finally, **HANOI** is called a second time to move the **N-1** discs from intermediate storage to the destination needle.

Exercises

Exercise 4.1: Write a function that prints all substrings of length **N** from a string **S**.

Exercise 4.2: The Fibonacci numbers **F(N)** are defined by the equations

```
F(0)    =    0
F(1)    =    1
F(N+1)  =    F(N) + F(N-1)
```

Define a function **F** such that the value of **F(N)** is the **N**th Fibonacci number.

Exercise 4.3: Define a function that converts algebraic expressions into Polish notation. Let the definition of expression include the binary operator **!** for exponentiation in addition to the operators **+**, **-**, *****, and **/**. Assume that exponentiation associates to the right.

Exercise 4.4: Define a function **NOT** such that **NOT(P)** matches the null string if **P** fails to match, and fails if **P** matches.

CHAPTER 5

Arrays, Tables, and Defined Data Types

5.1 Arrays

An array is an indexed aggregate of variables, called elements. Arrays are created by the execution of the primitive function **ARRAY**.   **ARRAY(p,e)** returns an array whose bounds and dimensions are described by the prototype **p**. Every element is initialized to the value of the expression **e**. For example,

> **VECTOR   =   ARRAY(10)**

assigns a one-dimensional array of length **10** to **VECTOR**. Since the second argument is omitted, each element of the array has the null string value. Indexing ordinarily starts at **1**. Other lower bounds may be specified by using a colon to separate the upper and lower limits.

> **LINE   =   ARRAY('-5:5')**

creates an array with lower bound **-5** and upper bound **5**.

Additional dimensions in a prototype are separated by commas. Thus,

> **BOARD   =   ARRAY('3,3','X')**

defines a three-by-three array with all elements having the value **X**.

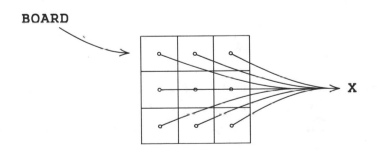

There is no intrinsic limit on the size or dimensionality of an array.

Warning: The first argument of **ARRAY** is the prototype, and the second is a value, which is given to each element of the resulting array. Thus,

        A   =   ARRAY('3,3')

creates a two-dimensional array with each element having the null string as value.

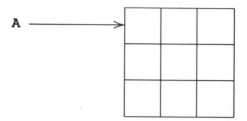

On the other hand,

        A   =   ARRAY(3,3)

creates a one-dimensional array with each element having the value **3**.

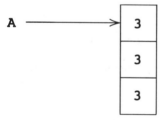

Each element of an array is given the same initial value. Consequently, execution of the instructions

        A1   =   ARRAY(5)
        A2   =   ARRAY(5,A1)

creates only two arrays. Each element of **A2** has the same array, **A1**, as value.

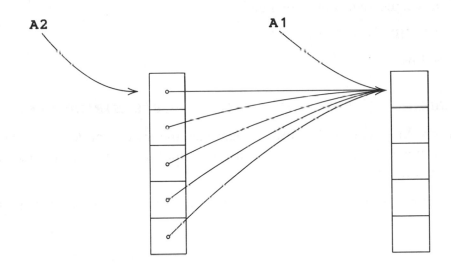

5.1.1 Array References

If the value of a variable is an array, as is the case with **VECTOR**, **BOARD**, **A**, **A1**, and **A2** above, an element in the array may be referenced through the variable. Angular brackets following the array-valued variable are used to specify the element. Array references such as **VECTOR<8>** or **BOARD<2,3>** are variables. For example,

        VECTOR<8>   =   EXP

assigns the value of **EXP** to the eighth element of **VECTOR**.

        OUTPUT   =   BOARD<2,3>

prints the value of the **2,3** element of **BOARD**.

        FIELD   =   BREAK(' ') . LINE<-3,4> ' '

defines a pattern that breaks out a field of data and assigns it to the **-3,4** element of **LINE**.

Each element of an array may have any type of data object as value. For example, the first element of an array may be an integer, the second a pattern, and so forth.

If an index referring to an element of an array falls outside the range of the array, the array reference fails. Thus,

        OUTPUT   =   VECTOR<12>

fails. This failure may be used to control iteration through the elements of an array without knowing its size. A function **SUM**, whose value is the sum of all the elements of an array, could have the defining statement

```
        DEFINE('SUM(ARRAY)N')
```

with the procedure

```
SUM        N     =    N + 1
           SUM   =    SUM + ARRAY<N>        :S(SUM)F(RETURN)
```

The summation loop continues until **N** exceeds the range of **ARRAY**. This function does not need to know the size of **ARRAY**, but only that it is a one-dimensional array with a lower bound of one.

Omitted trailing indices are taken to be zero. Specification of too many indices is an error.

Example - Bubble Sort

A simple application of one-dimensional arrays is illustrated in the following example that puts strings in lexical order. A bubble sort is much like an exchange sort. When two elements are found to be out of order, they are switched. However, the lexically smaller item is bubbled up to its proper place.

```
*                     BUBBLE SORT PROGRAM
           &TRIM   =    1
           DEFINE('SORT(N)I')
           DEFINE('SWITCH(I)TEMP')
           DEFINE('BUBBLE(J)')
*                     GET NUMBER OF ITEMS TO BE SORTED
           N       =    INPUT                         :F(ERROR)
           A       =    ARRAY(N)
*                     READ IN THE ITEMS
READ       I       =    I + 1
           A<I>    =    INPUT                         :F(GO)S(READ)
*                     SORT THE LIST
GO         SORT(N)
*                     PRINT SORTED LIST
           M       =    1
PRINT      OUTPUT  =    A<M>                          :F(END)
           M       =    M + 1                         :(PRINT)
*                     FUNCTIONS
SORT       I       =    LT(I,N - 1)  I + 1            :F(RETURN)
           LGT(A<I>,A<I + 1>)                         :F(SORT)
           SWITCH(I)
           BUBBLE(I)                                  :(SORT)
SWITCH     TEMP    =    A<I>
           A<I>    =    A<I + 1>
```

```
          A<I + 1>    =    TEMP                        :(RETURN)
BUBBLE    J           =    GT(J,1)   J - 1             :F(RETURN)
          LGT(A<J>,A<J + 1>)                           :F(RETURN)
          SWITCH(J)                                    :(BUBBLE)
END
```

For the input

```
15
ADDSIB
BUKINT
ADJTTL
BUCKET
ADREAL
BKSPCE
APDSP
ARRAY
BKSIZE
ALTERN
BRANCH
ADJUST
BUFFER
ADDSON
ADDLG
```

the output is

```
ADDLG
ADDSIB
ADDSON
ADJTTL
ADJUST
ADREAL
ALTERN
APDSP
ARRAY
BKSIZE
BKSPCE
BRANCH
BUCKET
BUFFER
BUKINT
```

One iteration of **SORT** is:

SWITCH   BUBBLE   INCREMENT
                                            I

Elements above **I** are properly ordered. If elements at **I** and **I + 1** are out of order, they are switched. The new element at **I**, which is **B**, is bubbled by means of interchanges to its proper place above **I**. **I** is incremented and the process continues.

5.2   Tables

A table is an aggregate of variables, similar to a one-dimensional array. However, a variable in a table can be referenced by any data object, unlike arrays that require integer references. A table can be thought of as an associative array.

A table is created by the **TABLE** function. For example,

        T   =   TABLE( )

creates a table and assigns it as the value of **T**. Variables in the table **T** may be subsequently referenced in much the same manner that array references are made. For example,

        T<'A'>   =   3

assigns the value **3** to the **A**th element of **T**.

The referencing argument can be any value of any data type. By simply using an argument, the appropriate variable in the table is referenced. If no such variable exists, one is created and given the null string as its initial value.

The **TABLE** function actually has two arguments, both of which can be omitted as in the introductory example above. The general form of the function is

> **TABLE(N,M)**

where **N** and **M** concern the size of the table. **N** determines the initial size of the table, indicating how many variables it can contain. **M** is the number of additional variables provided if more are required. For example,

> **TABLE(20,15)**

creates a tables of **20** variables. If more are required, the table size is increased to **35**. If this is not sufficient, the size is increased to **50**, and so on.

The default values for **N** and **M** are **10**. If either argument is omitted (or zero), the corresponding default is used. Efficient use of tables is obtained by choosing values of **N** and **M** appropriate to the expected use of the table.

Programmers are cautioned that each different argument references a different variable in a table. **T<1>** and **T<'1'>** reference different variables. Particular care must be taken when the referencing argument is not given explicitly, but rather results from the evaluation of an expression.

An example of the use of tables appears at the end of the next section.

5.3   Functions for Use with Arrays and Tables

5.3.1   COPY

The value of the **ARRAY** function is an object whose data type is **ARRAY**. This value may be assigned to one or more variables.

> **A   =   ARRAY(3)**
> **B   =   A**

A and **B** have the same array as value.

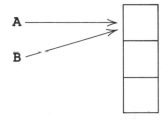

Thus,

```
B<2>    =    'SIX'
OUTPUT    =    A<2>
```

print **SIX**.

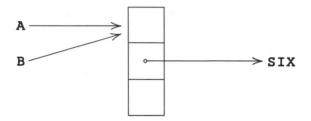

The **COPY** function produces a copy of an array. Executing the statements

```
A    =    ARRAY(3)
A<2>    =    'TWO'
B    =    COPY(A)
B<2>    =    'SIX'
```

creates distinct arrays. Unlike the previous example, assigning a value to **B<2>** does not affect the value of **A<2>**.

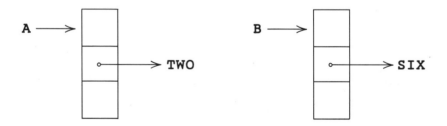

COPY may be used with other types of data, as described in Chapter 7. Tables cannot be copied, however.

5.3.2 PROTOTYPE

The value of the dimension or range of an array is sometimes needed. The primitive function **PROTOTYPE** returns the prototype used to define the array. **PROTOTYPE** has an array-valued argument and returns the prototype string. Thus, if

```
A    =    ARRAY('-5:5','X')
```

then the value of **PROTOTYPE(A)** is the string **-5:5**.

An example utilizing **PROTOTYPE** is the following function named **SQUARE**. The argument of **SQUARE** is any singly-dimensioned array. The value of **SQUARE** is a 2-dimensional square array whose dimensions equal that of the argument, and whose elements are null strings.

```
        DEFINE('SQUARE(A)')                              :(SQEND)
SQUARE  SQUARE  =  ARRAY(PROTOTYPE(A) ',' PROTOTYPE(A))  :(RETURN)
SQEND
```

The argument of **ARRAY** is a string formed from two occurences of **PROTOTYPE(A)** separated by a comma. Thus, the index range is the same for both dimensions of the new array.

5.3.3 ITEM

In order to reference an array or table element by means of angular brackets, the array must be the value of a known identifier. Sometimes this is not the case. For example,

```
    $X    =    ARRAY(10)
```

is an acceptable assignment statement. But **$X<2>** and **($X)<2>** do not reference the second element of the array. In the first expression, the unary **$** operates on the value of **X<2>**; the second is syntactically erroneous.

There are two ways to refer to an element of such an array. The array can be assigned to a known identifier:

```
    TEMP    =    $X
    TEMP<2>    =    'SIX'
```

Alternatively, the primitive function **ITEM** can be used. The value of **ITEM(A,i$_1$,...,i$_n$)** is the **(i$_1$,...,i$_n$)** element of the array **A**.

```
    ITEM($X,2)    =    'SIX'
```

assigns **SIX** to the second element of the array that is the value of **$X**.

Similarly, if

```
    A<1>    =    ARRAY(100)
```

is executed, the 50th item of this array may be referenced by **ITEM(A<1>,50)**. **ITEM** also may be used to reference tables.

If an index referring to an element of an array falls outside the range of the array, the call of **ITEM** fails. As with array and table references, extra arguments are erroneous.

5.3.4 Conversion between Arrays and Tables

Conversion between tables and arrays can be performed using the **CONVERT** function. If **T** is a table

```
A    =    CONVERT(T,'ARRAY')
```

assigns to **A** an array corresponding to the table **T**. The prototype of **A** is **n,2** where **n** is the number of variables in **T** that have nonnull values. A<I,1> is a referencing argument and A<I,2> is the value of the corresponding variable. Only variables with nonnull values are included. Conversion from **TABLE** to **ARRAY** fails if there is no variable with a nonnull value.

Conversion of a table to an array creates a 'fixed' representation of the table that can be accessed systematically by indexing through the resulting array. This ability is particularly useful when the variables of the table are not known, as illustrated by the example at the end of this section.

A rectangular array with a second dimension that has an extent of two can be converted to a table. For example, if **A** is an array with prototype **-3:3,2**,

```
T    =    CONVERT(A,'TABLE')
```

creates a table **T** with seven variables corresponding to A<I,1> (-3 ≤ I ≤ 3) and with values of these variables being A<I,2> respectively. A<I,1> is created even if the value of A<I,2> is the null string. If the second dimension does not have an extent of two, the call of **CONVERT** fails.

The value used for additional variables (corresponding to the second argument of **TABLE**) is the default, **10**.

Example - Word Counting

A simple application of tables is illustrated in the following example that counts the number of times that words occur in input text. A line of text is read in, printed, and decomposed into words, using a simple definition for word separation. Each word references a corresponding table variable used to keep the count. When the input text is exhausted, the table is converted into an array and the results printed.

```
        &ANCHOR    =    1
        SEPARATOR    =    ' .,;:?!-'
        END    =    BREAK(SEPARATOR)
        GAP    =    SPAN(SEPARATOR)
        TOKEN    =    END . WORD GAP
        COUNT    =    TABLE(20,10)
READ    LINE    =    INPUT                                    :F(PRINT)
        OUTPUT    =    LINE
        LINE    GAP    =
```

```
NEXTT   LINE    TOKEN   -                                          :F(READ)
        COUNT<WORD>   =    COUNT<WORD> + 1                         :(NEXTT)
PRINT   OUTPUT  =
        OUTPUT  =    'WORD COUNTS ARE:'
        OUTPUT  =
        COUNT   =    CONVERT(COUNT,'ARRAY')                        :F(END)
        I   =   1
NEXTC   OUTPUT  -    COUNT<I,1> ' = ' COUNT<I,2>                   :F(END)
        I   =   I + 1                                              :(NEXTC)
END
```

For input consisting of a fragment from the poem 'The Bells' by Edgar Allan Poe, the
output is

```
         ON THE FUTURE! - HOW IT TELLS
         OF THE RAPTURE THAT IMPELLS
       TO THE SWINGING AND THE RINGING
         OF THE BELLS, BELLS, BELLS, -
     OF THE BELLS, BELLS, BELLS, BELLS,
             BELLS, BELLS, BELLS, -
     TO THE RHYMING AND THE CHIMING OF THE BELLS!
```

```
WORD COUNTS ARE:

ON = 1
THE = 9
FUTURE = 1
HOW = 1
IT = 1
TELLS = 1
OF = 4
RAPTURE = 1
THAT = 1
IMPELLS = 1
TO = 2
SWINGING = 1
AND = 2
RINGING = 1
BELLS = 11
RHYMING = 1
CHIMING = 1
```

5.4 Programmer-Defined Data Types

SNOBOL4 allows the programmer to define his own types of data objects. A
programmer-defined data object is an ordered set of variables called fields. A call of
DATA(p) defines a new data type described by the prototype **p**. The prototype **p** is a

string denoting the name of the data type and the names of the fields. There is no intrinsic limit to the number of fields.

As an example of a programmer-defined data type, consider complex numbers. A complex number can be said to consist of two fields, the real and the imaginary. The call

```
DATA('COMPLEX(R,I)')
```

defines a data type `COMPLEX`, with two fields `R` and `I`.

To create an object with the data type `COMPLEX`, a call of the form

```
COMPLEX(e1,e2)
```

is made, where `e1` and `e2` are expressions with numerical values. For example, to assign the complex number '`1.5+2.0i`' to the variable `C`, the statement

```
C  =  COMPLEX(1.5,2.0)
```

is executed. Each call of the function `COMPLEX` creates two new variables corresponding to the real and imaginary parts. These variables may be referenced by using the field name as a function. After executing the statement above, the value of `C` is a complex number; the real part is referenced by `R(C)` and the imaginary part by `I(C)`. Thus,

```
A  =  R(C)
```

assigns the value `1.5` to `A`. Since `R(C)` is a variable, it may be assigned a value. If

```
R(C)  =  3.2
```

is executed, the complex number '`3.2+2.0i`' is assigned to `C`.

Operations on complex quantities can be defined using programmer-defined functions. A function to compute the sum of two complex quantities is

```
        DEFINE('SUM(C1,C2)')                           :(SUM.END)
SUM     SUM  =  COMPLEX(R(C1) + R(C2),I(C1) + I(C2))   :(RETURN)
SUM.END
```

If `C` has the value '`3.2+2.0i`', execution of the statement

```
C  =  SUM(C,COMPLEX(1.0,1.0))
```

assigns '`4.2+3.0i`' to `C`.

Example - Text Processing

There is no intrinsic limit to the length of a string in SNOBOL4, but there is often a practical limit. For example, scanning a string for a pattern can be time consuming if the string is long. However, many string applications require reading in and retaining long passages of text. For such cases, a new data type called `TEXT` can be defined.

```
DATA('TEXT(LINE,N,NEXT)')
```

The first field is a line of text, the second field indicates the line number, and the third field points to the next line of text.

A passage of text is read as follows:

```
        I   =   1
        HEAD    =   TEXT(INPUT,I)                    :F(EMPTY)
        CURRENT  =   HEAD
LOOP    I   =   I + 1
        NEXT(CURRENT)  =   TEXT(INPUT,I)             :F(DONE)
        CURRENT  =   NEXT(CURRENT)                   :(LOOP)
DONE
```

The resulting data structure has the form:

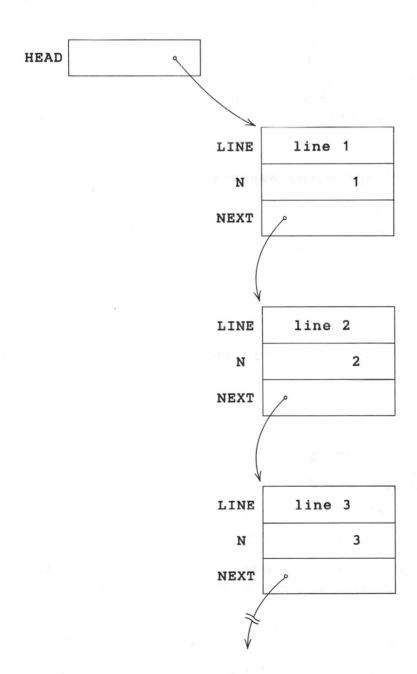

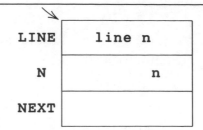

The statement

```
        LINE(HEAD)    'EVERY'                              :S(YES)F(NO)
```

examines the first line for the word **EVERY**.

The following section of program prints the lines and line numbers where **EVERY** occurs.

```
        CURRENT   =   HEAD
TEST    LINE(CURRENT)   'EVERY'                       :F(BUMP)
        OUTPUT  =  N(CURRENT)   ': '   LINE(CURRENT)
BUMP    CURRENT   =   NEXT(CURRENT)
        IDENT(CURRENT)                                :F(TEST)
```

The same field names may exist for several data types. Thus,

```
        DATA('LIST(VALUE,NEXT)')
```

defines a data type **LIST** which can coexist with the previous definition of the data type **TEXT**. Although **NEXT** is a field name for both **TEXT** and **LIST**, **NEXT(X)** is not ambiguous because the data type of the argument **X** indicates the usage.

5.4.1 VALUE

VALUE is a primitive field function defined on strings and names which refers to their value. If

```
        RADIX    =     'HEX'
```

then

```
        V    =    VALUE('RADIX')
```

assigns the string **HEX** to **V**. Similarly,

```
        VALUE('RADIX')    =    'DEC'
```

assigns the string **DEC** as the value of **RADIX**.

VALUE is supplied so that a programmer may define the field **VALUE** on programmer-defined data types, and then apply **VALUE** to strings and names as well as the defined types. This permits a uniform treatment of 'value' without the necessity for checking data type. If

```
DATA('LIST(VALUE,TEXT)')
DATA('NODE(FATHER,LSON,RSTB,VALUE)')
```

are used to define the data types **LIST** and **NODE**, then **VALUE** can be applied to objects with data type **LIST** and **NODE** as well as names and strings.

Exercises

Exercise 5.1: One way to represent a directed graph is with an array of arrays. Suppose the nodes of a graph are numbered 1 through **N**, and node **I** has **S(I)** successors. The graph can be represented by an **N*2** array. The **I,1** element is a one-dimensional array of successors with **S(I)** elements. The **I,2** element can be used for a value associated with the **I** th node.

   Write a program to read in and construct a graph. The first data card should contain the number of nodes. Each subsequent card should contain a node number and a list of successors.

Exercise 5.2: A path between two nodes can be represented by a string of node numbers separated by commas. Write a function **PATH(I,J)** that finds a path between the nodes **I** and **J**. If there is no path, the function should fail.

Exercise 5.3: Assume the statements in an assembly language program have three fields: label, operation, and operand. They are in free format and the label field is optional. The branch statement has the form

[label]   BRANCH   label

Write a program that analyzes an assembly language source deck and produces a flow table that lists the labels and the numbers of the statements that branch to each label.

Exercise 5.4: Define a function **MUL** that computes the product of two complex numbers. Redefine multiplication so that if either operand is complex the result is complex. Otherwise, the product should be the usual result.

CHAPTER 6

Keywords, Names, and Code

6.1 Keywords

The unary operator ampersand, &, when applied to certain identifiers called keywords, provides access to information used internally by the SNOBOL4 system. Some keywords permit internal values to be changed. Thus

&ANCHOR   =   1

turns on the anchored pattern matching mode. Another example of a keyword is &STCOUNT whose value is the number of statements that have been executed. If the statement

GT(&STCOUNT,40000)   :S(CLEAN.UP)

is executed, transfer to the statement labelled CLEAN.UP is made if more than 40000 statements have been executed. The value of &STCOUNT is automatically incremented as statements are executed. The programmer cannot assign a value to &STCOUNT, and an attempt to do so is an error. Such a keyword is *protected.* Keywords to which the programmer can assign values (such as &ANCHOR) are *unprotected.*

6.1.1 Protected Keywords

There are fifteen protected keywords.

&ALPHABET: The value of &ALPHABET is a string of all the characters of the machine on which SNOBOL4 is implemented. The characters are ordered according to their internal coding.

&ABORT: The value of &ABORT is the same as the initial value of ABORT. The value of ABORT can be changed, but the value of &ABORT cannot. There are corresponding protected keywords for the other primitive patterns.

&ARB: The value of &ARB is the same as the initial value of ARB.

&BAL: The value of &BAL is the same as the initial value of BAL.

&ERRTYPE: When a program error occurs, an integer code identifying the error is

128

assigned to &ERRTYPE. See the discussion of errors in Chapter 10. The initial value of &ERRTYPE is zero, indicating no error has occured.

&FAIL: The value of &FAIL is the same as the initial value of FAIL.

&FENCE: The value of &FENCE is the same as the initial value of FENCE.

&FNCLEVEL: The value of &FNCLEVEL is the level of programmer-defined function calls. The initial value of &FNCLEVEL is zero. &FNCLEVEL is incremented by one each time a programmer-defined function is called, and decremented with each return.

&LASTNO: The compiler assigns a number to each statement. These numbers are used primarily for diagnostic purposes. The value of &LASTNO is an integer corresponding to the number of the last (previous) statement executed. See also &STNO.

&REM: The value of &REM is the same as the initial value of REM.

&RTNTYPE: The value of &RTNTYPE is the string RETURN, FRETURN, or NRETURN, corresponding to the type of return made by the last programmer-defined function to return. The initial value of &RTNTYPE is the null string.

&STCOUNT: The value of &STCOUNT is an integer corresponding to the number of statements executed. The value of &STCOUNT is incremented when execution of a statement begins.

&STFCOUNT: The value of &STFCOUNT is an integer corresponding to the number of statements that have failed. &STFCOUNT is incremented when a statement fails.

&STNO: The value of &STNO is an integer corresponding to the number of the statement currently being executed. See &LASTNO.

&SUCCEED: The value of &SUCCEED is the same as the initial value of SUCCEED.

6.1.2   Unprotected Keywords

There are thirteen unprotected keywords to which a programmer can assign integer values.

&ABEND: If &ABEND is nonzero, indicating a request for an abnormal ending, a system core dump is given following program termination. When an abnormal end is forced in this manner on the IBM 360, the user completion code is the value of &ABEND (modulo 4096).

&ANCHOR: If &ANCHOR is nonzero, pattern matching is performed in the anchored mode. See Chapter 2. The initial value of &ANCHOR is zero.

&CODE: The value of &CODE is returned to the operating system on program completion. On the IBM 360, the value of &CODE is returned as the condition code for that job step. The initial value of &CODE is zero.

&DUMP: If &DUMP is nonzero at program termination, the values of natural variables and unprotected keywords are listed at the end of the program printout. The initial value of &DUMP is zero.

&ERRLIMIT: The value of &ERRLIMIT controls the handling of certain program errors. See the description of program errors in Chapter 10. The initial value of &ERRLIMIT is zero.

&FTRACE: If &FTRACE is greater than zero, diagnostic tracing information is provided on calls to and returns from all programmer-defined functions. See Chapter 8. The initial value of &FTRACE is zero.

&FULLSCAN: If &FULLSCAN is nonzero, pattern matching is performed in the fullscan mode. See Chapter 2. The initial value of &FULLSCAN is zero.

&INPUT: If &INPUT is nonzero, input occurs automatically for input-associated variables (such as INPUT). If &INPUT is zero, input does not occur. The initial value of &INPUT is one.

&MAXLNGTH: The value of &MAXLNGTH limits the length of strings that can be formed. If an attempt is made to form a string with more characters than &MAXLNGTH, a program error occurs. The initial value of &MAXLNGTH is 5000, but this value can be changed. All types of string formation are governed by &MAXLNGTH: concatenation, replacement, value assignment as a result of pattern matching, and string input.

&OUTPUT: If &OUTPUT is nonzero, output occurs automatically whenever a value is assigned to an output-associated variable. If &OUTPUT is zero, output does not occur. The initial value of &OUTPUT is one.

&STLIMIT: The value of STLIMIT is the limit on the number of statements that can be executed (see &STCOUNT). The initial value of &STLIMIT is 50000. Exceeding the limit on statement execution causes program termination.

&TRACE: Diagnostic tracing facilities are available if &TRACE is greater than zero. See Chapter 8. The initial value of &TRACE is zero.

&TRIM: If &TRIM is nonzero, trailing blanks are trimmed on input. The initial value of &TRIM is zero.

6.2   Names

A variable can be assigned a value during an assignment statement or by pattern matching through use of the unary cursor position operator ə or the binary value assignment operators . and $. In SNOBOL4, variables fall into two major classes, natural variables and created variables.

A natural variable is any variable whose name is a nonnull string. Thus,

```
A
$'AB'
$',,,('
```

are examples of natural variables, whose names, respectively, are the strings

```
A
AB
,,,(
```

The variable `,,,(` cannot appear explicitly in an assignment statement such as

```
,,,(  =  'X'
```

because it is syntactically incorrect. However,

```
$',,,('  —  'X'
```

is syntactically correct and performs the desired assignment. Every string except the null string is the name of a natural variable. Natural variables are available at the start of a program without any conscious act of creation on the part of the programmer. All natural variables with the exception of **ABORT**, **ARB**, **BAL**, **FAIL**, **FENCE**, **REM**, and **SUCCEED** have the null string as their initial value.

Created variables are generated during execution of a program when, for example, an array is created. The statement

```
A  =  ARRAY(10)
```

creates an array of ten variables. These variables are referenced by A<1>, A<2>, ..., A<10>.

Some expressions yield variables when evaluated. Such variables are called generated variables, and values can be assigned to them in the same manner that values can be assigned to variables that appear explicitly. In the statements

```
M  =  2
$('N' M)  =  'INVOICE'
```

the subject `$('N' M)` generates the variable **N2** which is assigned the value **INVOICE**. Array and table references, field functions on programmer-defined data objects, and programmer-defined functions that return by **NRETURN** are examples of expressions that generate variables.

Other expressions, for example arithmetic operations, yield values but not variables. Thus, execution of the statement

```
(A + B)  =  2
```

is an error.

Gotos require natural variables. These natural variables may also be generated. The indirect goto

```
:S($TRIM(INPUT))
```

is an example.

Some expressions, such as indirect references, always yield variables. Others, such as literals, always yield only values. Some expressions may or may not yield variables. For example,

        F(X)   =   2

may or may not be erroneous, depending on the function **F**. To allow for such cases, the syntax of SNOBOL4 permits any kind of expression as the subject of assignment. Statements such as

        2   =   3

are syntactically acceptable even though they are erroneous if executed.

6.2.1 Passing Names

Consider a function **BUMP** which increments the value of any variable by **1**. If the value of variable **N** is to be incremented, the call

        BUMP(N)

is not suitable because the value of **N**, not the name **N**, is passed to the procedure for **BUMP**. The form of the call must be

        BUMP('N')

which passes the string **N** to the **BUMP** procedure. Since the string **N** is the name of the variable **N**, indirect referencing may be used to increment the value.

The defining statement and procedure for **BUMP** are:

        DEFINE('BUMP(VAR)')
            .
            .
            .
BUMP $VAR = $VAR + 1   :(RETURN)

6.2.2 The Unary Name Operator

Suppose **BUMP** is to increment the value of a created variable, such as the second element of the array **A**. The call

        BUMP(A<2>)

is not suitable, since only the value of **A<2>** is passed. The call

        BUMP('A<2>')

is not suitable either, since the string **A<2>** is passed, and

> **$'A<2>'**

is a natural variable that bears no relation to the array element. The difficulty arises because there is no explicit name for created variables. However, implicit names for created variables can be obtained through use of a unary name operator.

The unary name operator **.** applied to any variable returns as its value the name of that variable. Thus, the value of

> **.A<2>**

is the created name of the second array element. The call

> **BUMP(.A<2>)**

passes the name of the second array element to **BUMP**, so that incrementing is done properly.

The name operator serves much the same purpose for created variables as quotation marks do for natural variables. Furthermore, the name operator applied to a natural variable behaves the same as quotation marks. Thus, the value of

> **.LINE**

is the string **LINE**. Both of the following pairs of statements assign the value **2** to **MAY**.

```
WORD  =   'MAY'
$WORD  =   2

WORD  =   .MAY
$WORD  =   2
```

If the argument of the name operator is a natural variable, the value returned by the name operator is a string which is an explicit name. If the argument of the name operator is a created variable, the value returned is an created name. If the argument is not a variable, an error occurs. For example,

> **.SIZE(X)**
> **.(A + B)**
> **.+A**

are erroneous because the arguments are not variables. If **A** and **B** are integers or numeral strings,

> **.$(A + B)**

is valid because **$(A + B)** is a natural variable.

6.2.3   Returning a Variable

When returning from a programmer-defined function via **RETURN**, the value of the function name becomes the value of the function call. If **NRETURN** is used, the value of the function name is returned as a variable, not as a value. Such a function call may thus be used freely in any context that requires a variable.

Consider, for example, the function **NEXT** which returns the first unused element of an array. The array is given as an argument and is assumed to have a zeroth element which indicates the last used element.

```
          DEFINE('NEXT(A)')                          :(NEXT.END)
*
NEXT      A<0>  =  A<0> + 1
          NEXT  =  .A<A<0>>
                                                     :S(NRETURN)F(FRETURN)
*
NEXT.END
```

Thus, executing the four statements

```
B     =   ARRAY('0:100')
NEXT(B)   =   'A'
NEXT(B)   =   'THE'
'STILL'   'T'   REM . NEXT(B)
```

assigns to **B<0>** through **B<3>** values **3**, **A**, **THE**, and **ILL**, respectively.

When **NEXT** returns, the value of **NEXT** is **.B<B<0>>**, which is the name of the first available array element. **NEXT(B)** becomes the variable **B<B<0>>**.

6.3   Gotos, Labels, and Code

Flow of control is governed by unconditional, success, and failure gotos. In the goto field, variables indicate the next statement to which control is passed based on the outcome of the current statement.

If a variable is used as a statement label, a label attribute pointing to the statement is assigned to the variable. This label attribute is independent of the value of the variable. Thus, a variable can be used in the label field and the goto field, as well as in the subject field of a single statement. The statement

```
DELAY     DELAY  =  LT(DELAY,N)  DELAY  +  1      :S(DELAY)F(ONWARD)
```

is acceptable and unambiguous.

If a variable has no label attribute, its use in a goto field is erroneous.

It is possible, as illustrated in the next section, to change the label attribute of a variable. In this way, a particular label variable, such as that appearing in

```
                    :S(LOOP)
```

may cause transfer to one statement at the beginning of execution and an entirely different statement later on.

6.3.1   Creation and Execution of Code

In the first phase of a SNOBOL4 run (compilation), the source program is converted into Polish-prefix object code. In the second (execution) phase this object code is interpreted. Object code is a type of data just as are strings, patterns, and arrays. During the execution phase, it is possible, using the primitive function **CODE(string)**, to convert a string of characters into object code. The argument to **CODE** is a string representing one or more SNOBOL4 statements. The value of a call to **CODE** is executable object code.

A string to be compiled into object code consists of SNOBOL4 statements separated by semicolons. For example, if the variable **GET** has a string value assigned by

```
        GET   =   '          &TRIM   =   1;'
+                 '          N   =   10;'
+                 '          LINE   =   ;'
+                 'LOOP      N   =   GT(N,0)   N   -   1        :F(OUT);'
+                 '          LINE   =   LINE   INPUT            :(LOOP)'
```

then

```
        NUCODE   =   CODE(GET)
```

causes the statements in the value of **GET** to be compiled. The value of **CODE(GET)** becomes the value of **NUCODE**.

Execution of statements in the value of **NUCODE** can be accomplished in two ways:

   (1) transfer to a labelled statement appearing in **NUCODE**, and

   (2) execution of a direct goto which passes control to the first statement in **NUCODE**, whether labelled or not.

Thus, execution of the goto

```
                :(LOOP)
```

causes transfer to the statement labelled **LOOP** inside of **NUCODE**, even if the original program had a statement labelled **LOOP**.

Blanks are as important in strings to be converted to code as they are in the program itself. A statement without a label must begin with a blank.

A direct goto is a special construction in the goto field, permitting transfer directly to the beginning of a block of object code rather than through a label. The direct goto uses enclosing angular brackets rather than parentheses. The expression enclosed in the angular brackets must be code-valued. Execution of the direct goto

```
                    :<NUCODE>
```

causes transfer to the first statement

```
          &TRIM    =    1
```

Flowing off the end of a block of compiled object code results in normal termination, just as if there were an end statement. If the label **END** is encountered in the string being compiled, compilation ceases at that point.

The following statement illustrates the use of the function **CODE** in the goto itself.

```
          :<CODE(' OUTPUT  =  "RECOMPILED"  :(RESTART)')>
```

The angular brackets indicate transfer to the beginning of the newly compiled block of **CODE**, which prints **RECOMPILED** and transfers to the statement labelled **RESTART**.

The primitive function **CODE** fails if its argument has a syntactic error.

It is a compilation error for the same label to appear more than once in the source program. Statements compiled using **CODE**, however, may have the same labels as statements compiled earlier. The label attribute for the corresponding variable references the new statement. For example, the following program segment is used to call a function **PROCESS(N)** with various values of **N**.

```
BEGIN      N  =  5
LOOP       N  =  LT(N,10)  N  +  1                    :F(OUT)
           PROCESS(N)                                 :(LOOP)
OUT
           NEWLOOP  =  'LOOP   N  =  GT(N,0)   N  -  1  :F(END)'
           CODE(NEWLOOP)                              :(BEGIN)
           .
           .
           .
END
```

Within the two-statement loop, **PROCESS(N)** is called with **N** having values **6**, **7**, **8**, **9**, **10** before control passes to the statement labelled **OUT**. At that point, a new block of code is compiled consisting of the statement

```
LOOP       N  =  GT(N,0)  N  -  1          :F(END)
```

It is intended that **PROCESS(N)** be called for **N** with values **4**, **3**, **2**, **1**, and **0**, but this is not the case. The original statement labelled **LOOP** is still in the program. It is not overwritten by the compilation. The label attribute of **LOOP** no longer points to it. The label attribute now points at the newly compiled statement. The new compilation is a second program which can freely communicate with the original. Execution of the program proceeds as if the following programs were compiled.

```
BEGIN      N  =  5
           N  =  LT(N,10)  N  +  1                    :F(OUT)
           PROCESS(N)                                 :(LOOP)
OUT
```

```
            NEWLOOP  =  'LOOP     N  =  GT(N,0)    N  -  1   :F(END)'
            CODE(NEWLOOP)                               :(BEGIN)
         .
         .
         .
END


LOOP    N  -  GT(N,0)   N  -  1  :F(END)
END
```

After compilation of NEWLOOP, transfer to BEGIN causes N to be assigned the value 5. Control flows into the statement originally labelled LOOP, which increments N to 6. PROCESS(N) is called and, on completion, control passes to the new statement labelled LOOP. N is decremented to 5, but PROCESS cannot be called as intended, since the new statement does not overwrite the old, and no way is provided for getting back to the original program.

The program segment can be rewritten to perform as intended by using explicit gotos to control program flow rather than relying on the sequence of statements to control flow.

```
BEGIN    N  =  5                                        :(LOOP)
LOOP     N  =  LT(N,10)   N  +  1                        :F(OUT)
PROC     PROCESS(N)                                      :(LOOP)
OUT

         NEWLOOP  =  'LOOP     N  =  GT(N,0)    N  -  1  :F(END)S(PROC)'
         CODE(NEWLOOP)                                   :(BEGIN)
      .
      .
      .

END
```

Following compilation of NEWLOOP, execution proceeds as if the following programs were compiled.

```
BEGIN    N  =  5                                        :(LOOP)
         N  =  LT(N,10)   N  +  1                        :F(OUT)
PROC     PROCESS(N)                                      :(LOOP)
OUT

         NEWLOOP  =  'LOOP     N  =  GT(N,0)    N  -  1  :F(END)S(PROC)'
         CODE(NEWLOOP)                                   :(BEGIN)
      .
      .
      .

END


LOOP    N  =  GT(N,0)   N  -  1  :F(END)S(PROC)
END
```

After assigning **5** to **N**, control passes from the statement labelled **BEGIN** to the new statement labelled **LOOP**. **N** is properly decremented to **4** and control passes to the statement labelled **PROC** which calls **PROCESS**. The loop continues until **N** is **0**.

Exercises

Exercise 6.1: A pushdown list can be implemented by means of an array. Let the first element in the array be the index of the top of the list. Define three unary operators that push onto the list and return a variable, pop from the list and return a value, and return a variable at the top of the list.

Exercise 6.2: Write a program that reads in another SNOBOL4 program, forms it into a string of statements separated by semicolons, converts it to code, and executes it. Assume the program to be read in is terminated by a card containing **EOF**, rather than an actual end of file. Test this program by using a copy of the program as input data.

CHAPTER 7

Types of Data

Most programs do not require any particular attention to types of data. Any variable can have any type of data as value, and most conversions between data types are performed automatically, without the need for any action on the part of the programmer.

In some situations, however, it is necessary to give more attention to data types. Explicit conversion from one data type to another may be necessary. Sometimes the details of the automatic, implicit conversions must be understood. This chapter covers these matters in some detail.

7.1 Data Type Representations

Data objects are classified by type. The string used to refer to the data type is called the formal identification of the data type. The types of data are:

Data Type	Formal Identification
string	`STRING`
integer	`INTEGER`
real number	`REAL`
pattern structure	`PATTERN`
array	`ARRAY`
table	`TABLE`
created name	`NAME`
unevaluated expression	`EXPRESSION`
object code	`CODE`
programmer-defined	Data type name (e.g. `COMPLEX`)
external	`EXTERNAL`

For notational convenience, the formal identification is sometimes abbreviated to the first letter, with **D** standing for defined data types and **X** standing for `EXTERNAL`.

The function `DATATYPE` can be used to obtain the formal identification of the data type of an object. The call `DATATYPE(object)` returns the formal identification. For example,

```
DATATYPE(LEN(1))
```

returns the value **PATTERN**. Similarly,

```
DATATYPE(37)
DATATYPE(.A<I>)
DATATYPE(*P)
```

return

> **INTEGER**
> **NAME**
> **EXPRESSION**

respectively.

The **DATA** function can be used to define a data type with the same formal identification as another data type. For example,

```
DATA('STRING(FIRST,LAST)')
```

defines a new data type with formal identification **STRING**. The two data types **STRING** are correctly distinguished by the SNOBOL4 system, but they cannot be differentiated during program execution by their formal identifications.

7.2 Explicit Conversion of Data Types

In some cases, it is reasonable to convert an object of one data type into a corresponding object of another data type. This can be accomplished by using the **CONVERT** function, introduced earlier in connection with tables and arrays.

7.2.1 CONVERT

A call of the **CONVERT** function has the form **CONVERT(object,datatype)** where the object is to be converted to the given data type, expressed as a formal identification. For example, the real number **2.5** can be converted into an integer by the statement

```
I   =   CONVERT(2.5,'INTEGER')
```

In **REAL**-to-**INTEGER** conversion, the fractional part is discarded, and **I** has the value **2**.

Any data object can be converted to a string by **CONVERT**. In most cases conversion to **STRING** simply returns the formal identification of the data type of the object to be converted, and in this way behaves like **DATATYPE**. In four cases, **INTEGER**, **REAL**, **ARRAY**, and **TABLE**, special conversions are performed to provide more meaningful representations of the object converted. In general, the result of converting any data object to **STRING** is referred to as the *string representation* of that object.

In conversion from **INTEGER** to **STRING**, leading zeroes are suppressed and a sign is provided only if the integer is negative. Thus the value of

        CONVERT(+00732,'STRING')

is the string **732**.

In conversion from **REAL** to **STRING**, at least one digit is provided before the decimal point. A sign is provided only if the real number is negative.

In conversion from **ARRAY** to **STRING**, the formal identification **ARRAY** is given, followed by the array prototype enclosed in parentheses. For example, if an array **A** is created by the statement

        A   =   ARRAY('0:10',3)

the value of

        CONVERT(A,'STRING')

is **ARRAY('0:10')**.

If the prototype is longer than 20 characters, only the formal identification, **ARRAY**, is given.

In conversion from **TABLE** to **STRING** the formal identification, **TABLE**, is given, followed by the current size of the table and its secondary extent enclosed in parentheses. For a typical table, **T**, the value of

        CONVERT(T,'STRING')

might be **TABLE(300,10)**.

The following table summarizes the data type conversions that can be performed using **CONVERT**.

Data Type of Argument	*Data Type of Object Returned*										
	S	I	R	P	A	T	N	E	C	D	X
STRING	*	F	F					F	F		
INTEGER	S	*	C								
REAL	S	F	*								
PATTERN	I			*							
ARRAY	S				*	F					
TABLE	S				F	*					
NAME	I						*				
EXPRESSION	I							*			
CODE	I								*		
defined type	I									(*)	
external type	I										(*)

In this table, the symbols have the following meaning:

(1) * indicates that no conversion is performed, and the first argument is simply returned as value. In the case of defined and external data types, the enclosing parentheses indicate that conversion is successful only in converting an object to its own data type. An object of one defined or external type cannot be converted to a different type.

(2) F indicates the conversion may fail. For example, the string A cannot be converted to an integer.

(3) I indicates the formal identification is returned.

(4) C indicates the conversion always succeeds.

(5) S indicates the string representation is returned.

If an attempt is made to perform a conversion that is not available, the CONVERT function fails.

7.3 Data Types of Functions and Operations

In many contexts, conversion from one type of data to another is performed implicitly as required by the functions and operations involved. A typical example is the conversion of strings to integers in arithmetic contexts. Another example is the conversion of any data type to its string representation on output.

Unlike many programming languages, SNOBOL4 permits any variable to have any type of data as value (keywords are the only exception). Furthermore, any expression, however complicated, can appear wherever a value is required. It is the result of evaluating an expression that is important. For example, the two statements

```
X    =    SIZE('ABCDEF')
X    =    SIZE('A' 'BCD' 'EF')
```

produce the same effect since in both cases the result of evaluating the argument of SIZE is the string ABCDEF. The way the string is created is irrelevant, but it is important that the argument be a string. Throughout the language, values may be constructed in any way, but individual functions and operations often require their arguments to have certain data types.

To simplify programming, automatic data type conversion is performed in many circumstances. Consider, for example, the statement

```
Y  =   SIZE(1376)
```

Here the argument of SIZE is an integer. This integer is automatically converted to a string, however, and the value 4 is assigned to Y.

In most cases, the problem of data type conversion can be ignored since conversion is automatically provided in the most common situations. Care must be observed, however, in the use of **IDENT** and **DIFFER** where no conversions are performed. There are occassional hazards of conversion. For example, the value of

```
SIZE(+00732)
```

is **3** because of the normalization performed during conversion, as described in a preceding section.

Specific information concerning expected data types and automatic conversions is given in the following sections.

7.3.1 Primitive Functions

The following table lists all primitive functions, including some described in later chapters. This table indicates the data types expected for each argument and the data type of the value returned. The following notation is used.

(1) Upper case letter abbreviations are used for formal identification of data types. For example, **S** stands for **STRING**.

(2) The letter **x** indicates that any data type is possible.

(3) The letter **y** indicates several data types are possible. Refer to the description of the individual function for details.

(4) The letter **n** indicates a number, either integer or real, is possible.

(5) The symbols •S indicate the null string.

(6) The letter **v** indicates a variable. Where a variable results from return by name, the resultant data type is indicated. For example **x←v** indicates a variable whose value may be of any data type.

Function Call	Return	Function Call	Return
ANY(S or E)	P	INPUT(S or N,I,I)	•S
APPLY(S,x,...,x)	x	INTEGER(x)	•S
ARBNO(P)	P	ITEM(A,I,...,I)	x←v
ARG(S,I)	S	ITEM(T,x)	x←v
ARRAY(S,x)	A	LE(n,n)	•S
BACKSPACE(I)	•S	LEN(I or E)	P
BREAK(S or E)	P	LGT(S,S)	•S
CLEAR(x)	•S	LOCAL(S,I)	S
CODE(S)	C	LT(n,n)	•S
COLLECT(I)	I	NE(n,n)	•S
CONVERT(x,S)	x	NOTANY(S or E)	P
COPY(y)	y	OPSYN(S,S,I)	•S
DATA(S)	•S	OUTPUT(S or N,I,S)	•S
DATATYPE(x)	S	POS(I or E)	P
DATE(x)	S	PROTOTYPE(A)	S
DEFINE(S,S)	•S	REMDR(I,I)	I
DETACH(S or N)	•S	REPLACE(S,S,S)	S
DIFFER(x,x)	•S	REWIND(I)	•S
DUMP(I)	•S	RPOS(I or E)	P
DUPL(S,I)	S	RTAB(I or E)	P
ENDFILE(I)	•S	SIZE(S)	I
EQ(n,n)	•S	SPAN(S or E)	P
EVAL(S or E)	x	STOPTR(S or N,S)	•S
EVAL(I)	I	TAB(I or E)	P
EVAL(R)	R	TABLE(I,I)	T
FIELD(S,I)	S	TIME(x)	I
GE(n,n)	•S	TRACE(S or N,S,S,S)	•S
GT(n,n)	•S	TRIM(S)	S
IDENT(x,x)	•S	VALUE(S or N)	x←v

7.3.2 Unary Operators

A unary operator is essentially the same as a function with one argument, but with a more compact syntactic representation. A table of expected data types and values returned for the defined unary operators follows. The previous notation is used with two additions:

(1) S^1 indicates strings that are protected keywords.
(2) S^2 indicates strings that are unprotected keywords.

Call	Return
¬x	•S
?x	•S
$(S or N)	x←v
.S	S
.v	N
*x	E
+n	n
−n	n
ə(v or E)	P
&S[1]	y
&S[2]	I←v

7.3.3   Binary Operators

A binary operator is essentially the same as a function of two arguments. A table of expected data types and values returned for the defined binary operators follows.

Call	Return
(P $ v)	P
(P . v)	P
(n ** n)	n
(n * n)	n
(n / n)	n
(n + n)	n
(n − n)	n
(x •S)	x
(•S x)	x
(S S)	S
(P P)	P
(P | P)	P

If either argument of concatenation is the null string, the other argument is returned as value. Automatic conversion of other data types is described in following sections.

7.3.4   Statement Components

In addition to functions and operators, there are three other constructions in which data types are important:

(1) assignment,
(2) pattern matching, and
(3) pattern matching with replacement.

For assignment, the expected data types are simple:

subject	=	*object*
V	=	X
εS^2	=	I

Thus the only restriction on the object of assignment occurs when assignment is made to an unprotected keyword. The same restriction applies to assignment performed as a result of pattern matching in which components contain conditional or immediate value assignment operators.

In pattern matching, the situation is even simpler. The expected data types are:

subject	*pattern*
S	S
S	P

Pattern matching with replacement can be considered in three steps:

(1) Pattern matching determines the string matched, and hence the initial and terminal unmatched parts of the subject string.

(2) Concatenation of the initial part, the replacement object, and the terminal part forms a new object.

(3) This new object is assigned to the subject variable.

Thus, the many possible cases of replacement can be analyzed using the preceding information. A typical form of replacement is

subject	*pattern*	=	*object*
S←V	S	=	S
S←V	P	=	S

where the resulting data type of the subject is a string. A number of special cases can be determined also. For example, if the pattern matches the entire string, the initial and terminal parts are null strings, and as described in the discussion of concatenation, the replacement object may have any data type. Similarly, if the subject is an unprotected keyword, the resulting replacement must be an integer.

7.4　Implicit Conversion of Data Types

The previous sections detail the data types expected by the various functions and operations. As indicated earlier, automatic conversion is provided in many contexts. The following sections describe such conversion in detail.

7.4.1　Conversion to **STRING**

Conversion to **STRING** is one of the most frequent of all implicit conversions. The string representation, which includes the conversion of all data types, is provided in the following situations:

(1) On output.

(2) Where required in trace printout (see Chapter 8).

(3) In dumps of variables, both from **DUMP(N)** (see Chapter 8) and after program termination (see Chapter 10).

INTEGER-to-**STRING** conversion is provided in the following situations:

(1) Where **STRING** is an expected data type.

(2) Where **STRING** is specified for the argument of an external function.

REAL-to-**STRING** conversion is performed in a few contexts:

(1) Where **STRING** is expected in concatenation, including concatenation performed in replacement statements.

(2) Where **STRING** is expected as the subject of pattern matching.

(3) Where **STRING** is specified for the argument of an external function.

7.4.2   Conversion to PATTERN

Although there is no explicit conversion to PATTERN, implicit conversion occurs in many circumstances. Conversion from INTEGER, REAL, STRING, and EXPRESSION to PATTERN is provided wherever PATTERN is specified as an expected data type in the preceding sections. A typical example of conversion to PATTERN is the concatenation of a string with a pattern.

7.4.3   Conversion to INTEGER

STRING-to-INTEGER conversion is frequently required. It is provided in the following situations:

(1) Where INTEGER is an expected data type. This includes arithmetic contexts that accept reals as well as integers.

(2) Where INTEGER is specified for the argument of an external function. This conversion includes conversion of numeral string reals in addition to the regular conversion.

REAL-to-INTEGER conversion is provided only for arguments of external functions.

7.4.4   Conversion to REAL

INTEGER-to-REAL and STRING-to-REAL conversion is provided in the following situations:

(1) Where REAL is an expected data type. This includes arithmetic contexts that accept integers as well as real numbers. Both numeral string integers and numeral string reals are converted.

(2) Where REAL is specified for an argument of an external function.

CHAPTER 8

Tracing

Tracing facilities are provided to permit the programmer to get diagnostic information about the execution of his program without interfering with its logic or structure. The tracing mode is turned on by assigning a positive integer to the keyword &TRACE. When this mode is in effect, certain types of program actions can be sensed, causing corresponding messages to be printed. The types of actions sensed are:

(1) change in the value of a variable,
(2) call of a defined function,
(3) return from a defined function,
(4) transfer to a label, and
(5) change in the value of certain keywords.

8.1   Standard Trace Procedures

The **TRACE** function is used to make specific trace requests.

    TRACE(name,type,tag)

associates the **name** with the **type** of action for tracing purposes. The **tag** provides identifying information which is included in the trace printout if the name is not a natural variable. If the name is a natural variable, the tag is ignored. One trace association must be made for each name and type desired.

Trace printout includes the statement number in which the action occurs, the result of the action, and the time of the action in milliseconds measured from the beginning of program execution.

If &TRACE is not positive, there is no tracing, even though trace requests have been made. The value of &TRACE is decremented by one every time an action is traced, and tracing is automatically turned off when the value of &TRACE reaches zero. Therefore the value assigned to &TRACE may be chosen to limit the amount of trace printout.

8.1.1 Value Tracing

```
TRACE(name,'VALUE',tag)
```

causes trace printout whenever the value of **name** is changed. Consider the following
program.

```
*
*       PRINT PERMUTATIONS OF SIZE N OF A GIVEN STRING
*
        &TRIM   =   1;      &TRACE   =   100                           1
        TRACE('CH','VALUE');   TRACE('STRING','VALUE')                 3
        DEFINE('PERM(STRING,N,HEAD)CH,USED')                           5
        PERMREQ   =   BREAK(',') . STRING LEN(1) REM . N               6
*
READ    CARD   =   INPUT                              :F(END)          7
        CARD   PERMREQ                                :F(ERROR)        8
        OUTPUT   =   'THE PERMUTATIONS OF ' STRING ' TAKEN ' N         9
+                    ' AT A TIME ARE:'                                 9
        PERM(STRING,N)                               :(READ)          10
PERM    OUTPUT   =   EQ(N,0)   HEAD                   :S(RETURN)       11
PERMA   STRING   LEN(1) . CH   =                      :F(RETURN)      12
        USED   =                                                      13
+           PERM(STRING USED,N - 1,HEAD CH)   USED   CH  :(PERMA)     13
ERROR   OUTPUT   =   '*** ERROR IN ' CARD             :(READ)         14
END                                                                  15
```

The printed output for the input **ABCD,2** is

```
    STATEMENT 8: STRING = 'ABCD',TIME = 17
THE PERMUTATIONS OF ABCD TAKEN 2 AT A TIME ARE:
    STATEMENT 12: CH = 'A',TIME = 17
    STATEMENT 12: STRING = 'BCD',TIME = 17
    STATEMENT 12: CH = 'B',TIME = 34
    STATEMENT 12: STRING = 'CD',TIME = 34
AB
    STATEMENT 12: CH = 'C',TIME = 50
    STATEMENT 12: STRING = 'D',TIME = 50
AC
    STATEMENT 12: CH = 'D',TIME = 50
    STATEMENT 12: STRING = '',TIME = 67
AD
    STATEMENT 12: CH = 'B',TIME = 67
    STATEMENT 12: STRING = 'CD',TIME = 67
    STATEMENT 12: CH = 'C',TIME = 84
    STATEMENT 12: STRING = 'DA',TIME = 84
BC
    STATEMENT 12: CH = 'D',TIME = 100
    STATEMENT 12: STRING = 'A',TIME = 100
BD
```

```
      STATEMENT 12: CH = 'A',TIME = 100
      STATEMENT 12: STRING = '',TIME = 117
BA
      STATEMENT 12: CH = 'C',TIME = 117
      STATEMENT 12: STRING = 'D',TIME = 117
      STATEMENT 12: CH = 'D',TIME = 134
      STATEMENT 12: STRING = 'AB',TIME = 134
CD
      STATEMENT 12: CH = 'A',TIME = 150
      STATEMENT 12: STRING = 'B',TIME = 150
CA
      STATEMENT 12: CH = 'B',TIME = 150
      STATEMENT 12: STRING = '',TIME = 167
CB
      STATEMENT 12: CH = 'D',TIME = 167
      STATEMENT 12: STRING = '',TIME = 183
      STATEMENT 12: CH = 'A',TIME = 183
      STATEMENT 12: STRING = 'BC',TIME = 183
DA
      STATEMENT 12: CH = 'B',TIME = 200
      STATEMENT 12: STRING = 'C',TIME = 200
DB
      STATEMENT 12: CH = 'C',TIME = 200
      STATEMENT 12: STRING = '',TIME = 217
DC
```

Value tracing is the default type of tracing, and value tracing is assumed if the second argument to **TRACE** is omitted. Thus **TRACE('CH')** and **TRACE('STRING')** would be sufficient in the example above. Value tracing occurs whenever a value is assigned to a traced variable by an assignment statement or as a result of value assignment in pattern matching. Value tracing does not occur when a value is assigned as the result of input or when values are assigned to formal arguments and local variables in the call of a programmer-defined function.

If the name is not a natural variable, the tag is printed to identify the name being traced. For example, **TRACE(.SUM<3>, 'VALUE', 'SUM<3>')** traces the third element of the array **SUM**. Here the tag **SUM<3>** (chosen to correspond to the created variable **SUM<3>**) provides a string that identifies the name of the trace request. As an example, consider the following program, which forms sums in several bins as given on data cards. The trace association must appear after creation of the array **SUM**, since the name **.SUM<3>** does not exist before the array is created.

```
      &ANCHOR    =    1                                              1
      &TRIM    =    1                                                2
      &TRACE    =      1000                                          3
      CARDPAT    =     BREAK(' ') . BIN SPAN(' ') REM . NUMBER       4
*
*     THE FIRST CARD GIVES THE NUMBER OF BINS
```

```
*
        SUM     =     ARRAY(INPUT,0)                              :F(ERR)         5
*
*       TRACE THE THIRD BIN.
*
        TRACE(.SUM<3>,'VALUE','SUM<3>')                                           6
*
*       SUBSEQENT CARDS CONTAIN A BIN NUMBER FOLLOWED BY A BLANK AND THEN
*       THE NUMBER TO BE ADDED TO THE BIN.
*
READ    CARD    =     INPUT                                      :F(DISPLAY)      7
        CARD    CARDPAT                                          :F(ERR)          8
        SUM<BIN>    =     SUM<BIN> + NUMBER                      :S(READ)F(ERR)   9
*
*       PRINT OUT THE SUMS
*
DISPLAY                                                                          10
        I   =    1                                                               11
PRINT   OUTPUT   =    'SUM<' I '> = ' SUM<I>                     :F(END)         12
        I   =    I + 1                                          :(PRINT)         13
END                                                                             14
```

For the input data

```
10
3 25
1    27
9          -75
5 +65
3 77
7 -89
2 75
10 0
3 -756
7     499
2 76
4   23
1 456
5 87
2                 33
10 23
3       0025
8 657
3 +45
```

the printed output is

```
    STATEMENT 9: SUM<3> = 25,TIME = 0
    STATEMENT 9: SUM<3> = 102,TIME = 50
    STATEMENT 9: SUM<3> = -654,TIME = 83
```

```
        STATEMENT 9:  SUM<3> = -629,TIME = 166
        STATEMENT 9:  SUM<3> = -584,TIME = 183
SUM<1> = 483
SUM<2> = 184
SUM<3> = -584
SUM<4> = 23
SUM<5> = 152
SUM<6> = 0
SUM<7> = 410
SUM<8> = 657
SUM<9> = -75
SUM<10> = 23
```

8.1.2 Function Tracing

There are three types of tracing for programmer-defined functions: **CALL**, **RETURN**, and **FUNCTION**. **CALL** and **RETURN** cause trace printout on the call to and return from a function. **FUNCTION** causes trace printout for both call and return.

CALL tracing gives the level from which the call is made, the function name, and the value of its arguments. **RETURN** tracing gives the level to which the return is made. The following examples indicate the three types of tracing applied to a program that computes the number of combinations of N things taken M at a time.

```
            &TRACE    =      1000                                    1
            TRACE('C','CALL')                                        2
            NM    =   BREAK(',') . N ',' BREAK(' ') . M              3
            DEFINE('C(N,M)')                                         4
READ        INPUT    NM                           :F(END)           5
            OUTPUT    =    'C(' N ',' M ')=' C(N,M)        :(READ)   6
*
C           M  =  LT(N - M,M)  N - M                                 7
            C  =  EQ(M,0)  1                        :S(RETURN)       8
            C  =  N * C(N - 1,M - 1) / M  :(RETURN)                  9
END                                                                 10
```

For the input 15,6 the output is

```
        STATEMENT 6:  LEVEL 0 CALL OF C('15','6'),TIME = 16
        STATEMENT 9:  LEVEL 1 CALL OF C(14,5),TIME = 50
        STATEMENT 9:  LEVEL 2 CALL OF C(13,4),TIME = 50
        STATEMENT 9:  LEVEL 3 CALL OF C(12,3),TIME = 66
        STATEMENT 9:  LEVEL 4 CALL OF C(11,2),TIME = 66
        STATEMENT 9:  LEVEL 5 CALL OF C(10,1),TIME = 83
        STATEMENT 9:  LEVEL 6 CALL OF C(9,0),TIME = 83
C(15,6)=5005
```

If `TRACE('C','RETURN')` is used instead, the output is

```
STATEMENT 8: LEVEL 6 RETURN OF C = 1,TIME = 34
STATEMENT 9: LEVEL 5 RETURN OF C = 10,TIME = 34
STATEMENT 9: LEVEL 4 RETURN OF C = 55,TIME = 50
STATEMENT 9: LEVEL 3 RETURN OF C = 220,TIME = 50
STATEMENT 9: LEVEL 2 RETURN OF C = 715,TIME = 67
STATEMENT 9: LEVEL 1 RETURN OF C = 2002,TIME = 67
STATEMENT 9: LEVEL 0 RETURN OF C = 5005,TIME = 67
C(15,6)=5005
```

and if `TRACE('C','FUNCTION')` is used, the output is

```
STATEMENT 6: LEVEL 0 CALL OF C('15','6'),TIME = 16
STATEMENT 9: LEVEL 1 CALL OF C(14,5),TIME = 16
STATEMENT 9: LEVEL 2 CALL OF C(13,4),TIME = 33
STATEMENT 9: LEVEL 3 CALL OF C(12,3),TIME = 33
STATEMENT 9: LEVEL 4 CALL OF C(11,2),TIME = 50
STATEMENT 9: LEVEL 5 CALL OF C(10,1),TIME = 50
STATEMENT 9: LEVEL 6 CALL OF C(9,0),TIME = 66
STATEMENT 8: LEVEL 6 RETURN OF C = 1,TIME = 66
STATEMENT 9: LEVEL 5 RETURN OF C = 10,TIME = 66
STATEMENT 9: LEVEL 4 RETURN OF C = 55,TIME = 83
STATEMENT 9: LEVEL 3 RETURN OF C = 220,TIME = 83
STATEMENT 9: LEVEL 2 RETURN OF C = 715,TIME = 83
STATEMENT 9: LEVEL 1 RETURN OF C = 2002,TIME = 99
STATEMENT 9: LEVEL 0 RETURN OF C = 5005,TIME = 99
C(15,6)=5005
```

To facilitate the tracing of programmer-defined functions, the keyword &FTRACE is provided. When &FTRACE is a positive integer, all programmer-defined functions are traced on call and return. The value of &FTRACE is decremented by one each time a programmer-defined function is called or returns. When the value of &FTRACE reaches zero, function tracing stops. &TRACE and &FTRACE are independent, and both may be used at the same time. The following program illustrates the use of &FTRACE.

```
        &FTRACE   =   1000;   &TRIM   =   1                          1
*
*       THIS PROGRAM COMPUTES THE NUMBER OF SYMMETRIC BISECTIONS OF
*       A CHECKERBOARD OF EVEN ORDER.  THE PROBLEM IS DESCRIBED IN
*       MARTIN GARDNER'S "MATHEMATICAL GAMES" IN SCIENTIFIC AMERICAN
*       NOVEMBER, 1962.
*
        DEFINE('AXIS(X,Y)')                                          3
        DEFINE('RIGHT(X,Y)')                                         4
        DEFINE('LEFT(X,Y)')                                          5
        DEFINE('UP(X,Y)')                                            6
        DEFINE('DOWN(X,Y)')                                          7
        DEFINE('COUNT(X)')                                           8
```

```
READ        SUM    =    0                                                            9
            N   =    INPUT                                       :F(END)             10
            BOARD   =    ARRAY(-N ':' N ',' -N ':' N)                               11
            BOARD<0,0>   =    ':'                                                    12
            AXIS(0,0)                                                                13
            OUTPUT   =    'THERE ARE ' SUM ' SYMMETRIC BISECTIONS OF A ' 2 *         14
.           N ' BY ' 2 * N ' CHECKERBOARD'                       :(READ)            14
*
AXIS        X   =    X + 1                                                           15
            EQ(X,N) COUNT()                                      :S(RETURN)          16
            IDENT(BOARD<-X,-Y>)                                 :F(FRETURN)          17
            IDENT(BOARD<X,Y>)                                   :F(FRETURN)          18
            BOARD<X,Y>   =    ':'                                                    19
            AXIS(X,Y)                                                                20
            UP(X,Y)                                                                  21
            BOARD<X,Y>   =                                       :(RETURN)           22
*
RIGHT       X       =    X  +  1                                                     23
            EQ(X,N)    COUNT()                                   :S(RETURN)          24
            IDENT( BOARD<-X,-Y>)                                :F(FRETURN)          25
            IDENT(BOARD<X,Y>)                                   :F(FRETURN)          26
            BOARD<X,Y>   =    ':'                                                    27
            RIGHT(X,Y)                                                               28
            UP(X,Y)                                                                  29
            DOWN(X,Y)                                                                30
            BOARD<X,Y>   =                                       :(RETURN)           31
*
UP          Y       =    Y  +  1                                                     32
            EQ(Y,N)    COUNT()                                   :S(RETURN)          33
            IDENT(BOARD<-X,-Y>)                                 :F(FRETURN)          34
            IDENT(BOARD<X,Y>)                                   :F(FRETURN)          35
            BOARD<X,Y>   =    ':'                                                    36
            RIGHT(X,Y)                                                               37
            UP(X,Y)                                                                  38
            LEFT(X,Y)                                                                39
            BOARD<X,Y>   =                                       :(RETURN)           40
*
LEFT        X       =    X  -  1                                                     41
            EQ(X,-N)    COUNT()                                  :S(RETURN)          42
            IDENT(BOARD<-X,-Y>)                                 :F(FRETURN)          43
            IDENT(BOARD<X,Y>)                                   :F(FRETURN)          44
            BOARD<X,Y>   =    ':'                                                    45
            LEFT(X,Y)                                                                46
            UP(X,Y)                                                                  47
            DOWN(X,Y)                                                                48
            BOARD<X,Y>   =                                       :(RETURN)           49
*
DOWN        Y       =    Y  -  1                                                     50
```

```
            EQ(Y,-N)    COUNT()                                 :S(RETURN)      51
            IDENT(BOARD<-X,-Y>)                                 :F(FRETURN)     52
            IDENT(BOARD<X,Y>)                                   :F(FRETURN)     53
            BOARD<X,Y>    =    ':'                                               54
            RIGHT(X,Y)                                                          55
            LEFT(X,Y)                                                           56
            DOWN(X,Y)                                                           57
            BOARD<X,Y>      =                                    :(RETURN)      58
*
COUNT       SUM       =   SUM  +  1                             :(RETURN)      59
*
END                                                                             60
```

For an input value of 2, this program produces the following output.

```
    STATEMENT 13: LEVEL 0 CALL OF AXIS(0,0),TIME = 17
    STATEMENT 20: LEVEL 1 CALL OF AXIS(1,0),TIME = 34
    STATEMENT 16: LEVEL 2 CALL OF COUNT(''),TIME = 34
    STATEMENT 59: LEVEL 2 RETURN OF COUNT = '',TIME = 34
    STATEMENT 16: LEVEL 1 RETURN OF AXIS = '',TIME = 50
    STATEMENT 21: LEVEL 1 CALL OF UP(1,0),TIME = 50
    STATEMENT 37: LEVEL 2 CALL OF RIGHT(1,1),TIME = 50
    STATEMENT 24: LEVEL 3 CALL OF COUNT(''),TIME = 67
    STATEMENT 59: LEVEL 3 RETURN OF COUNT = '',TIME = 67
    STATEMENT 24: LEVEL 2 RETURN OF RIGHT = '',TIME = 67
    STATEMENT 38: LEVEL 2 CALL OF UP(1,1),TIME = 83
    STATEMENT 33: LEVEL 3 CALL OF COUNT(''),TIME = 83
    STATEMENT 59: LEVEL 3 RETURN OF COUNT = '',TIME = 83
    STATEMENT 33: LEVEL 2 RETURN OF UP = '',TIME = 100
    STATEMENT 39: LEVEL 2 CALL OF LEFT(1,1),TIME = 100
    STATEMENT 46: LEVEL 3 CALL OF LEFT(0,1),TIME = 117
    STATEMENT 46: LEVEL 4 CALL OF LEFT(-1,1),TIME = 117
    STATEMENT 42: LEVEL 5 CALL OF COUNT(''),TIME = 117
    STATEMENT 59: LEVEL 5 RETURN OF COUNT = '',TIME = 133
    STATEMENT 42: LEVEL 4 RETURN OF LEFT = '',TIME = 133
    STATEMENT 47: LEVEL 4 CALL OF UP(-1,1),TIME = 133
    STATEMENT 33: LEVEL 5 CALL OF COUNT(''),TIME = 150
    STATEMENT 59: LEVEL 5 RETURN OF COUNT = '',TIME = 150
    STATEMENT 33: LEVEL 4 RETURN OF UP = '',TIME = 150
    STATEMENT 48: LEVEL 4 CALL OF DOWN(-1,1),TIME = 167
    STATEMENT 52: LEVEL 4 FRETURN OF DOWN,TIME = 167
    STATEMENT 49: LEVEL 3 RETURN OF LEFT = '',TIME = 183
    STATEMENT 47: LEVEL 3 CALL OF UP(0,1),TIME = 183
    STATEMENT 33: LEVEL 4 CALL OF COUNT(''),TIME = 183
    STATEMENT 59: LEVEL 4 RETURN OF COUNT = '',TIME = 200
    STATEMENT 33: LEVEL 3 RETURN OF UP = '',TIME = 200
    STATEMENT 48: LEVEL 3 CALL OF DOWN(0,1),TIME = 200
    STATEMENT 52: LEVEL 3 FRETURN OF DOWN,TIME = 217
    STATEMENT 49: LEVEL 2 RETURN OF LEFT = '',TIME = 217
```

```
        STATEMENT 40: LEVEL 1 RETURN OF UP = '',TIME = 217
        STATEMENT 22: LEVEL 0 RETURN OF AXIS = '',TIME = 217
THERE ARE 6 SYMMETRIC BISECTIONS OF A 4 BY 4 CHECKERBOARD
```

8.1.3   Label Tracing

```
        TRACE(name,'LABEL')
```

causes trace printout whenever transfer is made to **name**. No printout occurs if the statement labelled with the name is flowed into, or is entered as a function entry point.

The following program, which converts numbers from hexadecimal form to decimal form, illustrates label tracing.

```
        &TRIM    =    1                                                        1
        &TRACE   =    100                                                      2
        TRACE('DEHEX1','LABEL')                                                3
        FINDNO   =    BREAK(*NO) . NO                                          4
        ONE    =    LEN(1) . NO                                                5
        L0    =    POS(0) SPAN('0')                                            6
*
        DEFINE('DEHEX(STR)NO')                         :(DEHEX.END)            7
*
DEHEX     STR    L0    =                                                       8
DEHEX1    STR    ONE    =                              :F(RETURN)              9
        DEHEX  =  INTEGER(NO)  16 * DEHEX + NO         :S(DEHEX1)             10
        'ABCDEF'    FINDNO                             :F(FRETURN)           11
        DEHEX = 16 * DEHEX + 10 + SIZE(NO)             :(DEHEX1)             12
DEHEX.END                                                                    13
*
*
READ      NUMBER    =    INPUT                          :F(END)              14
+         OUTPUT    =    'DEHEX(' NUMBER ') = ' DEHEX(NUMBER)                 15
+                                                      :S(READ)             15
        OUTPUT   =    'UNABLE TO CONVERT ' NUMBER       :(READ)              16
END                                                                          17
```

The output for the indicated input is

```
        STATEMENT 10: TRANSFER TO DEHEX1,TIME = 16
        STATEMENT 10: TRANSFER TO DEHEX1,TIME = 16
        STATEMENT 10: TRANSFER TO DEHEX1,TIME = 16
DEHEX(100) = 256
        STATEMENT 10: TRANSFER TO DEHEX1,TIME = 50
        STATEMENT 10: TRANSFER TO DEHEX1,TIME = 50
DEHEX(00011) = 17
        STATEMENT 12: TRANSFER TO DEHEX1,TIME = 66
DEHEX(000F) = 15
        STATEMENT 10: TRANSFER TO DEHEX1,TIME = 83
```

```
     STATEMENT 12: TRANSFER TO DEHEX1,TIME = 99
     STATEMENT 12: TRANSFER TO DEHEX1,TIME = 99
     STATEMENT 12: TRANSFER TO DEHEX1,TIME = 116
UNABLE TO CONVERT 1ABCG
     STATEMENT 10: TRANSFER TO DEHEX1,TIME = 133
     STATEMENT 12: TRANSFER TO DEHEX1,TIME = 133
     STATEMENT 12: TRANSFER TO DEHEX1,TIME = 149
     STATEMENT 12: TRANSFER TO DEHEX1,TIME = 149
DEHEX(1ABC) = 6844
     STATEMENT 12: TRANSFER TO DEHEX1,TIME = 199
     STATEMENT 12: TRANSFER TO DEHEX1,TIME = 199
     STATEMENT 12: TRANSFER TO DEHEX1,TIME = 199
     STATEMENT 12: TRANSFER TO DEHEX1,TIME = 216
DEHEX(000FACE) = 64206
```

8.1.4 Keyword Tracing

```
     TRACE(name,'KEYWORD')
```

causes trace printout when the value of the named keyword is changed. Only four keywords can be traced: **ERRTYPE**, **FNCLEVEL**, **STCOUNT**, and **STFCOUNT**. The following program, which converts numbers from decimal to hexadecimal form, illustrates keyword tracing.

```
          &TRACE   =   1000;          &TRIM   =   1                          1
          TRACE('STFCOUNT','KEYWORD')                                        3
          DEFINE('HEXER(N)Q,R')                                              4
          HIGITS = '0123456789ABCDEF'                                        5
          LOCATN   =   LEN(*N) LEN(1) . R                                    6
          LOCATR   =   LEN(*R) LEN(1) . R                                    7
READ      NUM   =   INPUT                              :F(END)              8
          OUTPUT = 'HEXER(' NUM ') = ' HEXER(NUM)       :S(READ)             9
          OUTPUT = 'UNABLE TO CONVERT ' NUM             :(READ)             10
*
*
HEXER     INTEGER(N)                                   :F(FRETURN)         11
          Q  = GT(N,15)  N / 16                         :F(HEX.END)         12
          R = N - Q * 16                                                   13
          N = Q                                                            14
          HIGITS   LOCATR                               :F(FRETURN)         15
          HEXER = R HEXER                               :(HEXER)            16
HEX.END   HIGITS   LOCATN                               :F(FRETURN)         17
          HEXER = R HEXER                               :(RETURN)           18
END                                                                        19
```

The printed output for the indicated input is

```
    STATEMENT 12: &STFCOUNT = 1,TIME = 17
HEXER(15) = F
    STATEMENT 12: &STFCOUNT = 2,TIME = 33
HEXER(6844) = 1ABC
    STATEMENT 11: &STFCOUNT = 3,TIME = 50
    STATEMENT 9: &STFCOUNT = 4,TIME = 67
UNABLE TO CONVERT 1239.0003
    STATEMENT 12: &STFCOUNT = 5,TIME = 83
HEXER(236) = EC
    STATEMENT 12: &STFCOUNT = 6,TIME = 100
HEXER(64206) = FACE
    STATEMENT 12: &STFCOUNT = 7,TIME = 133
HEXER(699050) = AAAAA
    STATEMENT 12: &STFCOUNT = 8,TIME = 150
HEXER(0) = 0
    STATEMENT 12: &STFCOUNT = 9,TIME = 166
HEXER(000) = 0
    STATEMENT 12: &STFCOUNT = 10,TIME = 183
HEXER(256) = 100
    STATEMENT 12: &STFCOUNT = 11,TIME = 266
HEXER(123456789) = 75BCD15
    STATEMENT 8: &STFCOUNT = 12,TIME = 266
```

Note that the keyword name, without the ampersand, is given in the call of **TRACE**.

8.1.5 Discontinuation of Tracing

Tracing is a global condition that depends upon the value of &TRACE. Regardless of trace requests made through the **TRACE** function, there is no trace output if &TRACE is not positive. The value of &TRACE may be set to zero explicitly, or may reach zero as it is decremented as the result of tracing. Individual trace associations may be cancelled, however, by executing

```
    STOPTR(name,type)
```

which cancels a single trace association for the **name** and **type**. Thus the tracing of statement failure is stopped by executing

```
    STOPTR('STFCOUNT','KEYWORD')
```

If an attempt is made to cancel a trace association that has not been made, the call of **STOPTR** fails.

8.2   Programmer-Defined Trace Functions

The `TRACE` function has an optional fourth argument that permits the programmer to supply procedures for tracing. The complete form of the function is

    TRACE(name,type,tag,function)

where `function` is a programmer-defined function.

When the traced action occurs, the function is called with `name` as its first argument and `tag` as its second argument. The keywords `&TRACE` and `&FTRACE` are automatically set to zero on entry to a programmer-defined trace procedure and restored on return. This prevents accidental tracing of a trace procedure. The programmer may change the values `&TRACE` and `&FTRACE` while in a trace procedure. Upon return from the function, the former values are restored.

8.2.1   Invoking Programmer-Defined Trace Procedures

The time at which a programmer-defined trace procedure is called depends on the type of trace.

(1) `VALUE` : just after assignment of the new value.

(2) `CALL` : just after evaluation of the arguments, but before execution of the first statement in the function.

(3) `RETURN` : just before the return is made.

(4) `FUNCTION` : same as for `CALL` and `RETURN`.

(5) `LABEL` : just before transfer to the label.

(6) `KEYWORD` : just after the keyword is changed.

8.2.2   Tools for Writing Programmer-Defined Trace Procedures

Special information is required for writing more elaborate programmer-defined trace procedures. Three keywords and three functions are provided expressly for this purpose.

1. `&STNO` is a protected keyword whose value is the statement number of the statement currently being executed.

2. `&LASTNO` is a protected keyword whose value is the statement number of the last statement executed.

3. &RTNTYPE is a protected keyword whose value is the type of return (RETURN, FRETURN, or NRETURN) made by the last defined function to return.

4. ARG(function,n) is a function whose value is the name of the n th argument of the programmer-defined function. ARG is useful in writing programmer-defined trace procedures that trace several functions and need to determine the names of the formal arguments of the functions being traced.

5. LOCAL(function,n) is a function whose value is the name of the n th local variable of the defined function.

6. FIELD(data type,n) is a function whose value is the name of the n th field of the programmer-defined data type.

The following example illustrates a programmer-defined function, VALTR, that prints a trace output only when a traced variable is assigned a specified value. KEY is a global variable. Trace output only occurs when a traced variable is assigned the value of KEY. If the variable being traced is not a string, the tag is used in the printed output. Use of this function is illustrated in the following program, which produces trace output when certain variables are assigned the value 25.

```
        POWER   =    ARRAY('25,5')                                          1
        KEY     =    25                                                     2
        DEFINE('VALTR(VAR,TAG)ST,TIME')                                     3
        &TRACE  =    1000                                                   4
        TRACE('I','VALUE',,'VALTR')                                         5
        TRACE(.POWER<5,2>,'VALUE','5 ** 2','VALTR')                         6
        TRACE(.POWER<25,1>,'VALUE','25 ** 1','VALTR')                       7
*
*       SET UP MATRIX OF INTEGER POWERS
*
        J       =    1                                                      8
NEXTI   I       =    0                                                      9
NEXTP   I       =    I + 1                                                 10
        POWER<I,J>    =    I ** J                         :S(NEXTP)        11
        J       =    LT(J,5) J + 1                        :S(NEXTI)F(END)  12
*
VALTR   ST      =    &LASTNO                                               13
        TIME    =    TIME()                                                14
        IDENT($VAR,KEY)                                   :F(RETURN)       15
        TAG     =    IDENT(DATATYPE(VAR),'STRING') VAR                     16
        OUTPUT  =    'KEY VALUE "' KEY '" ASSIGNED TO ' TAG                17
+                    ' IN STATEMENT ' ST ' AT TIME ' TIME                  17
+                                                         :(RETURN)        17
END                                                                        18
```

The printed output is

```
KEY VALUE "25" ASSIGNED TO I IN STATEMENT 10 AT TIME 67
KEY VALUE "25" ASSIGNED TO 25 ** 1 IN STATEMENT 11 AT TIME 83
KEY VALUE "25" ASSIGNED TO 5 ** 2 IN STATEMENT 11 AT TIME 117
KEY VALUE "25" ASSIGNED TO I IN STATEMENT 10 AT TIME 167
KEY VALUE "25" ASSIGNED TO I IN STATEMENT 10 AT TIME 250
KEY VALUE "25" ASSIGNED TO I IN STATEMENT 10 AT TIME 333
KEY VALUE "25" ASSIGNED TO I IN STATEMENT 10 AT TIME 416
```

8.3 Other Tracing Techniques

Only programmer-defined functions can be traced. Occasions arise, however, when it is desirable to trace primitive functions, or even operators. The effect of such a trace can be achieved by using programmer-defined functions in conjunction with **OPSYN**. Suppose, for example, a trace of the function **SIZE** is desired. Execution of the statements

```
OPSYN('SIZE.','SIZE')
DEFINE('SIZE(S)')
TRACE('SIZE','FUNCTION')
```

in conjunction with the procedure

```
SIZE    SIZE   =    SIZE.(S)           :(RETURN)
```

provides a suitable redefinition of **SIZE** that performs the same operation as the primitive function **SIZE**, and which can be traced as indicated.

Operators can be traced in a similar manner. Two applications of **OPSYN** are required as indicated in the following example that traces addition of data given on input cards.

```
        DEFINE('SUM(X,Y)')                                          1
        OPSYN('#','+',2)                                            2
        OPSYN('+','SUM',2)                                          3
        &TRIM   =    1;       &FTRACE   =    100                    4
*
ADD     TOTAL   =    TOTAL + INPUT            :S(ADD)               6
        OUTPUT  =     'THE TOTAL IS ' TOTAL                 :(END)  7
*
SUM     SUM   =    X # Y                                  :(RETURN) 8
*
END                                                                9
```

The printout, for the data indicated, is

```
    STATEMENT 6: LEVEL 0 CALL OF SUM('','123'),TIME = 17
    STATEMENT 8: LEVEL 0 RETURN OF SUM = 123,TIME = 17
    STATEMENT 6: LEVEL 0 CALL OF SUM(123,'4.92'),TIME = 33
    STATEMENT 8: LEVEL 0 RETURN OF SUM = 127.9199,TIME = 33
    STATEMENT 6: LEVEL 0 CALL OF SUM(127.9199,'87'),TIME = 50
```

```
STATEMENT 8:  LEVEL 0 RETURN OF SUM = 214.9199,TIME = 50
STATEMENT 6:  LEVEL 0 CALL OF SUM(214.9199,'0.05'),TIME = 66
STATEMENT 8:  LEVEL 0 RETURN OF SUM = 214.9699,TIME = 66
STATEMENT 6:  LEVEL 0 CALL OF SUM(214.9699,'3.17'),TIME = 83
STATEMENT 8:  LEVEL 0 RETURN OF SUM = 218.1399,TIME = 83
STATEMENT 6:  LEVEL 0 CALL OF SUM(218.1399,'20'),TIME = 100
STATEMENT 8:  LEVEL 0 RETURN OF SUM = 238.1399,TIME = 100
```

8.4 Dumping Natural Variables

A listing of natural variables and their values can be obtained by executing the function DUMP. A call of DUMP(N) provides this dump if N is a nonzero integer. The list of variables is not alphabetized, and variables that have null string values are omitted. If N is zero, no dump is given. Thus diagnostic dump statements can be placed in a program and the dumping turned on and off globally by assigning nonzero and zero values to the argument of DUMP.

Exercises

Exercise 8.1: Write a programmer-defined trace procedure that produces trace printout of the same form that is produced by standard value tracing.

Exercise 8.2: Write a programmer-defined trace procedure and use it to trace 50 variables, COLn (n=1,...,50), so that when COLn is assigned a value, a copy of the value is printed, indented n columns.

Exercise 8.3: Write a programmer-defined trace procedure that traces OUTPUT so that when EOF is assigned to OUTPUT, &OUTPUT is set to zero to stop further output.

CHAPTER 9

Input and Output

Input and output are accomplished by using variables associated with data sets (files). In the case of a variable associated in the output sense, each time the variable is assigned a value, a copy of the value is put out onto the associated data set. In the case of a variable associated in the input sense, each time the value of the variable is used, a new value is read from the associated data set and becomes the new value of the variable. Thus, input and output go on during program execution without any explicit I/O statements, as a result of I/O associations.

Details of the material contained in this chapter vary from machine to machine. Material appearing here refers specifically to the IBM System/360 operating under OS.

9.1 Printed Output

The variable **OUTPUT** is associated with the system print data set. Consequently, whenever **OUTPUT** is assigned a value, printout is generated. For example,

        OUTPUT = 'THE SELECTED VALUES ARE'

produces the output

THE SELECTED VALUES ARE

Output may also result from value assignment specified in patterns. For example,

        PEXP = BAL . EXP1 . OUTPUT '+' BAL . EXP2 . OUTPUT
          .
          .
          .
        EXP PEXP

prints the two terms in **EXP**, and assigns their values to **EXP1** and **EXP2**. This type of output is often useful for diagnostic purposes, and does not affect the pattern matching or the assignments made to **EXP1** and **EXP2**.

Ordinary printout is printed 132 characters per line, with as many lines as necessary being generated. Carriage control is provided to give single spacing. The null string is treated as a blank character and a blank line is printed for it. Strings are usually assigned to output variables. If an object other than a string is assigned to an output variable, the string representation of the object (as described in Chapter 7) is printed.

9.2   Punched Output

The variable **PUNCH** is associated with the standard punch data set. Consequently, whenever **PUNCH** is assigned a value, a punched card is generated. For example,

```
PUNCH   =   0
```

produces a card with zero punched in column one.

All the remarks about print output apply to punch output, except that 80 characters are punched per card, with additional cards punched as necessary for longer strings. The cards have no sequence numbering or identification unless provided in the strings that are punched.

9.3   Input

The variable **INPUT** is associated with the standard input data set. Whenever the value of **INPUT** is used, a card image is read from the input stream and becomes the new value of **INPUT**. For example,

```
OUTPUT   =   INPUT
```

reads a card image and prints it. Similarly,

```
INPUT   BAL . EXP
```

reads a card image and attempts to match a balanced string. If &TRIM is zero, all 80 columns of the card images are read, and the value of **INPUT** is an eighty character string. If &TRIM is nonzero, trailing blanks are automatically deleted.

Since each use of **INPUT** reads a card image, previous values of **INPUT** are lost unless they are assigned to other variables.

If the end of the input data set is encountered when a value of **INPUT** is requested, failure results. This failure can be used to detect the end of an input data set. For example, the following statements

```
        I   =   1
READ    DATA<I>   =   INPUT                          :F(OUT)
        I   =   I + 1                                :(READ)
OUT
```

read card images into the array **DATA** until the input data stream is exhausted (or **I** exceeds the range of **DATA**). Control is then transferred to **OUT**.

9.4 The I/O System

All input/output is handled by FORTRAN IV I/O routines. That is, SNOBOL4 I/O is done by the same system that does I/O for FORTRAN IV object programs. Consequently, the conventions and I/O concepts specified for the FORTRAN IV language also apply to SNOBOL4. In addition, the version of the language described here operates under OS/360. It is necessary to understand both the fundamentals of FORTRAN IV I/O [7,8] and job control language (JCL) [9] in order to use the I/O facilities of SNOBOL4 effectively.

In FORTRAN, data sets (files) have numbers (data set reference numbers). These numbers are referred to in source-language programs and are associated at run time with specific data sets by JCL statements. There are three standard data sets:

> normal input stream (5)
> normal print output (6)
> normal punch output (7)

DDNAMEs in JCL are used to associate the data set reference numbers with actual data sets. DDNAMEs for FORTRAN have the form **FTxxFyyy**, where **xx** corresponds to the data set reference number and **yyy** is a file sequence number for multifile data sets. The typical DD cards used in SNOBOL4 associate the standard data set reference numbers **5**, **6**, and **7** as follows:

```
//FT06F001 DD SYSOUT=A
//FT07F001 DD UNIT=PUNCH
//FT05F001 DD *
```

This JCL, or its equivalent, is contained in the SNOBOL4 cataloged procedure, and is supplied automatically when the cataloged procedure is used.

A wide range of devices and record structures can be specified on DD cards. By changing the DD cards, the data streams can be assigned to different data sets at run time. Thus,

```
//FT05F001 DD DSN=PROG1,VOL=SER=BTLXX1,UNIT=DISK,DISP=OLD
```

specifies an input stream from a data set **PROG1** on a disk file. Similarly,

```
//FT07F001 DD DSN=PUNCHER,VOL=SER=MYSAV1,UNIT=9TRACK,DISP=(,PASS),
//          DCB=(RECFM=FB,LRECL=80,BLKSIZE=800),LABEL(1,SL)
```

causes punched output to go onto a 9-track tape with a blocking factor of ten.

A complete discussion of DD statements is beyond the scope of this book, and is an involved and difficult subject. The important fact is that JCL permits the specification of a wide variety of devices and record structures. This specification is made when the program is run and requires no alteration of the program.

FORTRAN supports multifile data sets. The last three characters in the DDNAME specify the file number. When FORTRAN comes to the end of a file, it automatically opens the next file of the same data set reference number.

Thus, for example, input may come from several files.

```
//FT05F002 DD DSN=DATA2,UNIT=DISK,VOL=SER=BTLHO4,DISP=OLD
//FT05F001 DD *
       .
       .
       .
/*
```

With these DD cards, when the in-line data stream is exhausted, failure occurs. A subsequent attempt to input reads data from **DATA2**. In a multifile data set, failure occurs each time the end of a file is reached.

9.5   Output Associations

The variables **OUTPUT** and **PUNCH** have predefined output associations. Programmer-defined associations may be made using the function **OUTPUT**. The form of the function is

```
OUTPUT(name,number,format)
```

OUTPUT associates the name with the data set reference number according to the given format. The format is a string specifying a FORTRAN IV format. The following statements correspond to the associations for the variables **OUTPUT** and **PUNCH**:

```
OUTPUT('OUTPUT',6,'(1X,132A1)')
OUTPUT('PUNCH',7,'(80A1)')
```

Using the **OUTPUT** function, any variable can be associated with any data set reference number. For example,

```
PRFORM   =   '(1X,132A1)'
TEST   =   ARRAY('8,8')
OUTPUT(.TEST<1,1>,6,PRFORM)
OUTPUT(.TEST<8,8>,6,PRFORM)
```

associate the array elements **TEST<1,1>** and **TEST<8,8>** with the ordinary print data set and with the standard print format. As a result, whenever either **TEST<1,1>** or **TEST<8,8>** is assigned a value, the new value is printed.

Data set reference numbers are not restricted to 5, 6, and 7, but can range from 1 through 99. Associations can be made with data set reference numbers other than the standard ones. In this case, a DD statement for that number must be provided when the program is run. For example

```
        OUTPUT('TEXT',7,'(80A1)')
```

associates **TEXT** with the punch data set. On the other hand,

```
        OUTPUT('TEXT',20,'(80A1)')
```

and the DD statement

```
//FT20F001 DD DSN=NEWF,UNIT=TAPE,VOL=SER=MYSAV1,LABEL=(2,SL),
//   DISP=(,PASS),DCB=(RECFM=FB,BLKSIZE=800,LRECL=80)
```

allow the program to put card images onto the second file of a tape. The **LRECL** parameter of **80** and the format **(80A1)** relate the record size of the file to the record size in the format.

Formats used in output association must specify the conversion of at least one element by **A**-conversion. (Normally **nA1**-conversion is used.) Integers and reals are converted into strings by SNOBOL4. **F**- and **I**-conversion must not be used. In addition to **A**-conversion, quoted literals, **X**-, **H**-, **T**-, and **Z**-conversion may be specified [7,8]. Carriage control must be provided for printing; otherwise the first character of the string is consumed for this purpose. Consider

```
        OUTPUT('TITLE',6,'(1H1,132A1/(1X,132A1))')
```

When a value is assigned to **TITLE**, a page is ejected and the value titles the next page of output. The use of literals is illustrated by

```
        OUTPUT('SUM',6,"(' SUM=',128A1/(1X,132A1))")
```

which includes identifying information with the format. Subsequently,

```
        SUM    =    300
```

causes the printout

```
SUM=300
```

On the IBM 360, the largest number accepted in format statements is **255**. Larger numbers are reduced modulo **256**. Thus

```
        OUTPUT('OUT',10,'(400A1)')
```

is equivalent to

```
        OUTPUT('OUT',10,'(144A1)')
```

The effect of larger numbers can be obtained by using repetition. For example,

```
        OUTPUT('OUT',10,'(20(20A1))')
```

specifies **400**-character output.

The predefined associations can be changed. Thus,

```
        OUTPUT('OUTPUT',6,'(1X,120A1)')
```

shortens the line length for **OUTPUT** to **120** characters.

The second and third arguments of **OUTPUT** can be defaulted. If the second argument is zero or null, the standard output unit, **6**, is assumed. If the third argument is null, the standard print format, **(1X , 132A1)** , is assumed. Thus

      OUTPUT ('OUT')

provides the same association as is predefined for **OUTPUT**.

9.6   Input Associations

Programmer-defined input associations can be made using the function **INPUT**. The form of this function is

      INPUT (name , number , length)

INPUT associates the name with the data set reference number, and specifies that the resulting string is to have the given length. (Notice in particular that no format is specified.) **INPUT** has a predefined association equivalent to

      INPUT ('INPUT' , 5 , 80)

If the length is less than the record size on the data set being read, the last part of the record is lost. Hence,

      INPUT ('INPUT' , 5 , 72)

changes the association for **INPUT** so that only 72 columns are read. Columns 73 through 80 are lost if data set reference number **5** is associated with ordinary card input. A length longer than the record size should not be specified.

The second and third arguments of **INPUT** can be defaulted. If the second argument is zero or null, the standard input unit, **5**, is assumed. If the third argument is zero or null, the standard length of **80** is assumed. Thus

      INPUT ('IN')

provides the same association for **IN** as is predefined for **INPUT**.

9.7   Other I/O Functions

Several other functions are provided for I/O-related operations [7,8]. All of these functions return the null string as value.

9.7.1 BACKSPACE

`BACKSPACE(number)` backspaces one record on the data set associated with the number. For example,

    BACKSPACE(15)

backspaces a record on the data set associated with data set reference number **15**.

9.7.2 DETACH

`DETACH(name)` removes any input and output association that the name may have. For example,

    DETACH('OUTPUT')

terminates normal print output.

9.7.3 ENDFILE

`ENDFILE(number)` writes an end of file on (closes) the data set specified by the number. For example,

    ENDFILE(20)

closes the data set associated with data set reference number **20**.

9.7.4 REWIND

`REWIND(number)` repositions the data set associated with the number to the first file. For example,

    REWIND(10)

rewinds the data set associated with data set reference number **10**. Subsequently, reference to **10** refers to the beginning of the data set specified by **FT10F001** (even if **10** is a multifile data set).

9.8   Turning Off Input and Output

Input and output occur automatically as a result of associations with variables, provided &INPUT and &OUTPUT are nonzero. Both these keywords have initial default values of one.

In some circumstances, it may be desirable to turn off input or output, or both. This may be achieved by setting the corresponding keyword to zero. Normal automatic input and output can be restored by assigning nonzero values to the keywords.

CHAPTER 10

Running a SNOBOL4 Program

Most of this book is devoted to language features and how they are used in programming. This chapter is concerned with the running of a SNOBOL4 program.

A SNOBOL4 run consists of three parts:

(1) compilation,
(2) execution, and
(3) termination.

10.1 Compilation

During compilation, the SNOBOL4 system is initialized and the source program is converted into intermediate object code, which is in a form suitable for interpretation during execution. Compilation uses the same procedures that are used by the **CODE** function. Additional procedures are used to read the source program from the input data set, print a compilation listing on the output data set, and note errors detected in the source program.

10.1.1 Source-Program Input

Input to the compiler comes from the standard input stream associated with data set reference number **5**. On the IBM 360, the compiler begins reading the program from the data set associated with **FT05F001**. Only the first 72 characters of a line are processed by the compiler, and columns 73 through 80 can be used for sequential numbering or other identification.

The compiler continues to read until it encounters the end statement of the program. If an end of file is encountered before the end statement is found, the compiler goes to the next file for reference number **5**. The input program may therefore be in several sections given by **FT05F001**, **FT05F002**, etc. When the end statement is encountered, compilation stops. If the end statement is missing from the program, the compiler tries to find the next file, assuming more program remains to be compiled. When this file is not found, an error message is printed by the FORTRAN I/O system and the run is terminated.

10.1.2   Source Listing

A listing of the source program with identifying statement numbers is printed on the standard output data set. The format of this listing is illustrated by examples later in this chapter. These examples have been slightly modified to fit within the page width of this book, but are otherwise accurate.

10.1.3   Listing Control

Listing of the source program and placement of statement numbers is controlled by control lines appearing in the source program. A minus sign at the beginning of a line identifies that line as a control line. There are three controls: **LIST**, **UNLIST**, and **EJECT**.

LIST turns on listing of the source program and controls placement of the statement numbers. The control line

```
-LIST LEFT
```

causes placement of statement numbers at the left side of the listing. The control line

```
-LIST RIGHT
```

causes placement of statement numbers at the right. In the initial, default mode, the source program is listed with numbers at the right. The control line

```
-LIST
```

is equivalent to

```
-LIST RIGHT
```

The control line

```
-UNLIST
```

turns off listing of the source program. Listing may be restored by using **LIST**.

A page eject in the source listing may be obtained by the control line

```
-EJECT
```

Blanks may appear between the minus sign and the control word. One or more blanks must separate **LIST** from **LEFT** or **RIGHT**. Any characters other than **LEFT** following blanks on the **LIST** control line cause the same action as **RIGHT**. An erroneous control line is ignored.

10.1.4   Operator Precedence and Associativity

SNOBOL4 permits considerable flexibility during program execution. Functions can be defined then, data objects created, and operators redefined. The precedence and associativity of operators cannot be changed, however. Precedence and associativity are properties of the operator symbol and are used during compilation to determine the structure of expressions. For example, the statement

        P   =   A   B $ C   D | Q

is equivalent to

        P   =   ((A   (B $ C))   D) | Q

Of course, parentheses can always be used to override the built-in precedence and associativity. The statement

        P   =   (A   B) $ C   (D | Q)

is quite different than the previous statement.

For reference purposes, the precedence and associativity of the binary operators is listed in the following table.

Binary Operators

Graphic	*Definition*	*Associativity*	*Precedence*
¬	*none*	right	12
?	*none*	left	12
$	immediate value assignment	left	11
.	conditional value assignment	left	11
! ,**	exponentiation	right	10
%	*none*	left	9
*	multiplication	left	8
/	division	left	7
#	*none*	left	6
+	addition	left	5
−	subtraction	left	5
@	*none*	left	4
blank	concatenation	left	3
		alternation	left	2
&	*none*	left	1

10.1.5   Errors Detected during Compilation

Certain kinds of errors in the source program are detected during compilation. When an error is detected in a statement, compilation of that statement is terminated, and an error message is printed below the statement. A marker indicating the vicinity of the error is printed also. This marker indicates how much of the statement the compiler had accepted before detection of the error. Depending on the nature of the error, this marker may be before or after the point of the error. A typical error is failure to place blanks around a binary operator. An example, with the resulting error message, is

```
     X    =     A+B
          '
```

*** ILLEGAL CHARACTER IN ELEMENT

The compiler detects this error as an erroneous character (+) in an element, and refuses to accept the element as indicated by the marker.

Since compilation of a statement stops when an error is encountered, only the first error in any one statement is detected. Compilation continues with the next statement. However if more than fifty erroneous statements are encountered, compilation of the program ceases and the program is not executed.

10.1.6   Compilation Error Messages

A list of compilation error messages follows.

1. **BINARY OPERATOR MISSING OR IN ERROR**. This error indicates an erroneous binary operator or a missing blank between expressions. Some examples are

```
     X    =     F(X)*** 2
     TEXT    =     '('TEXT ')'
     M    =     (A B)N
```

2. **ERRONEOUS INTEGER**. This error occurs if an integer literal in a statement exceeds the magnitude of the largest possible integer. On the IBM 360, the largest integer is $2^{31}-1$.

3. **ERRONEOUS LABEL**. This error occurs if the first character of a statement is not a blank, integer, letter, *, or −.

4. **ERRONEOUS OR MISSING BREAK CHARACTER**. This error occurs if a break character appears in an erroneous context, or if a nested expression is not closed. Some examples are

```
     X    =     (A,B)
     A<1,2)    =    5
     F(G(X)                :S(LOOP)
```

5. **ERRONEOUS REAL NUMBER**. This error occurs if a real literal that is too large or too

small appears in a statement. On the IBM 360, reals have the approximate range 10^{-78} to 10^{75}.

6. **ERRONEOUS SUBJECT**. This error occurs if an erroneous construction appears in the subject field. An example is

```
,   =    2
```

7. **ERROR IN GOTO**. This error occurs when a syntactic error is found in the goto field. Some typical errors are

```
:S(L1)S(L2)
:S(A1)     :F(A2)
:<CODE)
```

8. **ILLEGAL CHARACTER IN ELEMENT**. This error typically occurs when blanks are not provided where required. Some examples are

```
X   =    3:
E   =    3.5P
```

9. **IMPROPERLY TERMINATED STATEMENT**. This error occurs when a statement terminates before a construction is complete. An example is

```
N   =    M +
```

10. **PREVIOUSLY DEFINED LABEL**. This error occurs when a duplicate label is encountered. The first occurrence of a label holds, and subsequent occurrences are erroneous.

11. **UNCLOSED LITERAL**. This error occurs when a closing quotation mark is omitted. Examples are

```
LETTER   =    'A
TEXT    =    'HE YELLED STOP"
```

10.2   Execution

Execution of the compiled program begins when compilation is complete. Ordinarily, program execution begins with the first statement of the program. Program execution can be started with any labelled statement by specifying that label in the end statement. The label of the first statement to be executed is placed in the position of the subject. For example,

```
END INIT
```

causes program execution to begin with the statement labelled **INIT**. The end statement

```
END END
```

has the effect of a compile-only run.

10.2.1   The Sequence of Evaluation

An understanding of the sequence of evaluation requires an understanding of the overall evaluation of a statement in terms of its major components. There are three major types of statements: assignment, pattern matching, and replacement. These have the forms:

```
label   subject    =   object    goto
label   subject    pattern   goto
label   subject    pattern   =   object    goto
```

Labels and gotos are optional. The object may be explicitly omitted, in which case the object is taken to be an expression that has the null string as value.

There are two degenerate statement forms as well:

```
label   subject    goto
label   goto
```

Labels and gotos are optional in these forms as well. Thus a blank line is an acceptable statement. The replacement statement is the most complicated and general form and is used for illustration. All other statement forms can be considered formally as degenerate replacement statements, and the evaluation of the degenerate forms can be understood from the evaluation of the replacement statement by skipping the missing components. The sequence of evaluation is:

1. The label requires no evaluation, and in fact is not part of the statement at all. It merely serves to identify the statement.

2. The subject is evaluated first. If the evaluation of the subject fails, the statement fails, the goto is processed, and evaluation of all other components is skipped. If no failure goto is specified, control passes to the next statement.

3. The pattern is evaluated next. If this evaluation fails, the statement fails and the goto is processed as in the case of subject failure.

4. The pattern match is performed next. If the pattern match fails, the statement fails, conditional value assignment is not performed, the replacement is skipped, and the goto is processed. Immediate value assignment, and other effects which occur dynamically during pattern matching, may take place before the pattern match fails. If pattern matching succeeds, conditional value assignment is performed for those components that matched.

5. The object is evaluated. If this evaluation fails, the statement fails, no replacement is performed, and the goto is processed.

6. The replacement is performed.

7. The goto is processed. Goto processing depends on the structure of the goto and whether or not the statement fails. If the statement succeeds, only an unconditional or success goto in the statement is evaluated. If the statement fails, only an unconditional goto or failure goto in the statement is evaluated. Transfer is made to the evaluated goto,

if there is one, or control is passed to the next statement. Failure in evaluation of a goto is an error.

Any of the components of a statement may be arbitrarily complicated and may invoke many kinds of processes. Calls to programmer-defined functions can occur, for example, in any component of a statement (except the label), and even take place in the middle of pattern matching as the result of the evaluation of unevaluated expressions.

Within an expression, the order of evaluation depends on the order of the components and the operations performed on them. Evaluation of the components of an expression is from left to right. In complicated expressions, components are nested, and the order of evaluation may be determined by examining the fully parenthesized form of the expression as determined from the rules of precedence and association. Consider the expression

```
(K    L    F(A + B * C))
```

which has the fully parenthesized form

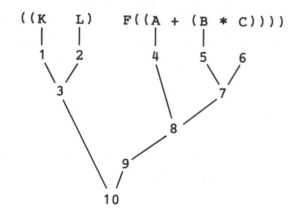

The order of evaluation of this expression is as indicated. If **F** is a programmer-defined function, its evaluation involves the execution of other statements and may in itself be very complicated.

In order to understand how failure is handled, it is important to know what operations can fail.

   1. Obtaining the value of a variable fails if the variable has an input association and an end-of-file condition is encountered. An attempt to read occurs only if the value of the variable is required, not merely because the variable appears in a statement. Thus, neither

```
INPUT    =    '0'
```

nor

```
LT(N,M)         :S(INPUT)
```

requires the value of **INPUT** and hence no attempt is made to read.

2. Primitive predicates fail if the stated condition is not met. The unary negation operator, for example, fails only if its operand does not fail.

3. The primitive functions **ARG**, **CODE**, **COLLECT**, **CONVERT**, **DUPL**, **EVAL**, **FIELD**, **LOCAL**, **REPLACE**, and **STOPTR** fail in certain circumstances.

4. Array references fail if an index is out of bounds.

5. Pattern matching may fail for a variety of reasons.

6. Programmer-defined functions fail by transferring to **FRETURN**.

Failure is a condition that causes a process to terminate and return to the process that called it, which in turn terminates and passes the failure condition back, until eventually the statement itself fails. The exception is the unary negation operator that converts a failure condition into successful evaluation, and converts successful evaluation into a failure condition. A statement fails if failure occurs in the evaluation of its subject or pattern, if pattern matching fails, or if failure occurs in evaluation of its object.

Details of function evaluation deserve special note. All the arguments to a programmer-defined function are evaluated before the function is called. If too many arguments are provided to the call of a programmer-defined function, the extra arguments are evaluated, but not passed. If the evaluation of any argument fails, a failure condition is returned and the function is not entered.

Primitive functions are called before their arguments are evaluated, and each function evaluates its own arguments. Too many arguments in the call of a primitive function is an error. If too few arguments are provided in the call of a primitive function, null strings are provided for the omitted arguments. An exception to this rule concerns functions invoked by **APPLY** or called through an **OPSYN**ed synonym. Such calls must contain the correct number of arguments.

10.2.2   Error Conditions

As indicated throughout this book, there are a number of errors that may occur during program execution. Some errors are relatively insignificant, while others are so severe that continued program execution is impossible. Error conditions are therefore divided into two categories:

(1) conditionally fatal, and
(2) unconditionally fatal.

The handling of conditionally fatal errors is controlled by two keywords. &ERRLIMIT limits the number of conditionally fatal errors that are allowed. If a conditionally fatal error occurs and the value of &ERRLIMIT is greater than zero, the value of ERRLIMIT is decremented by one, and failure occurs in the expression with the error. If the value of &ERRLIMIT is zero, program execution terminates with an error message. For example,

        &ERRLIMIT   =   10

permits ten conditionally fatal errors. The eleventh error causes error termination. The initial, default value of &ERRLIMIT is zero, so that any error causes error termination unless the value of &ERRLIMIT is changed.

Each error has a number. When the error occurs, this number becomes the value of the protected keyword &ERRTYPE, serving to identify the error. ERRTYPE can be traced, permitting diagnosis of conditionally fatal errors under program control.

10.2.3   Program Error Messages

A list of errors follows. Errors 1 though 16 are conditionally fatal. Errors 17 through 28 are unconditionally fatal and cause error termination regardless of the value of &ERRLIMIT.

1. **ILLEGAL DATA TYPE**. This error is one of the most frequent to occur. A typical example is

        X   =   X + 'A'

since **A** is not a numeral string.

2. **ERROR IN ARITHMETIC OPERATION**. This error occurs if an attempt is made to divide by zero, raise zero to a nonpositive power, or if the result of an arithmetic operation exceeds the magnitude for integers or reals. On the IBM 360, integers have the range of -2^{31} to $2^{31}-1$ and reals have the approximate range 10^{-78} to 10^{75}.

3. **ERRONEOUS ARRAY OR TABLE REFERENCE**. This error occurs if the value of the variable given in a reference is not an array or a table, or if the first argument of **ITEM** is not an array or table. An example is

        ITEM('A',3)

4. **NULL STRING IN ILLEGAL CONTEXT**. This error occurs in a variety of situations. A typical one is

        A   = $X

where the value of **X** is the null string.

5. **UNDEFINED FUNCTION OR OPERATION**. This error occurs if an attempt is made to call a function or use an operator that has no definition. For example,

    A   =   X # Y

produces this error if # is not given a definition by using **OPSYN**.

6. **ERRONEOUS PROTOTYPE**. This error occurs when **ARRAY**, **DATA**, **DEFINE**, or **LOAD** is called with a prototype that is syntactically erroneous. An example is

    DEFINE('F(X')

7. **UNKNOWN KEYWORD**. This error occurs if the unary operator & is applied to a string that is not a keyword.

8. **VARIABLE NOT PRESENT WHERE REQUIRED**. Assignment and goto require variables. The following statement illustrates this error.

    3   =   2

9. **ENTRY POINT OF FUNCTION NOT LABEL**. The entry point for a defined function given in **DEFINE** need not be a label, but must be by the time the defined function is first called. Otherwise this error occurs.

10. **ILLEGAL ARGUMENT TO PRIMITIVE FUNCTION**. This error occurs when certain primitive functions are called with illegal arguments. Specific cases are in the first argument of **ARG**, **FIELD**, and **LOCAL**, the second argument of **TRACE** and **STOPTR**, and the third argument of **OPSYN**.

11. **READING ERROR**. This error occurs when an error condition is encountered during an attempt to read a record.

12. **ILLEGAL I/O UNIT**. If a negative data set reference number (unit) is given as an argument to **BACKSPACE**, **ENDFILE**, or **REWIND**, or as the second argument to **INPUT** or **OUTPUT**, this error occurs.

13. **LIMIT ON DEFINED DATA TYPES EXCEEDED**. This limit on the number of different defined data types is 899. This error occurs if that limit is exceeded.

14. **NEGATIVE NUMBER IN ILLEGAL CONTEXT**. Several functions require nonnegative integer arguments. A negative number causes this error. The specific cases are in the arguments to **LEN**, **POS**, **RPOS**, **RTAB**, and **TAB**, and in the third argument of **INPUT**.

15. **STRING OVERFLOW**. This error occurs if a string longer than the value of &MAXLNGTH is formed. The initial, default value of &MAXLNGTH is 5000.

16. **OVERFLOW DURING PATTERN MATCHING**. This error occurs if an internal stack overflows during pattern matching. Such overflow may be caused by a looping pattern, or excessively recursive one.

17. **ERROR IN SNOBOL4 SYSTEM**. This error occurs if an internal error or inconsistency is detected by the SNOBOL4 system. Such an error indicates an implementation problem, and listings should be sent to the authors.

18. **RETURN FROM ZERO LEVEL**. This error occurs if a transfer to **RETURN**, **FRETURN**, or **NRETURN** is made outside the call of a programmer-defined function.

19. **FAILURE DURING GOTO EVALUATION**. This error occurs if failure occurs in the process of computing a label for a transfer. An example is

$$:(\$(IDENT(X,Y) \ X \ Y))$$

if **X** and **Y** are not identical.

20. **INSUFFICIENT STORAGE TO CONTINUE**. This error occurs when there is not enough storage available for continued operation of the SNOBOL4 system.

21. **STACK OVERFLOW**. This error occurs if the internal stack used by the SNOBOL4 system overflows. This error is usually the result of excessive recursion in programmer-defined functions. Stack overflow may also occur during storage regeneration.

22. **LIMIT ON STATEMENT EXECUTION EXCEEDED**. This error occurs if the number of statements executed exceeds the value of **&STLIMIT**. The initial default value of **&STLIMIT** is **50000**.

23. **OBJECT EXCEEDS SIZE LIMIT**. This error occurs if an attempt is made to create an object larger than the maximum possible size. On the IBM 360, this maximum size is $2^{24}-1$ bytes.

24. **UNDEFINED OR ERRONEOUS GOTO**. This error occurs if an attempt is made to transfer to a label that does not occur in the program, or if the result of evaluating the goto field is not a natural variable. An example is

$$:('LOOP' \ N)$$

25. **INCORRECT NUMBER OF ARGUMENTS**. This error occurs if a primitive function is called with an incorrect number of arguments. In the case of explicit function calls, this error results only from too many arguments, since null strings are automatically provided for omitted trailing arguments. In the case of functions **OPSYN**ed to primitive functions, or invoked by **APPLY**, this error is also caused by too few arguments.

26. **LIMIT ON COMPILATION ERRORS EXCEEDED**. Up to 50 erroneous statements are permitted during compilation of a SNOBOL4 program. If that number is exceeded, this error occurs. Note that this error occurs during compilation and prevents program execution.

27. **ERRONEOUS END STATEMENT**. This error occurs if there is a syntactic error in the end statement of a program, or if the label specified in the end statement does not occur in the program. This error prevents program execution.

28. **EXECUTION OF STATEMENT WITH A COMPILATION ERROR**. This error occurs if an attempt is made to execute a statement in which an error was detected during compilation.

Two kinds of failure occur in pattern matching as a result of conditionally fatal errors. If Error 16 occurs, the entire pattern match fails, as if **ABORT** had been encountered. Any other error causes the pattern component involved to fail to match, as if **FAIL** had been encountered.

10.3   Termination

There are three principal kinds of program termination:

(1) normal,
(2) error, and
(3) cancellation.

10.3.1   Normal Termination

Normal termination occurs when the program transfers to **END** or flows into the end statement. Various information is printed at the end of the listing, including counts of certain program operations and timing information. If the value of &DUMP is nonzero at program termination, a listing of the values of natural variables and unprotected keywords is provided. Only natural variables with nonnull values are included in the listing.

The following program illustrates the printout produced by a program that terminates normally.

```
SNOBOL4 (VERSION 3.0, DEC. 17, 1969)
BELL TELEPHONE LABORATORIES, INCORPORATED



            &DUMP   =   1;    &TRIM   =   1
*
*            THIS PROGRAM IS THE ALGORITHM BY HAO WANG (CF. 'TOWARD
*        MECHANICAL MATHEMATICS', IBM JOURNAL OF RESEARCH AND
*        DEVELOPMENT 4(1) JAN 1960 PP.2-22.)  FOR A PROOF-DECISION
*        PROCEDURE FOR THE PROPOSITIONAL CALCULUS.  IT PRINTS OUT A
*        PROOF OR DISPROOF ACCORDING AS A GIVEN FORMULA IS A THEOREM
*        OR NOT.  THE ALGORITHM USES SEQUENTS WHICH CONSIST OF TWO
*        LISTS OF FORMULAS SEPARATED BY AN ARROW (--*).  INITIALLY, FOR
*        A GIVEN FORMULA F THE SEQUENT
*
*                --* F
*
*        IS FORMED.  WANG HAS DEFINED RULES FOR SIMPLIFYING A FORMULA
*        IN A SEQUENT BY REMOVING THE MAIN CONNECTIVE AND THEN
*        GENERATING A NEW SEQUENT OR SEQUENTS.  THERE IS A TERMINAL
```

```
*           TEST FOR A SEQUENT CONSISTING OF ONLY ATOMIC FORMULAS:
*
*              A SEQUENT CONSISTING OF ONLY ATOMIC FORMULAS IS VALID IF
*              THE TWO LISTS OF FORMULAS HAVE A FORMULA IN COMMON.
*
*           BY REPEATED APPLICATION OF THE RULES, ONE IS LED TO A SET OF
*           SEQUENTS CONSISTING OF ATOMIC FORMULAS.  IF EACH ONE OF THESE
*           SEQUENTS IS VALID THEN SO IS THE ORIGINAL FORMULA.
*
*
*
           UNOP     =   'NOT'                                           3
           BINOP    =   'AND' | 'IMP' | 'OR' | 'EQU'                    4
           FORMULA  =   ' ' UNOP . OP '(' BAL . PHI ')'  |              5
+                       ' ' BINOP . OP '(' BAL . PHI ',' BAL . PSI ')'  5
           ATOM     =   ( ' ' BAL ' ' ) . A                            6
*
           DEFINE('WANG(ANTE,CONSEQ)PHI,PSI')                          7
*
READ       EXP   =    INPUT                          :F(END)           8
           OUTPUT  =                                                   9
           OUTPUT  =   'FORMULA: ' EXP                                 1
           OUTPUT  =                                                   1
*
           WANG(,' ' EXP)                            :F(INVALID)       1
           OUTPUT  =   'VALID'                        :(READ)          1
INVALID OUTPUT    =   'NOT VALID'                     :(READ)          1
*
WANG       OUTPUT  =   ANTE ' --* ' CONSEQ                             1
           ANTE    FORMULA  =                         :S( $('A' OP) )   1
           CONSEQ  FORMULA  =                         :S( $('C' OP) )   1
           ANTE    =   ANTE  ' '                                       1
           CONSEQ  =   ' '  CONSEQ  ' '                                1
TEST       ANTE    ATOM  =                            :F(FRETURN)      2
           CONSEQ  A                                  :S(RETURN)F(TEST) 2
*
*
ANOT       WANG(ANTE,CONSEQ ' ' PHI)                  :S(RETURN)F(FRETURN) 2
*
AAND       WANG(ANTE ' ' PHI ' ' PSI,CONSEQ)          :S(RETURN)F(FRETURN) 2
*
AOR        WANG(ANTE ' ' PHI,CONSEQ)                  :F(FRETURN)      2
           WANG(ANTE ' ' PSI,CONSEQ)                  :S(RETURN)F(FRETURN) 2
*
*
AIMP       WANG(ANTE ' ' PSI,CONSEQ)                  :F(FRETURN)      2
           WANG(ANTE,CONSEQ ' ' PHI)                  :S(RETURN)F(FRETURN) 2
*
```

```
AEQU      WANG(ANTE ' ' PHI ' ' PSI,CONSEQ)              :F(FRETURN)                  28
          WANG(ANTE,CONSEQ ' ' PHI ' ' PSI)              :S(RETURN)F(FRETURN)         29
*
CNOT      WANG(ANTE ' ' PHI,CONSEQ)                      :S(RETURN)F(FRETURN)         30
*
CAND      WANG(ANTE,CONSEQ ' ' PHI)                      :F(FRETURN)                  31
          WANG(ANTE,CONSEQ ' ' PSI)                      :S(RETURN)F(FRETURN)         32
*
COR       WANG(ANTE,CONSEQ ' ' PHI ' ' PSI)              :S(RETURN)F(FRETURN)         33
*
CIMP      WANG(ANTE  ' ' PHI,CONSEQ ' ' PSI)             :S(RETURN)F(FRETURN)         34
*
CEQU      WANG(ANTE ' ' PHI,CONSEQ ' ' PSI)              :F(FRETURN)                  35
          WANG(ANTE ' ' PSI,CONSEQ ' ' PHI)             :S(RETURN)F(FRETURN)         36
END                                                                                  37
```

NO ERRORS DETECTED IN SOURCE PROGRAM

FORMULA: IMP(NOT(OR(P,Q)),NOT(P))

```
 --*  IMP(NOT(OR(P,Q)),NOT(P))
NOT(OR(P,Q)) --*  NOT(P)
 --*  NOT(P) OR(P,Q)
P --*  OR(P,Q)
P --*  P Q
VALID
```

FORMULA: NOT(IMP(NOT(OR(P,Q)),NOT(P)))

```
 --*  NOT(IMP(NOT(OR(P,Q)),NOT(P)))
IMP(NOT(OR(P,Q)),NOT(P)) --*
NOT(P) --*
 --*  P
NOT VALID
```

FORMULA: IMP(AND(NOT(P),NOT(Q)),EQU(P,Q))

```
 --*  IMP(AND(NOT(P),NOT(Q)),EQU(P,Q))
AND(NOT(P),NOT(Q)) --*  EQU(P,Q)
NOT(P) NOT(Q) --*  EQU(P,Q)
NOT(Q) --*  EQU(P,Q) P
 --*  EQU(P,Q) P Q
P --*  P Q Q
Q --*  P Q P
VALID
```

```
FORMULA: IMP(IMP(OR(P,Q),OR(P,R)),OR(P,IMP(Q,R)))

 --*  IMP(IMP(OR(P,Q),OR(P,R)),OR(P,IMP(Q,R)))
 IMP(OR(P,Q),OR(P,R)) --*  OR(P,IMP(Q,R))
 OR(P,R) --*  OR(P,IMP(Q,R))
 P --*  OR(P,IMP(Q,R))
 P --*  P IMP(Q,R)
 P Q --*  P R
 R --*  OR(P,IMP(Q,R))
 R --*  P IMP(Q,R)
 R Q --*  P R
 --*  OR(P,IMP(Q,R)) OR(P,Q)
 --*  OR(P,Q) P IMP(Q,R)
 --*  P IMP(Q,R) P Q
 Q --*  P P Q R
VALID


NORMAL TERMINATION AT LEVEL  0

LAST STATEMENT EXECUTED WAS     8


DUMP OF VARIABLES AT TERMINATION

NATURAL VARIABLES

A = ' Q '
ABORT = PATTERN
ARB = PATTERN
ATOM = PATTERN
BAL = PATTERN
BINOP = PATTERN
EXP = 'IMP(IMP(OR(P,Q),OR(P,R)),OR(P,IMP(Q,R)))'
FAIL = PATTERN
FENCE = PATTERN
FORMULA = PATTERN
INPUT = 'IMP(IMP(OR(P,Q),OR(P,R)),OR(P,IMP(Q,R)))'
OP = 'IMP'
OUTPUT = 'VALID'
REM = PATTERN
SUCCEED = PATTERN
UNOP = 'NOT'
```

UNPROTECTED KEYWORDS

&ABEND = 0
&ANCHOR = 0
&CODE — 0
&DUMP = 1
&ERRLIMIT = 0
&FTRACE = 0
&FULLSCAN = 0
&INPUT = 1
&MAXLNGTH = 5000
&OUTPUT = 1
&STLIMIT = 50000
&TRACE = 0
&TRIM = 1

SNOBOL4 STATISTICS SUMMARY-
          1731 MS. COMPILATION TIME
           349 MS. EXECUTION TIME
           163 STATEMENTS EXECUTED,   34 FAILED
             0 ARITHMETIC OPERATIONS PERFORMED
            63 PATTERN MATCHES PERFORMED
             0 REGENERATIONS OF DYNAMIC STORAGE
             5 READS PERFORMED
            45 WRITES PERFORMED
          2.14 MS. AVERAGE PER STATEMENT EXECUTED

10.3.2   Error Termination

Error termination occurs if an unconditionally fatal error occurs, or if a conditionally fatal error occurs when &ERRLIMIT is zero. A message identifying the error is printed, and then statistics and dumps are provided as for normal termination.

The following example illustrates error termination. In this example, the input data was removed, causing failure in statement 3. The resulting attempt to transfer to ERR is erroneous since ERR does not occur as a label in the program.

```
SNOBOL4 (VERSION 3.0, DEC. 17, 1969)
BELL TELEPHONE LABORATORIES, INCORPORATED



        &ANCHOR    =    1                                                    1
        CARDPAT    =    BREAK(' ') . BIN LEN(1) BREAK(' ') . NUMBER          2
*       THE FIRST CARD GIVES THE NUMBER OF BINS
        SUM   =    ARRAY(TRIM(INPUT),0)                        :F(ERR)       3
```

```
          &TRACE    =    1000                                                  4
          TRACE(.SUM<3>,'VALUE','SUM<3>')                                      5
*         SUBSEQENT CARDS CONTAIN A BIN NUMBER FOLLOWED BY A BLANK AND THEN
*         THE NUMBER TO BE ADDED TO THE BIN.
READ      CARD   =    INPUT                              :F(DISPLAY)           6
          CARD   CARDPAT                                 :F(ERR)               7
          SUM<BIN>   =    SUM<BIN> + NUMBER              :S(READ)F(ERR)        8
*         PRINT OUT THE SUMS
DISPLAY                                                                        9
          I    =    1                                                         10
PRINT     OUTPUT    =    'SUM<' I '> = ' SUM<I>          :F(END)              11
          I    =    I + 1                                :(PRINT)             12
END                                                                          13
```

NO ERRORS DETECTED IN SOURCE PROGRAM

ERROR 24 IN STATEMENT   3 AT LEVEL   0

UNDEFINED OR ERRONEOUS GOTO


```
SNOBOL4 STATISTICS SUMMARY-
          1148 MS. COMPILATION TIME
            50 MS. EXECUTION TIME
             3 STATEMENTS EXECUTED,         1 FAILED
             0 ARITHMETIC OPERATIONS PERFORMED
             0 PATTERN MATCHES PERFORMED
             0 REGENERATIONS OF DYNAMIC STORAGE
             1 READS PERFORMED
             0 WRITES PERFORMED
         16.67 MS. AVERAGE PER STATEMENT EXECUTED
```

Another form of error termination occurs when an error is detected by the FORTRAN I/O routines. In this case, an error message is printed by the I/O routines, followed by the message CUT BY SYSTEM.

This type of error is illustrated by the following program in which no failure exit is provided on the statement reading data. Eventually data is exhausted, and a subsequent attempt to read causes the I/O routines to attempt to read from the second file for data set reference number 5. This file does not exist, and on the IBM 360 the error message IHC219I is printed.

```
SNOBOL4 (VERSION 3.0, DEC. 17, 1969)
BELL TELEPHONE LABORATORIES, INCORPORATED


        &TRIM    =    1                                                    1
        FINDNO   =    BREAK(*NO) . NO                                      2
        ONE   =    LEN(1) . NO                                            3
        L0   =    POS(0) SPAN('0')                                        4
*
        DEFINE('DEHEX(STR)NO')                       :(DEHEX.END)          5
*
*
DEHEX    STR    L0   =                                                     6
DEHEX1   STR    ONE   =                              :F(RETURN)            7
        DEHEX  =  INTEGER(NO)   16 * DEHEX + NO      :S(DEHEX1)            8
        'ABCDEF'   FINDNO                            :F(FRETURN)          9
        DEHEX = 16 * DEHEX + 10 + SIZE(NO)           :(DEHEX1)           10
DEHEX.END                                                                11
*
*
READ     NUMBER   =    INPUT                                             12
        OUTPUT                                                          13
        OUTPUT   =   'DEHEX(' NUMBER ') = ' DEHEX(NUMBER)              13
+                                            :S(READ)                   13
        OUTPUT  =   'UNABLE TO CONVERT ' NUMBER   :(READ)              14
END                                                                     15
```

NO ERRORS DETECTED IN SOURCE PROGRAM


```
DEHEX(100) = 256
DEHEX(00011) = 17
DEHEX(000F) = 15
UNABLE TO CONVERT 1ABCG
DEHEX(1ABC) = 6844
DEHEX(000FACE) = 64206
DEHEX(000FACE) = 64206
```


IHC219I

CUT BY SYSTEM IN STATEMENT 12 AT LEVEL   0

```
SNOBOL4 STATISTICS SUMMARY-
           1048 MS. COMPILATION TIME
            216 MS. EXECUTION TIME
            111 STATEMENTS EXECUTED,        28 FAILED
             59 ARITHMETIC OPERATIONS PERFORMED
             52 PATTERN MATCHES PERFORMED
              0 REGENERATIONS OF DYNAMIC STORAGE
              8 READS PERFORMED
              7 WRITES PERFORMED
           1.95 MS. AVERAGE PER STATEMENT EXECUTED
```

The message **CUT BY SYSTEM** may also occur if an error in the SNOBOL4 system causes a program interrupt.

10.3.3   Cancellation Termination

On the IBM 360, job cancellation prevents the SNOBOL4 system from regaining control. A system completion code is given, but no further output is printed. Statistics and dumps are lost, and it is not possible, in general, to determine where the program was when it was cancelled. In fact, program output may not be completely printed because of buffered output.

A typical cause for cancellation is a program loop, causing execution to exceed specified limits. Since some printed output may be lost, the program listing may be misleading. It is possible, for example, for a program to be cancelled in an execution loop, even though the compilation listing is incomplete, giving the erroneous impression of cancellation during compilation.

CHAPTER 11

Programming Details and Storage Management

This chapter is concerned with efficient programming techniques and good utilization of storage. The material that follows is intended for experienced programmers and individuals who have difficulties in running SNOBOL4 programs that are very large and time-consuming.

The most efficient programming and best use of the SNOBOL4 language requires considerable experience and sophistication. A student just learning the language should not attach too much importance to the material in this chapter. The various interdictions and comparisons will only obscure the underlying structure of SNOBOL4.

11.1   Implementation Overview

The key to efficient use of SNOBOL4 is an understanding of its implementation. The implementation is in itself a very large and involved topic. Only the most superficial description is attempted here.

The SNOBOL4 system consists of three main parts: A compiler, an interpreter, and a storage allocator.

The compiler analyzes the source program and converts it to a form of object code. In the analysis, each language element is converted into a suitable internal representation consisting of numbers, pointers, and flags. The object code is put in a Polish prefix form suitable for interpretation.

During the execution phase, the compiled object code is interpreted; functions are called, arguments fetched, and the resulting language operations are performed. Because of the nature of SNOBOL4, procedures are implemented in a recursive way.

Storage allocation occurs frequently during both compilation and interpretation. Strings identified by the compiler are entered into a storage area. During execution, storage is also allocated for new strings, patterns, arrays, and so forth. SNOBOL4 is unusual in this sense. In most languages, data objects are identified by declarations handled during compilation and hence little, if any, allocation is required during execution. Allocation of new data objects typically continues throughout execution of a SNOBOL4 program. As a result of continued allocation, available storage may be exhausted. Storage regeneration, which discards old, unneeded objects to make more space available, is therefore an important function of the storage allocator.

11.2   Strings

Handling strings is fundamental to the operation of the language. SNOBOL4 supports operations on strings of essentially unlimited length, without requiring any attention on the part of the programmer. This is particularly important in string formation where strings of any length can be assigned to any variable.

More important to the internal operation of the language is the fact that any nonnull string can be used as a variable. Some natural variables are explicit in the source program. Indirect referencing permits any string to be used as a variable, and hence have an assigned value. The statement

```
$INPUT    =    X
```

is an extreme example in which a string is read in and used as a variable.

To support the use of any nonnull string as a variable, every newly formed string is created as a variable. Space is provided for the value of that variable, and the null string is provided as the initial value. Proper functioning of the language requires that those natural variables be unique. Otherwise two different copies of the variable might have different values. In SNOBOL4 these problems are handled by assuring that each string occurs exactly once in storage. When a new string is formed, a search must be performed to determine whether that string already exists. Since string formation is a frequent operation, special techniques are used to make the search efficient. A combination of hash addressing [10,11] and a linked-bin structure is used. Each string, once it is formed, is uniquely represented by a pointer (address). The value of a natural variable is obtained by referencing the location to which it points. In the statement

```
      X    =    Y    Z
```

the variables **X**, **Y**, and **Z** are represented by pointers. Values of **Y** and **Z** are easily obtained. Assuming these values are strings, concatenation is performed, resulting in a new string. A search for this string is then performed. If it already exists as a variable, a pointer to it is returned. If the string is new, space is allocated for it, and a pointer to the new variable is returned. Assignment of this pointer as the value of **X** is now simple. This example illustrates a general characteristic of strings. Obtaining and assigning values is a simple operation. Creation of a new string is relatively more time consuming.

From the discussion, it should be evident that indirect referencing is a relatively efficient operation. Since natural variables are represented by pointers, an indirect reference only requires going from a pointer to the value to which it points.

11.3   Other Variables

Strings are only one kind of variable. Others are array and table references, fields of programmer-defined data objects, and keywords.

To reference an array, the variable is computed from the given indices. This operation is relatively simple and efficient. A similar operation is required for fields.

Table references are more complicated, and require a search of the table for the referencing item. This search is linear, but only requires comparison of pointer-type quantities. No string comparison is required since strings are represented by pointers. The time required to reference a table depends on the size of the table and the location of the referencing item within the table.

A typical alternative to tables is indirect referencing. The statements

        T<N>   =   X

and

        $('L' N)   =   X

are representative of the two choices. Generally speaking, the two take similar amounts of time. The time spent searching the table T is similar to the time taken to perform the concatenation and locate the corresponding natural variable. The space required for many natural variables with the prefix L is much greater than the space required for the table T, however.

On the other hand, if no prefix is required,

        $N   =   X

is more efficient than the table reference. Of course tables can be referenced with objects of any data type, while indirect referencing is limited to strings. Another consideration is whether a list of referenced items must be kept if indirect referencing is used. Conversion from **TABLE** to **ARRAY** provides such a list in a simple, efficient manner if tables are used.

Keyword references also require a linear search through a small table. Since keyword references are infrequent and the search small, keywords can be considered on a par with natural variables.

11.4   Patterns and Pattern Matching

A pattern is a data object, and may be very large if the pattern is complicated. The construction of a pattern is an involved process. For these reasons, it is more efficient to construct patterns outside of pattern matching statements, rather than to construct them repetitiously with each execution of the pattern matching statements. Unevaluated expressions make it possible to avoid construction of patterns in pattern matching statements, even if components of the pattern vary. An unevaluated expression amounts to a pointer to another pattern, which is accessed during pattern matching when the unevaluated expression is encountered.

Chapter 2 describes pattern matching in some detail, and much information about efficiency can be obtained by considering the bead diagrams and operation of the scanner. Several simple rules are worth remembering:

(1) Use the anchored mode if possible.
(2) Use **BREAK** instead of **ARB** if possible.
(3) Use **ANY** instead of alternation if possible.
(4) Avoid use of **ARBNO**.
(5) Use conditional rather than immediate value assignment if possible.
(6) Use the quickscan mode if possible.

Many programs can execute entirely in the anchored mode, avoiding much useless, time-consuming searching during pattern matching. In the unanchored mode, individual patterns can be anchored by using **FENCE** or **POS(0)** as their first component.

Where a known delimiter is sought, **BREAK** should be used. **ARB**, as its bead diagram illustrates, matches each character individually, which may be very inefficient.

Where one of a number of single characters is sought, **ANY** should be used. Alternation requires a large pattern with many components that must be matched one at a time. The time required for **ANY** to match is independent of the order in which the characters in its argument appear. In alternation, as indicated by the bead diagrams, the time depends strongly on the order of the alternatives.

ARBNO should be used only where its function is really needed. **SPAN** often will do, and is much more efficient.

Immediate value assignment often performs several assignments in the course of pattern matching. These additional operations should be avoided unless the dynamic effects of immediate assignment are really needed.

As illustrated in Chapter 2, the quickscan mode is designed to improve the efficiency of pattern matching by avoiding alternatives that cannot lead to successful matching. The fullscan mode, on the other hand, permits attempts to match, however futile they may be. For this reason, the fullscan mode may cause pattern matching to take much longer than the quickscan mode. The fullscan mode should be used only when pattern matching involves dynamic effects resulting from unevaluated expressions or immediate value assignment. If fullscan is needed only in a few statements, it is worth changing modes for these statements rather than running the entire program in the fullscan mode.

11.5   Input and Output

Automatic input and output occurs because of variables associated with data sets. If &OUTPUT is nonzero, output association is checked by a table lookup for every assignment of value to every variable. The time required to determine whether a particular variable is output-associated depends on the number of output-associated variables. This checking can be bypassed entirely by setting the value of &OUTPUT to zero during periods of program execution where output is not required. Input is handled in a similar manner, although checking is usually more frequent because it is required for every use of every variable. &INPUT can also be set to zero if input is not required.

Trimming of trailing blanks by setting &TRIM to a nonzero value has the benefit of creating shorter strings on input. Space is not allocated for the trailing blanks. Automatic trimming on input should be used, where appropriate, rather than explicit application of the TRIM function. TRIM applied to INPUT results in two strings: one consisting of the full input line, and another consisting of the trimmed result.

11.6   Storage Management

Dynamic storage is continually allocated during program compilation and execution. All forms of programmer data reside in allocated storage and compete for available space. This includes object code, strings, patterns, arrays, and so forth. Some data, depending on its use, is transient and may be discarded. Other data is always accessible to program and must be kept.

When available space is exhausted, the storage allocator regenerates storage, collecting all needed data and discarding all data inaccessible to the program. This process occurs automatically and usually does not concern the programmer directly. Statistics indicating a large number of regenerations suggest potential trouble. Repetitious construction of patterns and manipulation of very long strings are the most common causes of frequent storage regeneration. The amount of time required to regenerate storage depends on many factors and no specific figures can be given. A rough rule of thumb is that storage regeneration takes about 20 to 100 times as long as the execution of a typical statement. Thus storage regeneration is not a factor in program efficiency unless it occurs frequently.

11.6.1   Forcing Storage Regeneration

In special circumstances, a programmer may want to force storage regeneration or find out how much storage is available. This is done with the function COLLECT, which forces storage regeneration. COLLECT returns as value the amount of storage available (in bytes on the IBM 360) after regeneration. COLLECT(N) fails if less than N bytes remain.

11.6.2 Clearing Variable Values

Some programs are organized to process several sections of data independently, making it possible or necessary to remove residual data between sections. The function **CLEAR** assists in this manner. A call of **CLEAR( )** sets the values of all natural variables to the null string. **CLEAR** does not affect the values of keywords, created variables, I/O associations, or function definitions. Furthermore, values are cleared only at the level at which **CLEAR** is called. If values are saved by a call to a programmer-defined function, these values are restored when the function returns. This fact may be used to save the values of selected variables by calling **CLEAR** in a function in which these variables are formal arguments. If the values of **X**, **Y**, **Z**, and **PAT** are to be saved, a function **RESET** could have the defining statement

```
      DEFINE('RESET(X,Y,Z,PAT)')
```

with the procedure

```
RESET   CLEAR( )                   :(RETURN)
```

The values of **X**, **Y**, **Z**, and **PAT** (and **RESET**) are saved when **RESET** is called, and restored when it returns. All other natural variables are cleared.

CLEAR applies to the natural variables **ABORT**, **ARB**, **FAIL**, **FENCE**, **REM**, and **SUCCEED**, and clears their primitive pattern values. The corresponding keywords **&ABORT**, **&ARB**, **&FAIL**, **&FENCE**, **&REM**, and **&SUCCEED**, which are not affected by **CLEAR**, can be used to restore primitive patterns.

APPENDIX A

Syntax of SNOBOL4

This formal description of the syntax of SNOBOL4 is given in a syntax notation used in many IBM manuals [10]. Rules explaining this notation follow.

(1) A class of elements is denoted by a notation variable, which consists of lower case letters and periods and must begin with a letter.

(2) Literal characters are denoted by capital letters or special characters. Lower case letters and syntactic symbols are underlined when they represent literals. A lone underscore stands for itself.

(3) A syntactic unit is defined as one of the following:
    a. a notation variable,
    b. literal characters, or
    c. any collection of variables, literals, and syntax notation surrounded by braces or brackets.

(4) Braces { } denote a grouping.

(5) Square brackets [ ] denote an option. Anything enclosed within brackets may appear or be omitted.

(6) Vertical stacking of syntactic units and the vertical stroke | denote alternatives.

(7) Three dots ... denote optional repetition of the immediately preceding syntactic unit one or more times.

(8) Footnotes are used where restrictions apply to notation variables.

A.1 Syntax of Statements

The following notation variables define the components of a statement, leading to the definition of a statement itself.

```
digit:   0|1|2|3|4|5|6|7|8|9

letter:   A|B|C|D|E|F|G|H|I|J|K|L|M|N|O|P|Q|R|S|T|U|V|W|X|Y|Z

alphanumeric:   letter|digit

identifier:   letter [alphanumeric|.|_]...

blanks:   one or more blank characters

integer:   digit [digit]...

real:   integer . [integer]

operator:   ¬|?|$|.|!|%|*|/|#|+|-|ə|⊥|ε

unary:   operator

binary:   blanks [[operator|**] blanks]

string:   zero or more EBCDIC characters

sliteral:   '{string}¹'

dliteral:   "{string}²"

literal:   sliteral|dliteral|integer|real

element:   [unary]...  ⎧identifier    ⎫
                       ⎪literal        ⎪
                       ⎨function.call ⎬
                       ⎪reference      ⎪
                       ⎩( expression )⎭

operation:   element binary {element|expression}

expression:   [blanks] [element|operation] [blanks]

arg.list:   expression [, expression]...

function.call:   identifier ( arg.list )

reference:   identifier < arg.list >

label:   {alphanumeric {string}³}⁴

subject.field:   blanks element

pattern.field:   blanks expression
```

```
object.field:  blanks expression

equal:  blanks =

goto:  {( expression )|< expression >}

goto.field:  blanks : [blanks] ⎛goto
                               ⎜S goto [blanks] [F goto]⎞
                               ⎝F goto [blanks] [S goto]⎠

eol:    end of line

eos:    [blanks] {;|eol}

assign.statement:   [label] subject.field equal [object.field]
                    [goto.field] eos

match.statement:   [label] subject.field pattern.field [goto.field] eos

repl.statement:   [label] subject.field pattern.field equal
                  [object.field][goto.field] eos

degen.statement:   [label] [subject.field] [goto.field] eos

end.statement:   END [blanks [label|END]] eos

statement:   assign.statement|match.statement|repl.statement|
             degen.statement|end.statement
```

The following notes apply to the syntax given above:

[1] not including a single quote '
[2] not including a double quote "
[3] not including a blank or semicolon
[4] but not **END**. (**RETURN**, **FRETURN**, and **NRETURN** are syntactically acceptable, but do not override the standard function returns.)

A.2 Syntax of Programs

A SNOBOL4 program consists of a sequence of statements terminating with an end statement. Interspersed among these statements may be comment lines and control lines.

```
comment.line:  * string eol

control.line:  - [blanks] ⎛LIST blanks [LEFT|RIGHT]  [blanks] eol⎞
                          ⎜UNLIST                              ⎟
                          ⎝EJECT                               ⎠
```

A statement begins immediately following the preceding statement, i.e. at the beginning of a line or following a semicolon. A statement may be continued on the next line by using a continue line.

```
continue.line:   {+|.} remainder of statement
```

Comment, control, and continue lines must begin at the beginning of a line. They may not start in the interior of a line following a semicolon. A statement may be broken over a line boundary anywhere a blank is optional in the syntax. If a statement has the form

```
part1 [blanks] part2
```

it may be continued as

```
part1 [blanks] eol
{+|.}   [blanks] part2
```

where the + or . begins a new line as indicated, and takes the place of the optional blank.

A.3   Syntax of Prototypes

Prototypes for arrays, programmer-defined functions, programmer-defined data types, and external functions are evaluated during program execution, not during compilation. These prototypes may be given explicitly as literals or may be computed in a variety of ways. When **ARRAY**, **DEFINE**, **DATA**, or **LOAD** is executed, the corresponding prototype is then analyzed. The syntax of these prototypes follows.

```
item:   [identifier]

item.list:   item [, item]...

data.prototype:   identifier ( item.list )

function.prototype:   identifier ( item.list ) item.list

external.prototype:   identifier ( item.list ) item

signed.integer:   [[+|-] integer]

dimension:   signed.integer [: signed.integer]

array.prototype:   dimension [, dimension]...
```

A.4   Syntax of Data Type Conversions

Conversion from **STRING** to another data type involves a syntactic analysis of the string to be converted. Explicit conversions are performed to **INTEGER**, **REAL**, **EXPRESSION**, and **CODE**. Implicit conversions are performed for **INTEGER** and **REAL**.

```
string.integer:   signed.integer

string.real:   [[+|-]real]

string.expression:   expression

string.code:   statement [; statement]...
```

A.5   Character Codes for Various Machines

The character codes and graphics for symbols used in SNOBOL4 vary from machine to machine. The graphics used in this book correspond to the IBM 360 implementation. The following table summarizes the card codes and graphics for other implementations, using the IBM 360 as the point of reference. Not included in this table are the RCA Spectra 70 and XDS Sigma 5/6/7 which have the same codes and graphics as the IBM 360. The PDP-10 characters are similar to the IBM 360 as noted below. Punched card codes and typical printer graphics are given. Internal codes vary, and communication terminals may have different graphics.

IBM 360		*CDC 6600*		*UNIVAC 1108*		*GE 635*	
,	0-3-8	,	0-3-8	,	0-3-8	,	0-3-8
:	2-8	:	2-8	:	5-8	:	5-8
;	6-8-11	;	7-8-12	;	6-8-11	;	6-8-11
"	7-8	≠	4-8		7-8-11	"	0-6-8
'	5-8	↑	5-8-11	'	4-8	'	7-8-11
(	5-8-12	(	0-4-8	(	0-4-8	(	5-8-12
)	5-8-11	)	4-8-12	)	4-8-12	)	5-8-11
<	4-8-12	[	7-8	[	5-8-12	[	2-8
>	0-6-8	]	0-2-8	]	5-8-11	]	4-8-12
=	6-8	=	3-8	=	3-8	=	0-5-8
¬	7-8-11	¬	6-8-12	\	0-6-8	\	7-8-12
?	0-7-8	↱	0-5-8	?	0-12	?	7-8
$	3-8-11	$	3-8-11	$	3-8-11	$	3-8-11

IBM 360		CDC 6600		UNIVAC 1108		GE 635	
.	3-8-12	.	3-8-12	.	3-8-12	.	3-8-12
!	2-8-11		none		none		none
%	0-4-8	≥	5-8-12	%	0-5-8	%	0-4-8
*	4-8-11	*	4-8-11	*	4-8-11	*	4-8-11
/	0-1	/	0-1	/	0-1	/	0-1
#	3-8	≤	5-8	#	7-8-12	#	3-8
+	6-8-12	+	12	+	12	+	0-12
−	11	−	11	−	11	−	11
@	4-8	↓	6-8-11	@	7-8	@	4-8
|	7-8-12	∨	0-11	!	0-11	!	0-7-8
ε	12	∧	0-7-8	ε	2-8	ε	12

Notes:

1. The PDP-10 has the same character set as the IBM 360, except ! is equivalent to | , and \ (card code 7-8) is equivalent to ¬.

2. The CDC 3600 and the rest of the CDC 6000 series have the same character set as the CDC 6600. Card code 2-8-11 can also be used for ∨.

A.6 Extended Syntax for the IBM 360 Implementation

On the IBM 360 implementation, alternatives for several syntactically significant characters are provided. The extended syntax permits the use of characters available from terminal input and for which there are graphics on some print trains. The following table illustrates the added characters available in addition to the standard ones. Lower-case letters are also available on the IBM 360 implementation.

Added	Hexadecimal Code	Language Use	Standard
tab	05	concatenation, separator	blank
[	AD	left bracket and left direct goto delimiter	<
]	BD	right bracket and right direct goto delimiter	>
←	4A	assignment	=
↑	9F	exponentiation	!
⌐	AC	comment line	*
|	4F	comment line	*
⌐	AB	comment line	*

Notes:

1. The tab character cannot be used in **OPSYN** to represent concatenation, and is not treated like a blank in trimming.

2. The PDP-10 implementation permits the use of [,] , tab, ←, and ↑ in the same way as the extended IBM syntax.

APPENDIX B

Versions 2 and 3 of SNOBOL4

The first edition of this book describes Version 2 of SNOBOL4. This edition describes Version 3, which became available in December of 1969. Differences between the two versions are significant, and are detailed in the following sections.

B.1 Running Version 2 Programs under Version 3

Since Version 3 supercedes Version 2, the most serious differences are those that require changes in Version 2 programs to run them under Version 3. These differences are minor, and almost all programs written to run under Version 2 will run properly under Version 3 without modification. Points of difference follow.

1. In Version 2, negative values of **&FTRACE** and **&TRACE** turn on the tracing modes. In Version 3, the tracing modes are only on for positive values of these keywords.

2. An improvement in pattern matching heuristics for patterns involving **LEN** may be detectable during pattern matching in the quickscan mode. Fewer alternatives are attempted in Version 3.

3. Data type checking in the pattern-valued functions causes detection of erroneous arguments when the functions are called. In Version 2 such errors are not detected until pattern matching takes place.

4. The **CONVERT** function now performs conversions to **STRING** and **INTEGER** that fail in Version 2.

5. The **DATATYPE** function does not fail on external data types in Version 3 as it does in Version 2.

6. Negative arguments to **COLLECT** are erroneous in Version 3, but not in Version 2.

7. The standard print line length in Version 3 is 132, as opposed to 131 in Version 2.

8. Several constructions that are erroneous in Version 2 are acceptable in Version 3. Mixed-mode arithmetic is typical.

9. Program listing formats and messages are somewhat different in the two versions.

10. Program timing typically varies between the two versions.

11. On the IBM 360, handling of program interrupts, FORTRAN I/O error conditions, and step termination differs in the two versions.

B.2   Running Version 3 Programs under Version 2

Version 3 contains a number of features not available in Version 2. For this reason, many Version 3 programs will not run under Version 2 without considerable modification. Principal differences follow.

1. Version 2 does not have tables, or any of the features relating to them.

2. Version 2 does not have error control. All errors are fatal.

3. Version 2 does not permit mixed-mode arithmetic, comparison of real numbers, automatic conversion to and from **REAL**, or **REAL**-to-**INTEGER** conversion.

4. Version 2 does not support exponentiation of reals.

5. Version 2 does not permit operator definition by **OPSYN**. The unary operators ! and | are lacking, as well as the binary operators ¬, ?, $, and !.

6. A string to be converted to **CODE** must end with a semicolon.

7. The following functions are not included in Version 2: **DUMP**, **DUPL**, **REMDR**, and **TABLE**.

8. The following keywords are not included in Version 2: **&CODE**, **&ERRLIMIT**, **&ERRTYPE**, **&INPUT**, **&OUTPUT**, and **&TRIM**.

There are many other minor differences, mainly relating to data type conversions.

APPENDIX C

Sample Programs

Sample Program 1

```
SNOBOL4 (VERSION 3.0, DEC. 17, 1969)
BELL TELEPHONE LABORATORIES, INCORPORATED


*
*           THIS PROGRAM USES ARRAYS, PROGRAMMER-DEFINED FUNCTIONS, AND
*           A VARIETY OF OUTPUT FORMATS TO PRODUCE SETS OF BRIDGE HANDS.
*           THE FUNCTION DEAL() USES A PSEUDO-RANDOM NUMBER GENERATOR [13]
*           TO DEAL CARDS INTO FOUR ARRAYS NORTH, EAST, SOUTH, AND WEST.
*           THE FUNCTION DISPLAY() PRINTS THE HANDS, ONE TO A PAGE.
*
           OUTPUT('TITLE',6,'(14H1THIS IS HAND ,110A1)')              1
           OUTPUT('DEALER',6,'(11H DEALER IS ,110A1)')                2
           OUTPUT('SKIP',6,'(A1)')                                    3
*
*                    FUNCTIONS
*
           DEFINE('DEAL()')                                           4
           DEFINE('DISPLAY()')                                        5
           DEFINE('LINE(STR1,COL1,STR2,COL2)BL1,BL2')                 6
           DEFINE('RANDOM(N)')                                        7
           DEFINE('SUITL(HAND,SUIT)N')                :(CONSTANT)      8
*
DEAL       DEALSEQ   DEALHAND                                         9
           DECK  =   COPY(NEWDECK)                                    10
           N =   51                                                  11
NLOOP      DEALSEQ   NXTHAND                                          12
           CARD  =   RANDOM(N + 1)                                    13
           DECK<CARD>  SUITRANK  =  NE(CARD,N)  DECK<N>               14
           ITEM($HAND,SUIT,RANK)  =  $RANK                           15
           N =   GT(N,0)  N - 1                    :S(NLOOP)F(RETURN) 16
*
DISPLAY    TITLE  =  NTHDEAL                                          17
```

```
          DEALER  =   DEALR                                             18
          SKIP = '          '                                          19
          OUTPUT  =   LINE('NORTH',40)                                 20
          OUTPUT  =                                                    21
          OUTPUT  =   LINE(SUITL(NORTH,'S'),40)                        22
          OUTPUT  =   LINE(SUITL(NORTH,'H'),40)                        23
          OUTPUT  =   LINE(SUITL(NORTH,'D'),40)                        24
          OUTPUT  =   LINE(SUITL(NORTH,'C'),40)                        25
          SKIP = '          '                                          26
          OUTPUT  =   LINE('WEST',20,'EAST',60)                        27
          OUTPUT  =                                                    28
          OUTPUT  =   LINE(SUITL(WEST,'S'),20,                         29
+                         SUITL(EAST,'S'),60)                          29
          OUTPUT  =   LINE(SUITL(WEST,'H'),20,                         30
+                         SUITL(EAST,'H'),60)                          30
          OUTPUT  =   LINE(SUITL(WEST,'D'),20,                         31
+                         SUITL(EAST,'D'),60)                          31
          OUTPUT  =   LINE(SUITL(WEST,'C'),20,                         32
+                         SUITL(EAST,'C'),60)                          32
          SKIP = '          '                                          33
          OUTPUT  =   LINE('SOUTH',40)                                 34
          OUTPUT  =                                                    35
          OUTPUT  =   LINE(SUITL(SOUTH,'S'),40)                        36
          OUTPUT  =   LINE(SUITL(SOUTH,'H'),40)                        37
          OUTPUT  =   LINE(SUITL(SOUTH,'D'),40)                        38
          OUTPUT  =   LINE(SUITL(SOUTH,'C'),40)                        39
+                                             :(RETURN)                39
*
*
LINE      BL  LEN(COL1 - 1) . BL1                                      40
          BL2 =  DIFFER(STR2)  DUPL(' ',COL2 - (COL1 + SIZE(STR1)))    41
LINE1     LINE =  DUPL(' ',COL1 - 1)  STR1  BL2  STR2  :(RETURN)       42
*
*
RANDOM    RAN.VAR  =   RAN.VAR * 1061 + 3251                           43
          RAN.VAR  RTAB(5)  =                                          44
          RANDOM  =   (RAN.VAR * N) / 100000        :(RETURN)          45
*
*
SUITL     SUITL  =   SUIT  '  '                                        46
SUITL1    SUITL  =   SUITL  HAND<$SUIT,N>                :F(RETURN)     47
          N  =  N + 1                                   :(SUITL1)      48
*
*              CONSTANTS
*
CONSTANT  S  =   1                                                     49
          H  =   2                                                     50
          D  =   3                                                     51
```

```
          C   =   4                                                        52
          $0  =   'A'                                                      53
          $1  =   'K'                                                      54
          $2  =   'Q'                                                      55
          $3  =   'J'                                                      56
          $4  =   '10'                                                     57
          $5  =   '9'                                                      58
          $6  =   '8'                                                      59
          $7  =   '7'                                                      60
          $8  =   '6'                                                      61
          $9  =   '5'                                                      62
          $10  =   '4'                                                     63
          $11  =   '3'                                                     64
          $12  =   '2'                                                     65
          DEALSEQ  =   'NORTH,EAST,SOUTH,WEST,NORTH,'                       66
          NXTHAND  =   *HAND ','  BREAK(',') . HAND                        67
          DEALHAND =   *DEALR ','  BREAK(',') . HAND . DEALR               68
          SUITRANK  =   LEN(1) . SUIT  REM . RANK                          69
          EMPTYHAND  =   ARRAY('4,0:12')                                   70
          NEWDECK  =   ARRAY('0:51')                                       71
          RAN.VAR  =   157                                                 72
          DEALMAX  =   3                                                   73
          NTHDEAL  =                                                       74
          DEALR  =   'WEST'                                                75
          N   =   0                                                        76
BLDDEK    I   =   I + 1                                                    77
          R   =   0                                                        78
BLDDK1    NEWDECK<N>  =   I R                                              79
          N  =  LT(N,51)  N + 1                       :F(NEWDEAL)          80
          R  =  LT(R,12)  R + 1                    :S(BLDDK1)F(BLDDEK)     81
*
*
NEWDEAL   NTHDEAL  =  LT(NTHDEAL,DEALMAX)  NTHDEAL + 1  :F(END)            82
          NORTH  =   COPY(EMPTYHAND)                                       83
          EAST   =   COPY(EMPTYHAND)                                       84
          SOUTH  =   COPY(EMPTYHAND)                                       85
          WEST   =   COPY(EMPTYHAND)                                       86
*
          DEAL()                                                          87
*
          DISPLAY()                                    :(NEWDEAL)          88
END                                                                       89


NO ERRORS DETECTED IN SOURCE PROGRAM
```

THIS IS HAND 1
DEALER IS NORTH

NORTH

S   AQ974
H   K5
D   AJ93
C   Q8

WEST

S   J83
H   A108
D   872
C   K1042

EAST

S   62
H   Q9732
D   K64
C   J96

SOUTH

S   K105
H   J64
D   Q105
C   A753

THIS IS HAND 2
DEALER IS EAST

NORTH

S   J
H   AKQJ95
D   J107
C   A83

WEST

S   Q852
H   10732
D   83
C   J75

EAST

S   AK974
H   86
D   AK42
C   96

SOUTH

S   1063
H   4
D   Q965
C   KQ1042

THIS IS HAND 3
DEALER IS SOUTH

NORTH

S J107
H Q
D A985
C K7653

WEST

S 954
H 864
D K7643
C J10

EAST

S AQ863
H J10952
D 10
C AQ

SOUTH

S K2
H AK73
D QJ2
C 9842

```
NORMAL TERMINATION AT LEVEL   0

LAST STATEMENT EXECUTED WAS    82


SNOBOL4 STATISTICS SUMMARY-
          2279 MS. COMPILATION TIME
          3295 MS. EXECUTION TIME
          3026 STATEMENTS EXECUTED,     142 FAILED
          1783 ARITHMETIC OPERATIONS PERFORMED
           516 PATTERN MATCHES PERFORMED
             0 REGENERATIONS OF DYNAMIC STORAGE
             0 READS PERFORMED
            69 WRITES PERFORMED
          1.09 MS. AVERAGE PER STATEMENT EXECUTED
```

Sample Program 2

```
SNOBOL4 (VERSION 3.0,  DEC. 17, 1969)
BELL TELEPHONE LABORATORIES, INCORPORATED


* * * * * * * * * * * * * * * * * * * * * * * * * * * * * * * * *
*                                                               *
*       THIS PROGRAM COMPUTES AND PRINTS A TABLE OF N FACTORIAL  *
*       FOR VALUES OF N FROM 1 THROUGH AN UPPER LIMIT "NX".      *
*                                                               *
*       IT DEMONSTRATES A METHOD OF MANIPULATING NUMBERS WHICH ARE  *
*       TOO LARGE FOR THE COMPUTER, AS STRINGS OF CHARACTERS.  THE  *
*       COMMAS IN THE PRINTED VALUES ARE OPTIONAL, ADDED FOR READING *
*       EASE.                                                    *
*                                                               *
* * * * * * * * * * * * * * * * * * * * * * * * * * * * * * * * *
*
*       INITIALIZATION.
*
        NX = 35                                                      1
*
        N = 1       ;    NSET = 1                                    2
        NUM = ARRAY(1000)                                           4
        NUM<1> = 1                                                   5
        FILL = ARRAY('0:3')                                         6
        FILL<0> = '000';   FILL<1> = '00';   FILL<2> = '0'          7
*
        OUTPUT = '             TABLE OF FACTORIALS FOR 1 THROUGH ' NX   10
        OUTPUT =                                                    11
*
*       COMPUTE THE NEXT VALUE FROM THE PREVIOUS ONE.
*
L1      I = 1                                                       12
L2      NUM<I> = NUM<I> * N                        :F(ERR)          13
        I = LT(I,NSET) I + 1                       :S(L2)           14
        I = 1                                                       15
L3      LT(NUM<I>,1000)                            :S(L4)           16
        NUMX = NUM<I> / 1000                       :F(ERR)          17
        NUM<I + 1> = NUM<I + 1> + NUMX             :F(ERR)          18
        NUM<I> = NUM<I> - 1000 * NUMX              :F(ERR)          19
L4      I = LT(I,NSET) I + 1                       :S(L3)           20
*
*       FORM A STRING REPRESENTING THE FACTORIAL.
*
L5      NSET = DIFFER(NUM<NSET + 1>) NSET + 1                       21
        NUMBER = NUM<NSET>                         :F(ERR)          22
        I = GT(NSET,1) NSET - 1                     :F(L7)          23
```

```
L6          NUMBER = NUMBER ',' FILL<SIZE(NUM<I>)> NUM<I>                    24
            I = GT(I,1) I - 1                              :S(L6)           25
*
*           OUTPUT A LINE OF THE TABLE.
*
L7          OUTPUT = N '!=' NUMBER                                          26
            N = LT(N,NX) N + 1                             :S(L1)F(END)     27
*
*           ERROR TERMINATION.
*
ERR         OUTPUT = N '! CANNOT BE COMPUTED BECAUSE OF TABLE OVERFLOW.'    28
            OUTPUT = '       INCREASE THE SIZE OF ARRAY "NUM".'             29
*
END                                                                        30


NO ERRORS DETECTED IN SOURCE PROGRAM
```

TABLE OF FACTORIALS FOR 1 THROUGH 35

```
1!=1
2!=2
3!=6
4!=24
5!=120
6!=720
7!=5,040
8!=40,320
9!=362,880
10!=3,628,800
11!=39,916,800
12!=479,001,600
13!=6,227,020,800
14!=87,178,291,200
15!=1,307,674,368,000
16!=20,922,789,888,000
17!=355,687,428,096,000
18!=6,402,373,705,728,000
19!=121,645,100,408,832,000
20!=2,432,902,008,176,640,000
21!=51,090,942,171,709,440,000
22!=1,124,000,727,777,607,680,000
23!=25,852,016,738,884,976,640,000
24!=620,448,401,733,239,439,360,000
25!=15,511,210,043,330,985,984,000,000
26!=403,291,461,126,605,635,584,000,000
27!=10,888,869,450,418,352,160,768,000,000
28!=304,888,344,611,713,860,501,504,000,000
29!=8,841,761,993,739,701,954,543,616,000,000
30!=265,252,859,812,191,058,636,308,480,000,000
31!=8,222,838,654,177,922,817,725,562,880,000,000
32!=263,130,836,933,693,530,167,218,012,160,000,000
33!=8,683,317,618,811,886,495,518,194,401,280,000,000
34!=295,232,799,039,604,140,847,618,609,643,520,000,000
35!=10,333,147,966,386,144,929,666,651,337,523,200,000,000
```

NORMAL TERMINATION AT LEVEL   0

LAST STATEMENT EXECUTED WAS   27

SNOBOL4 STATISTICS SUMMARY-
            1381 MS. COMPILATION TIME
            1747 MS. EXECUTION TIME
            1880 STATEMENTS EXECUTED,   274 FAILED
            1686 ARITHMETIC OPERATIONS PERFORMED
               0 PATTERN MATCHES PERFORMED
               0 REGENERATIONS OF DYNAMIC STORAGE
               0 READS PERFORMED
              37 WRITES PERFORMED
            0.93 MS. AVERAGE PER STATEMENT EXECUTED

Sample Program 3

```
SNOBOL4 (VERSION 3.0,  DEC. 8, 1969)
BELL TELEPHONE LABORATORIES, INCORPORATED


*
*          THIS PROGRAM USES PROGRAMMER-DEFINED DATA TYPES TO
*          REPRESENT AN ARBITRARILY LONG INTEGER AS A LINKED LIST
*          CALLED ALI.  OPSYN IS USED TO DEFINE A BINARY OPERATOR
*          AND TWO UNARY OPERATORS FOR MANIPULATING ALIS.
*
*          % APPENDS A NODE TO THE HEAD OF A LIST.  # AND / RETURN
*          THE VALUE OF THE HEAD OF THE LIST, AND THE LIST LINKED
*          FROM THE HEAD, RESPECTIVELY.
*
*          THE OPERATORS + AND * ARE GENERALIZED TO RETURN INTEGERS
*          IF THE OPERANDS ARE INTEGERS AND THE RESULT LESS THAN
*          MAX (10000).  IF THE RESULT IS GREATER THAN MAX, AN ALI
*          IS GENERATED WITH THE VALUE OF THE HEAD EQUAL TO THE LOW
*          ORDER DIGITS, AND THE LINK POINTING TO AN ALI WITH THE
*          HIGHER DIGITS.  IF EITHER OPERAND IS AN ALI, THE RESULT
*          IS AN ALI.
*
*          THE USE OF ALIS IS ILLUSTRATED BY COMPUTING THE FIRST K
*          POWERS OF AN INTEGER N.
*
*
           &ANCHOR    =   1                                            1
           OPSYN('SUM','+',2)                                         2
           OPSYN('PROD','*',2)                                        3
           DATA('ALI(V,L)')                                           4
           DEFINE('OUT(OUT)')                                         5
           DEFINE('APPEND(V,L)')                                      6
           DEFINE('ADD(I1,I2)C')                                      7
           DEFINE('MUL(I1,I2)C')                                      8
           DEFINE('VAL(VAL)')                                         9
           DEFINE('LINK(I)')                                         10
           OPSYN('+','ADD',2)                                        11
           OPSYN('*','MUL',2)                                        12
           OPSYN('%','APPEND',2)                                     13
           OPSYN('/','LINK',1)                                       14
           OPSYN('#','VAL',1)                                        15
           MAX        =   10000                                      16
           ADDFIX     =   RTAB(SIZE(MAX) - 1) . C  REM . ADD         17
           MULFIX     =   RTAB(SIZE(MAX) - 1) . C  REM . MUL         18
```

```
*                      FUNCTION DEFINITIONS
*
                                                    :(FEND)              19
*
APPEND     APPEND    =   ALI(V,L)                    :(RETURN)           20
*
*
ADD        ADD       =   IDENT(I2)  I1          :S(RETURN)              21
           ADD       =   IDENT(I1)  I2          :S(RETURN)              22
           ADD       =   SUM(#I1,#I2)                                   23
            LT(ADD,MAX)  INTEGER(I1)  INTEGER(I2)  :S(RETURN)           24
           ADD       =   LT(ADD,MAX)  ADD % (/I1 + /I2)    :S(RETURN)   25
           ADD       ADDFIX                                             26
           ADD       =   ADD % (C + (/I1 + /I2))    :(RETURN)           27
*
LINK       LINK      =   ¬INTEGER(I)  L(I)          :(RETURN)           28
*
VAL        VAL       =   ¬INTEGER(VAL)  V(VAL)      :(RETURN)           29
*
*
*
OUT        OUT       =   IDENT(/OUT)  #OUT          :S(RETURN)          30
           OUT       =   OUT(/OUT) DUPL('0',SIZE(MAX) - SIZE(#OUT) - 1) 31
+                                  #OUT             :(RETURN)           31
*
*
MUL        MUL       =   DIFFER(#I1) DIFFER(#I2) PROD(#I1,#I2) :F(RETURN) 32
            LT(MUL,MAX)  INTEGER(I1)   INTEGER(I2)    :S(RETURN)        33
           MUL       =   LT(MUL,MAX)   MUL % ( I1 * /I2  + I2 * /I1)    34
+                                         :S(RETURN)                    34
           MUL       MULFIX                                             35
           MUL       =   MUL % (C +  I1 * /I2  +  I2 * /I1)             36
+                                         :(RETURN)                     36
FEND                                                                    37
           N         =   256                                            38
           K         =   25                                             39
           P         =   1                                              40
           OUTPUT    =   'POWERS OF '  N                                41
           OUTPUT    =                                                  42
L          I         =   LT(I,K)  I + 1            :F(END)              43
           P         =   P * N                                          44
           OUTPUT    =   I ': '  OUT(P)            :(L)                 45
END                                                                    46
```

NO ERRORS DETECTED IN SOURCE PROGRAM

POWERS OF 256

```
1:  256
2:  65536
3:  16777216
4:  4294967296
5:  1099511627776
6:  281474976710656
7:  72057594037927936
8:  18446744073709551616
9:  4722366482869645213696
10:  1208925819614629174706176
11:  309485009821345068724781056
12:  79228162514264337593543950336
13:  20282409603651670423947251286016
14:  5192296858534827628530496329220096
15:  1329227995784915872903807060280344576
16:  340282366920938463463374607431768211456
17:  87112285931760246646238995025326621327 36
18:  22300745198530623141535718272648361505980416
19:  5708990770823839524233143877797980545530986496
20:  1461501637330902918203684832716283019655932542976
21:  374144419156711147060143317175368453031918731001856
22:  95780971304118053647396689196894323976171195136475136
23:  24519928653854221733733552434404946937899825954937634816
24:  6277101735386680763835789423207666416102355444464034512896
25:  1606938044258990275541962092341162602522202993782792835301376
```

NORMAL TERMINATION AT LEVEL   0

LAST STATEMENT EXECUTED WAS   43

SNOBOL4 STATISTICS SUMMARY-
```
         1514 MS. COMPILATION TIME
         5159 MS. EXECUTION TIME
         6511 STATEMENTS EXECUTED,    2782 FAILED
          762 ARITHMETIC OPERATIONS PERFORMED
          229 PATTERN MATCHES PERFORMED
            0 REGENERATIONS OF DYNAMIC STORAGE
            0 READS PERFORMED
           27 WRITES PERFORMED
         0.79 MS. AVERAGE PER STATEMENT EXECUTED
```

Sample Program 4

```
SNOBOL4 (VERSION 3.0, DEC. 17, 1969)
BELL TELEPHONE LABORATORIES, INCORPORATED


*          TOPOLOGICAL SORT
*
*   MAPS A PARTIAL ORDERING OF OBJECTS INTO A LINEAR ORDERING
*
*          A(1), A(2), ..., A(N)
*
*   SUCH THAT IF   A(S) < A(T) IN THE PARTIAL ORDERING,THEN S < T.
*   (CF. D.E.KNUTH, THE ART OF COMPUTER PROGRAMMING,VOLUME 1,
*   ADDISON-WESLEY,MASS.,1968, P.262)
*
           &DUMP      = 1                                          1
           &TRIM      = 1                                          2
           OUTPUT('OUT',6,'(121A1)')                              3
           PAIR       = BREAK('<') . MU LEN(1) BREAK(',') . NU LEN(1)   4
           DATA('ITEM(COUNT,TOP)')                                5
           DATA('NODE(SUC,NEXT)')                                 6
           DEFINE('DECR(X)')                                      7
*
*    SET UP A TABLE THAT ASSOCIATES WITH EACH OBJECT AN ITEM.
           X          =    TABLE(50)                              8
*
*   EACH ITEM HAS TWO FIELDS, (COUNT,TOP), WHERE
*       COUNT = NO. OF ELEMENTS PRECEEDING THE OBJECT.
*       TOP = TOP OF A LIST OF OBJECTS SUCCEEDING IT.
*
*   READ IN RELATIONS.
*
*   INITIALIZE THE ITEMS TO (0,NULL).
*
*    FOR EACH RELATION, MU < NU, INCREASE THE COUNT OF PREDECESSORS
*   OF NU AND ADD A NODE TO THE LIST OF SUCCESSORS OF MU.
*
T1A       OUT        = '0 THE RELATIONS ARE:'                     9
T2A       REL        =    INPUT ','                  :F(T3A)      10
          OUTPUT     = REL                                        11
T2        REL        PAIR  =                         :F(T2A)      12
          X<NU>      =    IDENT(X<NU>)  ITEM(0)                   13
          COUNT(X<NU>)  =   COUNT(X<NU>) + 1                      14
          X<MU>      =    IDENT(X<MU>)  ITEM(0)                   15
          TOP(X<MU>)  =   NODE(NU,TOP(X<MU>))        :(T2)        16
*
*    A QUEUE IS MAINTAINED OF THOSE ITEMS WITH ZERO COUNT FIELD.
```

```
*      THE LINKS FOR THE QUEUE, QLINK, ARE KEPT IN THE COUNT FIELD.
*      THE VARIABLES F,R POINT TO THE FRONT AND REAR OF THE QUEUE.
*
T3A        OPSYN('QLINK','COUNT')                              17
           Y      =  CONVERT(X,'ARRAY')                        18
           PROTOTYPE(Y)  BREAK(',') . N                        19
*
*      INITIALIZE THE QUEUE FOR OUTPUT.
*
           K          = 0                                      20
T4         K      =  ?Y<K + 1,1>  K + 1              :F(T8)    21
           F      =  EQ(COUNT(Y<K,2>),0)  Y<K,1>     :F(T4)    22
T4A        R      =  Y<K,2>                                    23
T4B        K      =  ?Y<K + 1,1>  K + 1              :F(T5)    24
           QLINK(R)  =  EQ(COUNT(Y<K,2>),0) Y<K,1>     :F(T4B)S(T4A)  25
*
*      OUTPUT THE FRONT OF THE QUEUE.
*
T5         OUT    =  '0   THE LINEAR ORDERING IS:'             26
T5A        OUTPUT =  DIFFER(X<F>)  F                 :F(T8)    27
           N      = N - 1                                      28
           P      = TOP(X<F>)                                  29
*
*      ERASE RELATIONS.
*
T6         IDENT(P)                                 :S(T7)    30
           DECR(.COUNT(X<SUC(P)>))                  :S(T6A)   31
*
*      IF COUNT IS ZERO ADD  ITEM TO QUEUE.
*
           QLINK(R)  =  SUC(P)                                 32
           R         = X<SUC(P)>                               33
T6A        P         = NEXT(P)                      :(T6)     34
*
*      REMOVE FROM QUEUE.
*
T7         F         = QLINK(X<F>)                  :(T5A)    35
*
*      FUNCTION DEFINITIONS.
*
DECR       $X     = GT($X,1)  $X - 1                :S(RETURN)  36
           $X     = 0                               :(FRETURN)  37
*
T8         OUTPUT = NE(N,0) 'THE ORDERING CONTAINS A LOOP.'    38
END                                                            39


NO ERRORS DETECTED IN SOURCE PROGRAM
```

```
   THE RELATIONS ARE:
LETTERS<ALPHANUM,NUMBERS<ALPHANUM,
BLANKS<OPTBLANKS,
NUMBERS<REAL,
NUMBERS<INTEGER,
LETTERS<VARIABLE,ALPHANUM<VARIABLE,
BINARY<BINARYOP,BLANKS<BINARYOP,
UNQALPHABET<DLITERAL,
UNQALPHABET<SLITERAL,
SLITERAL<LITERAL,DLITERAL<LITERAL,INTEGER<LITERAL,REAL<LITERAL,

   THE LINEAR ORDERING IS:
LETTERS
NUMBERS
BLANKS
BINARY
UNQALPHABET
INTEGER
REAL
ALPHANUM
OPTBLANKS
BINARYOP
SLITERAL
DLITERAL
VARIABLE
LITERAL
```

```
NORMAL TERMINATION AT LEVEL   0

LAST STATEMENT EXECUTED WAS      38


DUMP OF VARIABLES AT TERMINATION

NATURAL VARIABLES

ABORT = PATTERN
ARB = PATTERN
BAL = PATTERN
F = 0
FAIL = PATTERN
FENCE = PATTERN
INPUT = 'SLITERAL<LITERAL,DLITERAL<LITERAL,INTEGER<LITERAL,REAL<LITERAL'
K = 14
MU = 'REAL'
N = 0
NU = 'LITERAL'
OUT = '0   THE LINEAR ORDERING:'
OUTPUT = 'LITERAL'
PAIR = PATTERN
R = ITEM
REM = PATTERN
SUCCEED = PATTERN
X = TABLE(50,10)
Y = ARRAY('14,2')


UNPROTECTED KEYWORDS

&ABEND = 0
&ANCHOR = 0
&CODE = 0
&DUMP = 1
&ERRLIMIT = 0
&FTRACE = 0
&FULLSCAN = 0
&INPUT = 1
&MAXLNGTH = 5000
&OUTPUT = 1
&STLIMIT = 50000
&TRACE = 0
&TRIM = 1
```

```
SNOBOL4 STATISTICS SUMMARY-
          1847 MS. COMPILATION TIME
           349 MS. EXECUTION TIME
           310 STATEMENTS EXECUTED,      71 FAILED
            64 ARITHMETIC OPERATIONS PERFORMED
            25 PATTERN MATCHES PERFORMED
             0 REGENERATIONS OF DYNAMIC STORAGE
            10 READS PERFORMED
            25 WRITES PERFORMED
          1.13 MS. AVERAGE PER STATEMENT EXECUTED
```

Sample Program 5


```
SNOBOL4 (VERSION 3.0, DEC. 17, 1969)
BELL TELEPHONE LABORATORIES, INCORPORATED
```

```
    This program is a syntactic recognizer for SNOBOL4 statements.
    The extended graphics for the IBM 360 are used in the program
    and in the data.
```

1

```
    A series of patterns is built, culminating in a pattern that
    matches SNOBOL4 statements.
```

2

```
    Card images are then read in and processed.
```

3

```
        DEFINE('opt(pattern)')                                          3
        OPSYN('↑','opt',1)                                              4
        OPSYN('%','SPAN',1)                                             5
        OPSYN('#','ANY',1)                                              6
        leftbr    ← #'<['                                               7
        rightbr   ← #'>]'                                               8
        letters   ← 'ABCDEFGHIJKLNMOPQRSTUVWXYZabcdefghijklmnopqrstuvw'  9
    +                   'xyz'                                           10
        digits    ← '0123456789'                                       10
        alphanumerics   ← letters digits                               11
        blanks    ← %' '                                               12
        integer   ← %digits                                            13
        real    ← integer '.' ↑integer                                 14
        identifier    ← #letters ↑%(alphanumerics '._')                15
        opsyms    ←    '¬?$.!%*/#+-ə|ε'                                 16
        unary   ← #opsyms                                              17
        binarysyms    ←    #opsyms | '**'                              18
        unaryop   ←   %opsyms                                          19
        binaryop    ← blanks ↑(binarysyms blanks)                      20
        unqalpha    ← &ALPHABET                                        21
        unqalpha    '"'    ←                                           22
        unqalpha    "'"    ←                                           23
        dliteral    ← '"' ↑%(unqalpha '"') '"'                         24
        sliteral    ← "'" ↑%(unqalpha "'") "'"                         25
        literal    ← sliteral | dliteral | integer | real             26
        element    ← ↑unaryop (identifier | literal | *function_call | 27
    +                   '(' *expression ')' | *array_ref)             28
                                                                       28
```

```
        operation    ← *element binaryop (*element | *expression)        29
        expression   ← ↑blanks (*element | *operation | null) ↑blanks    30
        arglist   ← *expression ↑(',' *arglist)                          31
        function_call   ← identifier '(' *arglist ')'                    32
        array_rof   ← identifier leftbr *arglist rightbr                 33
        label   ← #alphanumerics (BREAK(' ;') | REM)                     34
        label_field   ← ↑label                                           35
        goto   ←   '(' expression ')' | leftbr expression rightbr        36
        goto_field   ← ↑(blanks ':' FENCE ↑blanks (goto | 'S' goto       37
                       | 'F' goto | 'S' goto ↑blanks 'F' goto | 'F' goto 37
+                      ↑blanks 'S' goto) ↑blanks)                        37
        eql     ← #'=←'                                                  38
        rule    ← ↑(blanks element (blanks eql ↑(blanks expression) |    39
+                  ↑(blanks expression ↑(blanks eql ↑(blanks expression)) 39
+                  )))                                                   39
        eos    ← RPOS(0) | ';'                                           40
        statement   ← label_field rule goto_field eos                    41
                                                                         42
```

```
 ┌─────────────────────────────────────────────────────────────────┐
 │  The recognizing program follows.  Comment and control cards      │
 │  are not processed.  If an erroneous statement is encountered      │
 │  in a string of statements separated by semicolons, subsequent    │
 │  statements in that string are not processed.                     │
 └─────────────────────────────────────────────────────────────────┘
```

```
                                                                         43
                                                                         44
        INPUT(.input,5,72)                                               45
        &ANCHOR    ← 1                                                   46
        &TRIM    ← 1                                                     47
        &FULLSCAN    ← 1                                                 48
        eof    ←                                                         49
        space    ← DUPL(' ',5)                                           50
        line    ←                                                        51
        comment    ← #'*-| ⌐L'                                          52
        continue   ← #'+.' . cc                                          53
readi   image   ← input                              :F(END)            54
        OUTPUT    ← space line                                          55
        image     comment                            :F(readc)S(readi)  56
nextst  IDENT(eof)                                   :F(END)            57
        OUTPUT    ← space line                                          58
        image   ← line                                                  59
readc   line   ← input                               :F(endgam)         60
        line     comment                             :S(print)          61
        line     continue   ←                        :F(anlyz)          62
        OUTPUT    ← space cc line                                       63
        image   ← image line                         :(readc)           64
anlyz   image    statement   ←                       :F(error)          65
        DIFFER(image)                                :S(anlyz)          65
+                                                    F(nextst)          65
```

```
error   OUTPUT    ← '<<< syntactic error >>>'            :(nextst)        66
print   OUTPUT    ← space line                           :(readc)         67
endgam  eof    ← 1                                       :(anlyz)         68
*
opt     opt    ← null | pattern                          :(RETURN)        69
END                                                                       70
```

NO ERRORS DETECTED IN SOURCE PROGRAM

```
            X    ←     Y+Z
<<< syntactic error >>>
            ELEMENT<I,J>← ELEMENT<I,-J> + ELEMENT<-I,J>
<<< syntactic error >>>
            A<X,Y,Z + 1>    ←     F(X,STRUCTURE.BUILD(TYPE,LENGTH + 1))
    SETUP    PAT1    ←    (BREAK(',:') $ FIRST | SPAN(' .') $ SECOND
    +                     . VALUE ARBNO(BAL | LEN(1))   :($SWITCH)
            DEFINE('F(X,Y)) .
<<< syntactic error >>>
            L    ←    LT(N,B<J> L + 1
<<< syntactic error >>>
    NEWONE.TRIAL    X    ←     ¬COORD<1,K> X * X
            TRIM(INPUT)    PAT1    :S(OK)  :F(BAD)
<<< syntactic error >>>
        X    ←    3.01; Y = 2.     ; Z    =    X * -Y
            RANDOM    ←    (RAN.VAR * N) / 10000
    LOOP    OUTPUT    =    LT(N,10)    :S(LOP
<<< syntactic error >>>
    LOOP    OUTPUT    =    LT(N,10)        :S(LOOP)
        OUTPUT    =    X    :(FAST)
        ?M<X>          :S(A1)F(A2)
    OUTPUT    =    ''
    F('',"",)    =
    F('',"",)    =         "'
<<< syntactic error >>>
```

NORMAL TERMINATION AT LEVEL   0

LAST STATEMENT EXECUTED WAS   56

SNOBOL4 STATISTICS SUMMARY–
         1930 MS. COMPILATION TIME
         3594 MS. EXECUTION TIME
          232 STATEMENTS EXECUTED,   56 FAILED
            0 ARITHMETIC OPERATIONS PERFORMED
           63 PATTERN MATCHES PERFORMED
            0 REGENERATIONS OF DYNAMIC STORAGE
           24 READS PERFORMED
           30 WRITES PERFORMED
     15.49 MS. AVERAGE PER STATEMENT EXECUTED

Sample Program 6

```
SNOBOL4 (VERSION 3.0,  DEC. 17, 1969)
BELL TELEPHONE LABORATORIES, INCORPORATED


*          WHEN THE OUTPUT ASSOCIATION FOR "SING" IS CHANGED TO
*          A DIGITAL-TO-ANALOG CONVERTER WITH THE PROPER MELODY
*          SYNTHESIZER, THIS PROGRAM SINGS THAT OLD CHRISTMASTIME
*          FAVORITE, "A PARTRIDGE IN A PEAR TREE."
*
*                                       M. D. SHAPIRO
*
           ACAPPELLA.CHOIR = 6 OR MORE PEOPLE SINGING IN TUNE        1
*
           DAYS = 'FIRST,SECOND,THIRD,FOURTH,FIFTH,SIXTH,'           2
+          'SEVENTH,EIGHTH,NINTH,TENTH,ELEVENTH,TWELFTH,'            2
           NEXT = BREAK(',') . WHICH LEN(1)                          3
*
           TRACE('SING','VALUE',,'SONG')                             4
           &TRACE = 1000                                             5
           DEFINE('SONG()')                            :(NEXT.DAY)   6
SONG       PAUSE IDENT(SING) OUTPUT('SING', ACAPPELLA.CHOIR,         7
+          "(' " PAUSE "',100A1)") = '   '              :(RETURN)    7
*
NEXT.DAY   DAYS NEXT =                                 :F(CODA)      8
           SING = (TAKE A BREATH)                                    9
           SING = 'ON THE ' WHICH ' DAY OF CHRISTMAS,'              10
           SING = 'MY TRUE LOVE GAVE TO ME,'           :($WHICH)    11
TWELFTH    SING = 'TWELVE LORDS A-LEAPING,'                         12
ELEVENTH   SING = 'ELEVEN LADIES DANCING,'                          13
TENTH      SING = 'TEN PIPERS PIPING,'                              14
NINTH      SING = 'NINE DRUMMERS DRUMMING,'                         15
EIGHTH     SING = 'EIGHT MAIDS A-MILKING,'                          16
SEVENTH    SING = 'SEVEN SWANS A-SWIMMING,'                         17
SIXTH      SING = 'SIX GEESE A-LAYING,'                             18
FIFTH      SING = 'FIVE GOLD RINGS,'                                19
FOURTH     SING = 'FOUR COLLY BIRDS,'                               20
THIRD      SING = 'THREE FRENCH HENS,'                              21
SECOND     SING = 'TWO TURTLEDOVES,'                                22
FIRST      SING = AND 'A PARTRIDGE IN A PEAR TREE.'                 23
           AND = IDENT(AND) 'AND '                     :(NEXT.DAY)  24
*
CODA       SING = INPUT                                :S(CODA)     25
*
END                                                                26


NO ERRORS DETECTED IN SOURCE PROGRAM
```

Sample Program 6 231

```
ON THE FIRST DAY OF CHRISTMAS,
MY TRUE LOVE GAVE TO ME,
A PARTRIDGE IN A PEAR TREE.

   ON THE SECOND DAY OF CHRISTMAS,
   MY TRUE LOVE GAVE TO ME,
   TWO TURTLEDOVES,
   AND A PARTRIDGE IN A PEAR TREE.

      ON THE THIRD DAY OF CHRISTMAS,
      MY TRUE LOVE GAVE TO ME,
      THREE FRENCH HENS,
      TWO TURTLEDOVES,
      AND A PARTRIDGE IN A PEAR TREE.

         ON THE FOURTH DAY OF CHRISTMAS,
         MY TRUE LOVE GAVE TO ME,
         FOUR COLLY BIRDS,
         THREE FRENCH HENS,
         TWO TURTLEDOVES,
         AND A PARTRIDGE IN A PEAR TREE.

            ON THE FIFTH DAY OF CHRISTMAS,
            MY TRUE LOVE GAVE TO ME,
            FIVE GOLD RINGS,
            FOUR COLLY BIRDS,
            THREE FRENCH HENS,
            TWO TURTLEDOVES,
            AND A PARTRIDGE IN A PEAR TREE.

               ON THE SIXTH DAY OF CHRISTMAS,
               MY TRUE LOVE GAVE TO ME,
               SIX GEESE A-LAYING,
               FIVE GOLD RINGS,
               FOUR COLLY BIRDS,
               THREE FRENCH HENS,
               TWO TURTLEDOVES,
               AND A PARTRIDGE IN A PEAR TREE.

                  ON THE SEVENTH DAY OF CHRISTMAS,
                  MY TRUE LOVE GAVE TO ME,
                  SEVEN SWANS A-SWIMMING,
                  SIX GEESE A-LAYING,
                  FIVE GOLD RINGS,
                  FOUR COLLY BIRDS,
                  THREE FRENCH HENS,
                  TWO TURTLEDOVES,
                  AND A PARTRIDGE IN A PEAR TREE.
```

```
ON THE EIGHTH DAY OF CHRISTMAS,
MY TRUE LOVE GAVE TO ME,
EIGHT MAIDS A-MILKING,
SEVEN SWANS A-SWIMMING,
SIX GEESE A-LAYING,
FIVE GOLD RINGS,
FOUR COLLY BIRDS,
THREE FRENCH HENS,
TWO TURTLEDOVES,
AND A PARTRIDGE IN A PEAR TREE.

   ON THE NINTH DAY OF CHRISTMAS,
   MY TRUE LOVE GAVE TO ME,
   NINE DRUMMERS DRUMMING,
   EIGHT MAIDS A-MILKING,
   SEVEN SWANS A-SWIMMING,
   SIX GEESE A-LAYING,
   FIVE GOLD RINGS,
   FOUR COLLY BIRDS,
   THREE FRENCH HENS,
   TWO TURTLEDOVES,
   AND A PARTRIDGE IN A PEAR TREE.

      ON THE TENTH DAY OF CHRISTMAS,
      MY TRUE LOVE GAVE TO ME,
      TEN PIPERS PIPING,
      NINE DRUMMERS DRUMMING,
      EIGHT MAIDS A-MILKING,
      SEVEN SWANS A-SWIMMING,
      SIX GEESE A-LAYING,
      FIVE GOLD RINGS,
      FOUR COLLY BIRDS,
      THREE FRENCH HENS,
      TWO TURTLEDOVES,
      AND A PARTRIDGE IN A PEAR TREE.

         ON THE ELEVENTH DAY OF CHRISTMAS,
         MY TRUE LOVE GAVE TO ME,
         ELEVEN LADIES DANCING,
         TEN PIPERS PIPING,
         NINE DRUMMERS DRUMMING,
         EIGHT MAIDS A-MILKING,
         SEVEN SWANS A-SWIMMING,
         SIX GEESE A-LAYING,
```

```
FIVE GOLD RINGS,
FOUR COLLY BIRDS,
THREE FRENCH HENS,
TWO TURTLEDOVES,
AND A PARTRIDGE IN A PEAR TREE.

ON THE TWELFTH DAY OF CHRISTMAS,
MY TRUE LOVE GAVE TO ME,
TWELVE LORDS A-LEAPING,
ELEVEN LADIES DANCING,
TEN PIPERS PIPING,
NINE DRUMMERS DRUMMING,
EIGHT MAIDS A-MILKING,
SEVEN SWANS A-SWIMMING,
SIX GEESE A-LAYING,
FIVE GOLD RINGS,
FOUR COLLY BIRDS,
THREE FRENCH HENS,
TWO TURTLEDOVES,
AND A PARTRIDGE IN A PEAR TREE.

       *
      ***
     *****
    *******
   *********
  ***********
      |||
```

```
NORMAL TERMINATION AT LEVEL   0

LAST STATEMENT EXECUTED WAS    25


SNOBOL4 STATISTICS SUMMARY-
          1149 MS. COMPILATION TIME
           565 MS. EXECUTION TIME
           276 STATEMENTS EXECUTED,     123 FAILED
             0 ARITHMETIC OPERATIONS PERFORMED
            25 PATTERN MATCHES PERFORMED
             0 REGENERATIONS OF DYNAMIC STORAGE
             9 READS PERFORMED
           121 WRITES PERFORMED
          2.05 MS. AVERAGE PER STATEMENT EXECUTED
```

APPENDIX D

Solutions to Exercises

Solution 1.1

```
R          OUTPUT     =    INPUT          :F(END)
           OUTPUT     '&'                 :S(R)
           PUNCH      =    OUTPUT         :(R)
END
```

Solution 1.2

```
           FRONT      =    LEN(8)
R          X          =    INPUT          :F(END)
           X     FRONT =
           OUTPUT     =    X              :(R)
END
```

Solution 1.3

```
           E          =    2.71828
           POWER      =    1
           OUTPUT     =    'POWERS OF E:'
LOOP       POWER      =    POWER * E
           OUTPUT     =    POWER
           SUM        =    SUM  +   POWER
           I          =    LT(I,9)  I  +  1    :S(LOOP)
           OUTPUT     =    'SUM: '    SUM
END
```

Solution 1.4

```
        &TRIM    =   1
        IN    =   'ABCDEFGHIJKLMNOPQRSTUVWXYZ,.:;!?0123456789+-*/ə% '
        CODE     =     '0123456789+-*/ə% ABCDEFGHIJKLMNOPQRSTUVWXYZ,.:;!?'
READ    OUTPUT   =   REPLACE(INPUT,IN,CODE)          :S(READ)
END
```

Solution 1.5

```
        &TRIM    =   1
        A        =   ARRAY(INPUT)
        I        =   1
READ    A<I>     =   INPUT             :F(PRINT)
        I        =   I  +  1           :(READ)
PRINT   I        =   I  -  1
        OUTPUT   =   A<I>              :S(PRINT)
END
```

Solution 1.6

```
        CH       =   LEN(1) . X
        HEX      =   TABLE(16)
        HEX<'0'> = 0; HEX<'1'> = 1; HEX<'2'> = 2; HEX<'3'> = 3
        HEX<'4'> = 4; HEX<'5'> = 5; HEX<'6'> = 6; HEX<'7'> = 7
        HEX<'8'> = 8; HEX<'9'> = 9; HEX<'A'> = 10; HEX<'B'> = 11
        HEX<'C'> = 12; HEX<'D'> = 13; HEX<'E'> = 14; HEX<'F'> = 15
*
        DEFINE('H(N)X')
                    .
                    .
                    .
H       N    CH   =                   :F(RETURN)
        H         =   DIFFER(HEX<X>)   16 * H + HEX<X>
+                                     :F(FRETURN)S(H)
END
```

Solution 1.7

```
PARTA    DATA('BNODE(VALUE,LSON,RSON)')
PARTB    N          =    BNODE('+',BNODE('X'),BNODE('Y'))
PARTC    DEFINE('LLIST(N)')
                    .
```

.
.
.

```
LLIST   OUTPUT    =   DIFFER(N)  VALUE(N)         :F(RETURN)
        LLIST(LSON(N))
        LLIST(RSON(N))                 :(RETURN)
END
```

Solution 2.1

```
        &TRIM    =    1
        COUNT    =    0
        PAT      =    POS(0)  LEN(*N)  BREAK('.,:;?!()"' "'") LEN(1) @N
READ    TEXT     =    INPUT          :F(PRINT)
        OUTPUT   =    TEXT
        N        =    0
C       TEXT     PAT              :F(READ)
        COUNT    =    COUNT + 1    :(C)
PRINT   OUTPUT   =
        OUTPUT   =    'THERE ARE ' COUNT ' PUNCTUATION MARKS.'
END
```

Solution 2.2

```
        P     =  ('C' | 'CR') $ OUTPUT ('O' | 'OO' | 'EE') $ OUTPUT
+                ('P' | 'PS') $ OUTPUT  RPOS(0)
```

Solution 2.3

```
        &TRIM    =    1
        WORD     =    BREAK(' ,.:;?') . W LEN(1)
        N        =    INPUT
        OUTPUT   =    ' WORDS OF LENGTH ' N ' ARE:'
READ    TEXT     =    INPUT  ' '    :F(END)
NEXTW   TEXT     WORD =            :F(READ)
        OUTPUT   =    EQ(SIZE(W),N)  W   :(NEXTW)
END
```

This program assumes the word length is given left justified on the first input card. Text on subsequent cards is assumed to be broken between words.

Solution 2.4

```
          LETTER      =   'ABCDEFGHIJKLMNOPQRSTUVWXYZ'
          DIGIT       =   '0123456789'
          LABEL    =   ' '  | ANY(LETTER) (SPAN(LETTER DIGIT) @N *LE(N,8)
+                        | NULL) ' '
          &ANCHOR     =   1
R         CARD        =   INPUT          :F(END)
          CARD     LABEL               :S(R)
          OUTPUT      =   CARD           :(R)
END
```

Solution 2.5

```
          QUOTE       =   ANY('"' "'")
          LITERAL     =   (QUOTE $ Q BREAK(*Q) LEN(1) )
```

Solution 2.6

```
          &TRIM       =   1   ;       &FULLSCAN    =    1
          ABC      =   POS(0) (SPAN('A') @N SPAN('B')
+                        POS(*(2 * N)) RPOS(*N) SPAN('C') RPOS(0))
READ      CARD        =   INPUT          :F(END)
          CARD     ABC                  :F(NO)
          OUTPUT      =   '"' CARD '" MATCHES.'   :(READ)
NO        OUTPUT      =   '"' CARD '" DOES NOT MATCH.'   :(READ)
END
```

Solution 2.7

```
          REP         =   POS(0) (LEN(1) ARB) $ X (RPOS(0) ABORT
+                        | ARBNO(*X) RPOS(0))
```

Solution 2.8

```
          HOL         =   POS(0)  BREAK('H') $ N LEN(*(N + 1)) RPOS(0)
```

Solution 2.9

```
          &FULLSCAN  =   1;     &TRIM    =   1
          PALIN      =   LEN(1) $ H aX (*GT(2 * X,SIZE(S)) |
+                          *RTAB(X) aY aZ (*H aZ | *EQ(Y,Z) ABORT) FAIL)
READ      S          =   INPUT            :F(END)
          S    PALIN                      :F(NO)
          OUTPUT     =   '"' S '"  IS A PALINDROME.'    :(READ)
NO        OUTPUT     =   '"' S '"  IS NOT A PALINDROME.'  :(READ)
END
```

Solution 3.1

```
          B2         =   '  '
          FIELDS     -   LEN(7) . LAB  LEN(8) . OP LEN(20) . OPER
+                          LEN(41) . COM
R         INPUT          FIELDS              :F(END)
          OUTPUT     = LAB B2 OP B2 OPER COM    :(R)
END
```

Solution 3.2

```
          &TRIM  =   1;     &ANCHOR  -   1
          BB         =   BREAK(' ');   SB   =   SPAN(' ')
          FIELDS     =   BB . F1 SB BB . F2  SB (BB . F3 SB REM . F4
+                          | REM . F3 NULL . F4)
READ      CARD       =   INPUT            :F(END)
          CARD           FIELDS            :F(ERROR)
          IMAGE      =   F1  DUPL(' ',9 - SIZE(F1)) F2 DUPL(' ',
+                          10 - SIZE(F2))  F3 DUPL(' ',20 - SIZE(F3)) F4
+                                            :F(ERROR)
          OUTPUT     =   LE(SIZE(IMAGE),80)  IMAGE      :F(ERROR)
          PUNCH      =   OUTPUT           :(READ)
ERROR     OUTPUT     =   '*** FORMAT ERROR IN: ' CARD        :(READ)
END
```

Solution 3.3

```
          &TRIM  =   1;     &ANCHOR  =   1
          BB         =   BREAK(' ');   SB   =   SPAN(' ')
          QL         =   ANY("'")   BREAK("'") LEN(1)
          FIELDS     =   BB . F1 SB BB . F2  SB ((QL | BB) . F3 SB REM . F4
+                          | REM . F3 NULL . F4)
```

```
           COMMENT   =   ( '*' REM) . OUTPUT
READ       CARD      =   INPUT            :F(END)
           CARD      COMMENT              :S(READ)
           CARD      FIELDS               :F(ERROR)
           IMAGE   =  F1  DUPL(' ',9 - SIZE(F1)) F2 DUPL(' ',
+                        10 - SIZE(F2))  F3 DUPL(' ',20 - SIZE(F3)) F4
+                                    :F(ERROR)
           OUTPUT    =   LE(SIZE(IMAGE),80)  IMAGE     :F(ERROR)
           PUNCH     =    OUTPUT      :(READ)
ERROR      OUTPUT    =   '*** FORMAT ERROR IN: '  CARD       :(READ)
END
```

Solution 3.4

```
           &TRIM     =   1
READ       X       =   INPUT             :F(PRINT)
           MAX       =   GT(X,MAX)  X  :(READ)
PRINT      OUTPUT    =   'MAXIMUM: '  MAX
END
```

Solution 3.5

```
           &TRIM     =   1
READ       N         =   INPUT          :F(END)
           FACT      =   INTEGER(N) GT(N)  1    :F(ERROR)
           I         =   1
L          I         =   LT(I,N)  I + 1       :F(PRINT)
           FACT      =   FACT * I      :(L)
PRINT      OUTPUT    =   N '! = ' FACT      :(READ)
ERROR      OUTPUT    =   '**** ERROR : '   N ' NOT A POSITIVE INTEGER.'
+                                    :(READ)
END
```

Solution 3.6

```
           &TRIM     =   1
READ       X         =   INPUT           :F(END)
           COUNT     =   ·1
           Y         =   INPUT           :F(END)
           Z         =   REPLACE(X,X,Y)
C          COUNT     =   DIFFER(Z,X)  COUNT + 1    :F(PRINT)
           Z         =   REPLACE(Z,X,Y)      :(C)
PRINT      OUTPUT    =   'THE PERMUTATION (' X ',' Y ') HAS INDEX '
```

```
+                   COUNT           :(READ)
END
```

This program assumes the members of the permutation are given left justified on successive cards.

Solution 3.7

```
READ        INPUT   LEN(7) . OUTPUT      :F(END)
            OUTPUT    =   REPLACE('ABCDEFG','GFEDCBA',OUTPUT)
            OUTPUT    =                 :(READ)
END
```


Solution 3.8

```
        OPSYN('#','SIZE',1)
```


Solution 3.9

```
        OPSYN('#','+',2)
```


Solution 4.1

```
        DEFINE('SUBSTR(S,N)')
                    .
                    .
                    .
SUBSTR   S          LEN(N) $ OUTPUT RPOS(0)     :(RETURN)
```

This function requires the unanchored mode.

Solution 4.2

```
        DEFINE('F(N)')
                    .
                    .
                    .
F           F       =   EQ(N)  0      :S(RETURN)
            F       =   EQ(N,1)  1    :S(RETURN)
            F       =   F(N - 1) + F(N - 2) :(RETURN)
```

Solution 4.3

```
          &ANCHOR  =  1
          EXPAT   =  BAL . X '!' . OP REM . Y
          PMPAT   =  (ARBNO(BAL ANY('+-')) $ X FAIL | *DIFFER(X)
+                        TAB(*(SIZE(X) - 1))) . X LEN(1) . OP REM . Y
          MDPAT   =  (ARBNO(BAL ANY('*/')) $ X FAIL | *DIFFER(X)
+                        TAB(*(SIZE(X) - 1))) . X LEN(1) . OP REM . Y
          STRIP   =  '(' BAL . POL ')' RPOS(0)
          DEFINE('POL(POL)X,Y,OP')
                          .
                          .
                          .
POL       POL   STRIP                      :S(POL)
          POL   PMPAT  =  OP  '(' POL(X) ',' POL(Y) ')'
+                                     :S(RETURN)
          POL   MDPAT  =  OP  '(' POL(X) ',' POL(Y) ')'
+                                     :S(RETURN)
          POL   EXPAT  =  OP  '(' POL(X) ',' POL(Y) ')'
+                                     :(RETURN)
```

Solution 4.4

```
          DEFINE('NOT(P)')
          &FULLSCAN  =  1
          DEFINE('FLAG()')
                      .
                      .
                      .
FLAG      FLAG.    =  1                 :(RETURN)
NOT       NOT      =  NULL $ FLAG. P *FLAG() FAIL
+                    |  *IDENT(FLAG.)    :(RETURN)
```

Solution 5.1

```
          &FULLSCAN  =  1
          &ANCHOR  =  1
          &TRIM  =  1
          DEFINE('INCR()')
          G        =  ARRAY(INPUT ',2')
          NUMBER   =  BREAK(' ')  . N SPAN(' ')
          NODE     =  BREAK(' ')  . X SPAN(' ')
          COUNT    =  @CT  @K SUCCEED TAB(*K)  BREAK(' ') *INCR()
+                     SPAN(' ')  @K  RPOS(0)
*
```

```
*
R         LINE      =    INPUT  ' '    :F(GO)
          OUTPUT    =    LINE
          LINE      NUMBER  =
          LINE      COUNT
          G<N,1>    =    ARRAY(CT)
          I         =    0
S         I  =  I  +  1
          LINE      NODE  =              :F(R)
          ITEM(G<N,1>,I)  =  X           :S(S)F(ERR)
GO        N         =    0
          BB        =    DUPL(' ',5)
GO1       N         =    N + 1
          X         =    G<N,1>        :F(END)
          OUTPUT    =    N
          I         =    DIFFER(G<N,1>)  0    :F(GO1)
GO2       I         =    I + 1
          OUTPUT    =    BB  X<I>      :S(GO2)F(GO1)
INCR      CT        =    CT + 1        :(RETURN)
END
```

The pattern **COUNT** counts the number of fields separated by blanks. Transfer to the undefined label **ERR** causes program termination with an error message.

Solution 5.2

```
P         DEFINE('PATH(I,J)K')    DEFINE('PATH1(I,J)S,L,K')
                    .
                    .
                    .
PATH      K         =    K + 1
          G<K,2>    =                    :S(PATH)
          PATH      =    PATH1(I,J)    :S(RETURN)F(FRETURN)
PATH1     S         =    DIFFER(G<I,1>)  G<I,1>      :F(FRETURN)
          G<I,2>    =    IDENT(G<I,2>)  1      :F(FRETURN)
PATH_T    L         =    L + 1
          K         =    S<L>          :F(PATH_D)
          PATH1     =    EQ(K,J)  I  ','  J    :F(PATH_T)S(RETURN)
PATH_D    L         =    0
PATH_A    L         =    L + 1
          K         =    S<L>          :F(FRETURN)
          PATH1     =    I  ','  PATH1(K,J)      :S(RETURN)F(PATH_A)
```

These functions supplement Solution 5.1.

Solution 5.3

```
                &DUMP       =   1
                &ANCHOR     =   1
                ALPHA       =   ANY('ABCDEFGHIJKLMNOPQRSTUVWXYZ')
                ALPHANUM    =   ANY('ABCDEFGHIJKLMNOPQRSTUVWXYZ0123456789')
                LABEL       =   (ALPHA  ARBNO(ALPHANUM)) . L  SPAN(' ')
                OUTPUT('EJECT',,'(1H1)')
                DEFINED     =   BREAK(':')
                FLOW        =   TABLE(10,10)
                BRANCH      =   (SPAN(' ') | NULL) 'BRANCH' SPAN(' ')
+                                   BREAK(' ') . L
R               LINE        =   INPUT               :F(LIST)
                OUTPUT      =   LINE
                STNO        =   STNO  + 1
                LINE        LABEL     =             :F(BRANCH)
                FLOW<L>     DEFINED               :S(MULTI)
                FLOW<L>     =   STNO  ':'  FLOW<L>
BRANCH          LINE        BRANCH                :F(R)
                FLOW<L>     =   FLOW<L>  STNO  ','          :(R)
MULTI           OUTPUT      =   '***** ERROR-MULTIDEFINED LABEL *****'  :(R)
LIST            LIST        =   CONVERT(FLOW,'ARRAY')
                EJECT       =
                OUTPUT      =  DUPL(' ',20)  'FLOW TABLE'
                OUTPUT      =
                I           =   0
LOOP            I           =   I + 1
                X           =   LIST<I,1>                   :F(END)
                LIST<I,2>  DEFINED                          :S(LIST1)
OUTPUT          =   '*** ' LIST<I,1>  ' IS UNDEFINED LABEL:'
+                                   LIST<I,2>               :(LOOP)
LIST1           OUTPUT      =   X  DUPL(' ',15 - SIZE(X))  LIST<I,2>    :S(LOOP)
                OUTPUT      =   X  DUPL(' ',5)  LIST<I,2>    :(LOOP)
END
```

In the flow table, each label is given with the defining statement number, followed by a list of statement numbers containing branches to the label.

Solution 5.4

```
                DATA('COMPLEX(R,I)')
                DEFINE('MUL(X,Y)')
                OPSYN('%','*',2)
                OPSYN('*','MUL',2)

                                            :(END)
MUL             MUL         = DIFFER(DATATYPE(X),'COMPLEX')
+                             DIFFER(DATATYPE(Y),'COMPLEX')
```

```
+                        X  %  Y                  :S(RETURN)
            MUL   =   DIFFER(DATATYPE(X),'COMPLEX')
+                       COMPLEX(X % R(Y),X % I(Y))        :S(OUT)
            MUL   =   DIFFER(DATATYPE(Y),'COMPLEX')
I                       COMPLEX(Y * R(X),Y * I(X))        :S(OUT)
            MUL   =   COMPLEX(R(X)  % R(Y) - I(X) % I(Y),
+                               R(X) % I(Y) + R(Y) % I(X))
OUT         MUL   =   EQ(I(MUL))  R(MUL)        :(RETURN)
```

An example of the use of this function would be the execution of the following statements:

```
A   =   COMPLEX(5,3)
B   =   COMPLEX(6,2)
PR  =   A * B
PR  =   4 * A
PR  =   B * 5
PR      =   5 * 4
```

Solution 6.1

```
DEFINE('PUSH(A)')
DEFINE('POP(A)')
DEFINE('TOP(A)')
OPSYN('%','PUSH',1)
OPSYN('#','POP',1)
OPSYN('!','TOP',1)
&TRIM = 1
              .
              .
              .
              .
PUSH  A<0> = A<0> + 1
      PUSH = .A<A<0>>                    :F(FRETURN)S(NRETURN)
*
POP   POP = A<A<0>>
      A<0> = GT(A<0>) A<0> - 1           :S(RETURN)F(FRETURN)
*
TOP   TOP = .A<A<0>>                     :(NRETURN)
```

A typical list could be defined by the statement

```
X = ARRAY('0:10',0)
```

Solution 6.2

```
        &ANCHOR = 1
        &TRIM = 1
        PROG =
        CONT = '+' | '.'
READ    STRING = INPUT                  :F(ERR)
        STRING  'EOF'                     :S(EXEC)
        STRING '*'                         :S(READ)
        STRING   CONT  =                 :S(CONTINUE)
        PROG  =  PROG ';' STRING       :(READ)
CONTINUE  PROG  =  PROG  STRING        :(READ)
EXEC       PROG  =  CODE(PROG)      :S<PROG>F(ERR)
END
```

Solution 8.1

```
        DEFINE('TR(VAL,TAG)NO,T,N,Q')
        OPSYN('D','DATATYPE')
        &TRACE     =   10000
                        .
                        .
                        .
TR      NO     =   &LASTNO
        T      =   TIME()
        N      =   IDENT(D(VAL),'NAME')  TAG          :S(TRA)
        N      =   IDENT(D(VAL),'STRING') VAL
TRA     Q      =   IDENT(D($VAL),'STRING')  "'"
        OUTPUT  =  'STATEMENT ' NO ':' N ' = '
+                   Q  CONVERT($VAL,'STRING')  Q
+                   ', TIME = ' T        :(RETURN)
```

Solution 8.2

```
        &TRIM     =   1
        &TRACE    =   1000
        DEFINE('PUT(V)I')
INIT    N         =   LT(N,50) N + 1      :F(TEST)
        TRACE('COL' N,,,'PUT')    :(INIT)
                        .
                        .
                        .
```

```
PUT        V      'COL'   REM . I         :F(ERR)
           OUTPUT    =   DUPL(' ',I)  $V  :(RETURN)
TEST
                      .
                      .
                      .
```

Solution 8.3

```
           &TRACE    =   10000
           DEFINE('OUTOFF(X)')
           TRACE('OUTPUT',,,'OUTOFF')
                    .
                    .
                    .
OUTOFF     IDENT($X,'EOF')      :F(RETURN)
           &OUTPUT   =   0   STOPTR('OUTPUT')          :(RETURN)
```

References

1. Farber, D. J., R. E. Griswold, and I. P. Polonsky. 'SNOBOL, A String Manipulation Language,' *Journal of the Association for Computing Machinery*, Vol. 11, No. 1 (January, 1964), pp. 21-30.

2. Farber, D. J., R. E. Griswold, and I. P. Polonsky. 'The SNOBOL3 Programming Language.' *Bell System Technical Journal*, Vol. XLV, No. 6 (July-August, 1966), pp. 895-944.

3. Forte, Allen. *SNOBOL3 Primer*, The MIT Press, Cambridge, Massachusetts, 1967.

4. Strauss, H. J. External Functions for SNOBOL4 (S4D10). Unpublished, 1968.

5. Lukasiewicz, Jan. *Aristotle's Syllogistic from the Standpoint of Modern Formal Logic*, Clarendon Press, Oxford, England, 1951, p.78.

6. Burks, A. W., D. W. Warren, and J. B. Wright. 'An Analysis of a Logical Machine Using Parenthesis-free Notation,' *Mathematical Tables and Other Aids to Computation*, Vol. VIII, 1954, pp. 53-57.

7. IBM System/360 Operating System. FORTRAN IV [G and H] Programmer's Guide. Form C28-6817-1, International Business Machines Corporation, 1969.

8. IBM System/360 FORTRAN IV Language. Form C28-6515-7, International Business Machines Corporation, 1968.

9. IBM System/360 Operating System. Job Control Language. Form C28-6539-7, International Business Machines Corporation, 1968.

10. Peterson, W. W. 'Addressing for Random-Access Storage,' *IBM Journal of Research and Development*, Vol. 1, No. 2 (1957), pp. 130-146.

11. Morris, R. 'Scatter Storage Techniques,' *Communications of the Association for Computing Machinery*, Vol. 11, No. 1 (1968), pp 38-44.

12. IBM System/360 PL/I [F] Language Reference Manual. Form C28-8201-2, International Business Machines Corporation, 1969, pp. 242-243.

13. Hammersley, J. M. and D. C. Handscomb. *Monte Carlo Methods*, Methuen & Co. Ltd., London, 1965, pp. 27-29.

Index